RISKTAKER, CARETAKER, SURGEON, UNDERTAKER

The Four Faces of Strategic Leadership

William E. Rothschild

John Wiley & Sons, Inc.

New York • Chichester • Brisbane • Toronto • Singapore

In recognition of the importance of preserving what has been
written, it is a policy of John Wiley & Sons, Inc. to have
books of enduring value published in the United States
printed on acid-free paper, and we exert our best efforts
to that end.

Copyright © 1993 by William E. Rothschild
Published by John Wiley & Sons, Inc.

All rights reserved. Published simultaneously in Canada.

Reproduction or translation of any part of this work
beyond that permitted by Section 107 or 108 of the
1976 United States Copyright Act without the permission
of the copyright owner is unlawful. Requests for
permission or further information should be addressed to
the Permissions Department, John Wiley & Sons, Inc.

This publication is designed to provide accurate and
authoritative information in regard to the subject
matter covered. It is sold with the understanding that
the publisher is not engaged in rendering legal, accounting,
or other professional services. If legal advice or other
expert assistance is required, the services of a competent
professional person should be sought. *From a Declaration
of Principles jointly adopted by a Committee of the
American Bar Association and a Committee of Publishers.*

Library of Congress Cataloging-in-Publication Data
Rothschild, William E.
    Risktaker, caretaker, surgeon, undertaker : the four faces of
strategic leadership / by William E. Rothschild.
        p. cm.
    Includes index.
    ISBN 0-471-53629-6
    1. Leadership. 2. Strategic planning. I. Title.
HD57.7.R687   1993
658.4'012—dc20   92-31531

Printed in the United States of America

10 9 8 7 6 5 4 3 2 1

This book is dedicated to the strategic leaders
of the future:

My children—Robert William, Stephen Michael,
Karen Ann, and William E., Jr.

My grandchildren—Robbie and Timmy

My daughters-in-law—Britta and Jayne.

I am proud of each of them and know they will
be leaders in the future.

Acknowledgments

I wish to thank all the leaders at General Electric that I have known and worked for. General Electric continues to be a major source of pride and learning.

Further I wish to thank all the clients with whom I have worked in my second career.

Finally I wish to thank my partner and my friend, my wife Alma. She has continued to provide encouragement and help throughout my career.

Contents

PART FIVE

PART SIX

Introduction

There is a leadership crisis in the world today. The 1992 U.S. presidential election has provided an excellent example of the desire of Americans to have a strong decisive leader. Voters were seeking an individual who is strong enough to take decisive actions to reduce the debt, solve the global conflicts, keep the environment clean, make the streets safe, and so on. In short they wanted a messiah. The same is true in the business world. Many would like to have the perfect leader, who can deal with all situations. They want the courage of the risktaker, the wisdom of the evolutionary caretaker, and the decisiveness of the surgeon and the compassion of an undertaker. They seek the "leader for all seasons."

Unfortunately, no one person can do it all. There is no leader for all seasons who can do everything and do it all equally well.

This book, which is about the reality of leadership, has two fundamental premises: First, the type of leader must change to reflect the maturity of the business or organization; second, the leader's abilities and talents will be the key to how the institution differentiates itself from its competitors. In simple terms, some leaders will excel at invention, others at selling, still others at problem solving, and some in just being able to make things better than anyone else. The key is to understand what the situation demands and then match those requirements to the strategic leader possessing the necessary unique talents.

For the past 30 years, I have been a student and practitioner of strategic management. I have witnessed and participated in many businesses in various phases of their life cycles. Some businesses have been young and growing rapidly, others have been mature, and several were nearing old age and death.

Because of this experience, I developed a strong awareness of the need for a different type of leader at each phase of the business life cycle. The leader who was successful at the inception and start-up of a business was not always able to make the transition into the mature stage. Likewise, winners in the mature stage often could not adjust their management patterns and implement what was necessary when a business needed the skill of the restructurer. Further, I witnessed and admired the skill of those leaders who were able to manage the final stages of the business's life and could make the decision to close or liquidate the firm or merge it with another.

This book is an integration of my own experiences, observations, and evaluations of leaders in all walks of life. Since I have spent my career in business, most of the illustrations will be from the business world. There are leaders in every facet of society, however, and the rules and premises should pertain to them as well.

THERE IS NO LEADER FOR ALL SEASONS

The distinctive requirements of a business, or society, at certain phases of its existence make it impossible for one leader to be best for all conditions at all times. Indeed, I will describe four definable leadership styles or types, which correspond to the "seasons" of the business or society.

First, there is the revolutionary: the creator, whose special talent is developing and leading new businesses or new institutions. These individuals have a vision and a commitment that allow them to gamble their entire career and personal wealth on making their dreams a reality. I call these leaders *risktakers*. They are needed when the business or institution is in its infancy and youth, a period of rapid growth.

As the business begins to grow slower, a different style of leadership is necessary to nurture a more orderly, evolutionary growth and long-term prosperity. These leaders add structure and stability to the organization. They don't get the glory of the risktakers, who usually precede them, but they are true leaders nonetheless. I call them *caretakers*.

When a mature business or institution slows down, it needs a different type of leader. These individuals can distance themselves from the past and from the folklore of the business. They are able to separate the strong from the weak and to focus on those parts that can survive and grow, while discarding the weak pieces that need to be pruned. These are the restructuring leaders who have become so prevalent today. I call such leaders *surgeons* because they must have a surgeon's skill if the patient is to survive the operation and prosper in the future.

Sometimes, however, the patient may be fatally ill. In business terms, the organization must either be systematically closed down or dismantled completely, so that its independent existence ceases. These leaders are skilled at gradually harvesting the business into its ultimate demise. But they do so with skill and compassion. They help the survivors live and even feel good while the death is gradually taking place. I call these individuals *undertakers* because their talent resembles the ability of the undertaker to "make the deceased look good" while helping the survivors get through their grief with a minimum of discomfort.

What is a leader?

Although leaders have different styles, which are appropriate at certain seasons of the business, they share many characteristics.

- *Leaders Are Committed to Having Their Organizations Survive and Prosper.* During the past decade, many books have been written about the need for leaders to become more shareholder oriented, but that should not be the major objective or goal of a leader. Market share, profitability, return of investment, increasing shareholder value are all means to the end. The objective of leadership—*long-term prosperity and growth.* (The length of time will vary from one type of leader to another. Obviously, the long term for the undertaker may be much briefer than that for the risktaker.) Objectives such as "quarter-by-quarter" profit goals are for portfolio managers, not leaders.

- *Leaders Focus on Making Their Institutions Unique.* They must find a way to distinguish their companies or organizations from the pack and position them to take advantage of these differences. Such efforts must be built on the leaders' unique talents, which are used to drive the entire organization. These "strategic drivers" focus on gaining and maintaining a competitive advantage. The areas of leader uniqueness include product innovation; problem-solving abilities; and skills in selling, producing, and creating massive systems and networks. Leaders must have unique talents to be successful.

- *Leaders Have a Rare Blend of Insight, Intuition, and Analytical Abilities.* They must be able to conceptualize and communicate an effective and sustainable "game plan." This game plan must be clear, simple, and easy to follow, because it guides team members in implementing the strategic driver. However, the game plan, as in sports, must be flexible and not overly quantitative; leaders manage strategically, not by the numbers.

- *Leaders Attract, Recruit, Motivate, and Maintain the Right Players on Their Team.* The type of player, as well as the depth and breadth of the team will vary from one leader to another. A risktaking team is significantly different from an evolutionary team. Further, those required to restructure or even gradually harvest over a long period of time differ from those who will be able to evolve growth. The deficit of this ability to motivate and retain the right team, especially the key players, has been a serious problem for businesses and institutions over the past decade and will continue to be a major challenge. Leaders must be personally engaged in this activity. Without the right team, they are not real leaders.

- *Leaders Are Consistent and Predictable.* They "do what they say, and say what they do." They avoid "management by slogan"; that is, they don't just make speeches using the latest management catch phrases. During the past decade, I have witnessed a number of slogan-obsessed managers with programs only an inch deep. Leaders are also consistent in all their actions, from defining the concept to game plan and team composition. There is no confusion about where they stand or where they want to go.

- *Leaders Not Only Know Where They Want to Go, They Realize When It Is Time to Get Out.* Actually, it would be more accurate to say they realize when to turn their organizations over to a more appropriate leader, for the next phase of the cycle. A major problem with leaders is their refusal to recognize that they can't lead forever.

There is no perfect leader. Some excel in one area and are weak in others, which is why they need a game plan and a team to implement it. Leaders complement and supplement their deficiencies. I believe that leaders are born and have innate talents. They can improve, but they can't be developed unless they have a natural ability to lead.

THE BOOK DESIGN

Part One focuses on the four faces of strategic leaders. It elaborates and illustrates the different types of leader, including when each is likely to be needed. A number of factors determine the "right" leader: the business's or organization's status on the life cycle, the type of customer and decision maker, the expectations and needs of the key stakeholders, the competitive environment, the technology, and external impactors. A leader must conform to these factors in varying degrees. Part One introduces the concept that leaders must excel at some aspect of the business.

Part Two focuses on product-oriented leaders, including the innovative risktakers who create new products or services that often become major markets or industries. Next are the evolutionary caretakers, who modify and adapt products that meet the changing needs of the users and customers. These growers build on the risktakers' innovations, making them viable for the longer term. Then there is a discussion of the surgeons and undertakers, who have the unenviable job of pruning or even overseeing the merciful closing down of some parts of the business or finding an "adopted" parent for others. These leaders have the skill to focus on what is the best for the institution without becoming so tied to the past that they lose their objectivity.

Part Three probes into the genius of the problem-solving leaders. There is a chapter dealing with the "risktakers of all risktakers," those who try to solve the major problems of society, health, science. The caretaking version of the problem solver is also discussed since such individuals are more likely to be found in the business and everyday world. These leaders begin with understanding the customer's perspective and so help the customer solve problems in an organized and efficient manner.

Part Four highlights leaders whose uniqueness is their ability to sell and market. Innovative risktaking sellers can be as creative as those who develop the products or solve major problems. These leaders get people to buy the products or accept the solutions, often by creating new ways of selling. This Part will describe both individuals who invented and those who made the invention into a sustainable organization. There will also be a discussion of many of the surgeon and undertaker leaders who have been prominent in sales and marketing in the past decade.

Part Five provides insights into individuals who may be overlooked in discussions of leaders. These are the risktakers who create systems, infrastructures, and production capabilities that work so well they are often taken for granted. These leaders have provided society with the roads, the parks, and the transportation, electrical, and communications systems that are vital but seldom appreciated, unless they fail to work properly.

Manufacturing people are the most unappreciated group in any business. These operations people are often not considered to be leaders. Yet many of them have provided the means to make an institution different and successful.

Leaders come in all shapes and forms, and it is unfair to ignore any group. Also, different skills will be required as a business develops and matures. Therefore, even though this book's title focuses on the leader's willingness and need to assume risk, the text analyzes these different kinds of experts in detail and then relates them to the four faces of strategic leaders.

Part Six, the final section of the book, does three things: It summarizes the lessons learned from the lack of leadership in the 1980s, provides some insights about the leaders who will be needed in the 1990s, and readdresses the issue of whether there has been or can be a leader for all seasons. The objective is to relate some of the current and future trends and problems with the type of leader that these conditions may require. This is not a futuristic thesis, but a practical guide to the qualities that will determine effective leadership.

In addition, this book will probe beyond the superficial aspects of leadership type. Each chapter will describe the preferred "game plan" for the type of leader being discussed. For instance, one chapter will describe how risktaker problem solvers must deal with clients in solving problems and how these leaders must think about protecting their solutions and using them in other situations. These practical actions will help determine whether a leader's game plan fits the preferred strategies. Each chapter also discusses the right team for the leader, emphasizing that leaders are not leaders unless they have a team with members who conform to the leader's strategic driver, degree of aggression, and game plan.

Timing is often the deciding factor between success and failure. Each chapter also includes a description of the situations that are most likely to enhance the leader's success.

To avoid the awkward repetition of "he or she," this book uses these pronouns alternately throughout the text. This convention is for ease of reading only. Unless the text explicitly states otherwise, all the material herein refers impartially to both men and women, who, needless to say, have equal capacity for leadership.

I hope that the insights in this book will challenge many of your beliefs about being a successful leader.

PART
ONE

THE FOUR FACES OF STRATEGIC LEADERSHIP

Chapter 1 describes management policies in the 1980s, which equated leaders with those who espoused "slogans." Real strategic leaders do more than give speeches.

Chapter 2 explains the need for different leadership types in the life cycle of businesses and organizations. Those required at the beginning are different from those needed in the growth, maturity, and decline of the business. However, leaders do have many similar characteristics.

In addition to fitting the life cycle position of the business, a leader must conform to other factors in the situation. Chapter 3 discusses the type of customer, type of competitors, expectations and needs of major stakeholders, and the dynamics of technology that must be evaluated in selecting the right leader.

Leaders must be the best at some function of the business. There are those who excel in inventing products, others in sales, others in problem solving and others in ability to make products or systems. A realistic game plan is vital for communicating and leading, and successful leaders must answer key questions that influence the game plan and the team selection.

1

Managing by Slogan Is Not Leadership

The 1980s were characterized not by strategic leadership but by single-dimensional thinking that I have termed "managing by slogans." Heads of corporations and other institutions were caught up in a desire to find catchy phrases or slogans that could represent themes for their organizations. Organizations were thus defined by "quality management" or by the desire to "empower the work force," to "be lean and mean," or to "be customer and market driven."

Such a theme or slogan might be a useful guide for members of an organization. It was often presented by management, however, as the answer to all the organization's problems. In fact, these slogans are only expressions of intent; management must move beyond slogans to implement long-term programs and to act consistently over time. It is action that truly defines an organization. Further, one theme or slogan might not be appropriate for all parts of a company, an issue that will be discussed in greater detail in a later chapter.

For now, I will elaborate a little on the management trends of the past decade and explain why the succeeding preoccupations with quality, productivity, cost cutting, restructuring, and customer service have not yielded the desired long-term results.

QUALITY

During the 1980s, book after book and article after article blamed lack of quality for the decline of the U.S. automotive and consumer electronics industries. They asserted, with some justification, that during the boom years of the 1950s and 1960s, American managers had been willing to sacrifice quality for "bookkeeping" efficiencies and short-term profits. Business authors pointed out that many chief executive officers (CEOs) would build products that didn't meet their own standards, then "ship and fix" them in the field or after the customers complained. The company number crunchers were able to demonstrate that this procedure made money, in the short run, for those firms that had already invested in extensive repair service operations and were thus able to fix the "small percentage" of less than perfect products. Such statistical quality control made sense in the short run because American consumers were willing to accept marginally defective products. Why? Because in those days, there was no alternative. The vast majority of industries, including automobiles and electronics, were dominated by U.S. firms, and they appeared dedicated to a strategy of short-run efficiencies.

The competitive picture began to change in the early 1970s, however, when Japanese consumer electronics and automobile companies entered the market with superior quality products. The Japanese approach was "zero defects." Because these manufacturers had to transport their merchandise long distances to the U.S. market and because they had no service network in place, they made their products right before they shipped them. Once American consumers learned they had a choice, they opted for higher levels of quality, giving the Japanese a major competitive advantage.

It took U.S. managers nearly a decade to catch on. Finally, they listened to their customers, recalculated the financials, and became believers. They read the literature, made trips to Japan, enrolled in "Quality Colleges," and spent heavily on improving quality. To their amazement, they discovered that they were learning *American* techniques. The Japanese had adopted the teachings of Deming and Juran, gurus of quality who had concentrated on teaching the Japanese their quality principles because they could not get a hearing in their native country. The difference: The Japanese were searching for a long-term approach; American managers are always looking for the quick fix and so move from one fad to another.

PRODUCTIVITY AND COST CUTTING

During the 1980s, the "lean and mean" school of management became popular. It was, however, another one-dimensional scheme, similar to the quality approach.

The argument was that U.S. firms were losing in the global market-place because American workers were not as productive as workers from other countries and the costs of their union wages and benefits were too high. The solution was to move production to nonunion areas, first in the United States, then in the Far East and Mexico. Plants in Detroit and the Northeast were closed, and jobs were lost forever. The once-mighty AFL/CIO unions, encumbered by aging leadership, were unable to halt the trend.

Initially, the results were improved costs and increased margins. This was not surprising. Any change can have a short-term positive impact, since it often takes time for the numbers to catch up with the moves. However, there proved to be no lasting competitive advantage. First, the wages of the nonunion and "undeveloped" laborers have increased. Second, the other costs—shipping, tariffs, lower quality—have begun to outstrip the benefits. Finally, when the competition made similar moves, the competitive differential disappeared.

But the productivity advocates were ready with a second simple solution: automation. American firms rushed to copy Japanese and other Far East producers by buying and installing robots and other forms of automated machine tools. They marched behind the banners of "the factory of the future" and "the workerless plant." Unfortunately, they discovered, often too late, that robots were not as capable as people and that automation might cost more and turn out products of lesser quality. Many firms caught up in the theme of the day gained no competitive advantage.

The next rationalization was, "Well, if we can't do it ourselves, let someone else do it." Thus, "outsourcing" emerged as a management fad. American companies sold "private label" or "OEM'ed" products made by foreign firms. Ford cars were made by Mazda, Chevrolets by Toyota, GE televisions by Hitachi, and so on. These and other products were sold under their U.S. brand names. As before, the strategy created short-term profits. But these disappeared as the sourcing companies moved into the market with their own products and their own brands. Indeed, when the foreign firms used their economies, which had been provided by the U.S. brands, to cut prices, margins disappeared.

Having failed to sustain profits by moving plants, automating, and outsourcing, management took its knife to itself. Or, rather, to its people. The goal was to reduce overhead by cutting administrative staff at headquarters. Middle- and even first-line supervisors were targeted. This step required a slight alteration in the slogan of the moment. Because many of the people on the chopping block were friends and neighbors of those doing the chopping, the catch phrase became "Lean, NOT mean." Kinder and gentler downsizing meant "golden handshakes," special buy-out packages, and early retirements. Throughout the nation, millions of managers and staff professionals left their jobs "voluntarily"; some retired, others began second or third careers. These are the new un(or under)employed of the 1990s.

Unfortunately, "lean and mean" has not advanced the competitive position of U.S. industry. In the continued search to reduce costs and increase productivity of resources, companies today find themselves cutting into the bone and not the fat. Further, they have mortgaged the future with heavy debt. In the meantime, the foreign competition has declined to follow this seductive path of short-term opportunism.

RESTRUCTURING

If the business is stagnating and profits are scarce, then maybe the solution is to get out—to sell while you can. The rationalization of American managers was that the primary and only real purpose of business was to "maximize shareholder value." In many cases, they were responding to the attacks of the LBOs (leveraged buy-outs), junk bond merchants, and "asset strippers." All this was an outgrowth of "portfolio planning," which itself is one of the steps in sound strategic thinking. I still advocate portfolio planning to help companies grow; I never anticipated it would be overused and actually kill firms.

Portfolio management began in the early 1970s as a device to help companies set priorities and focus on attractive and viable businesses. It was developed in response to a situation in which firms burdened with an overcrowded portfolio were milking good businesses to pay for those that were marginal or even unnecessary. These companies had gotten caught up in the "growth for the sake of growth" theme of the day. Portfolio strategy urged firms to analyze their business units critically, in terms of "reason for being and relative attractiveness to the total company." The message was that since companies could no longer "be all things to all people," they needed to select and then pay attention to the best business units. Once determined, these units should be allocated most of the resources. The poor performers (or "dogs," as the Boston Consulting Group affectionately called them) should be harvested or divested.

This theory has considerable merit within the context of the big picture. The expectation of portfolio management was that other firms would acquire the discarded business units (give the poor dog a home) and lavish them with the special attention that would turn them into winners. Poor producers for one company would be reallocated to another and revived, not simply used up and abandoned. However, many managers discovered that it was more profitable to harvest and sell off assets than to grow or take risks by adding to their portfolio. Portfolio management was never intended to be just a game of reduction.

Portfolio managers were analogous to the rich playboy who had inherited a large amount of real estate and found that if he systematically converted his holdings into cash, he could spend his inheritance and live the good life. Unfortunately, both the playboy and the manager found that selling assets is a short-term game. If the proceeds are not reinvested in assets that will grow, the game is over. We had fun, but now we're poor, and nothing is left for the next generation. Some view the United States as now living off the liquidation of its assets, with the same sad future for all of us.

Many managers who liquidated company assets without reinvesting for the future simply took the money and ran. That is, they paid themselves handsome salaries and bonuses while depleting their companies. In addition, outsiders recognized the value of purchasing these discarded pieces and selling them at huge profits. Simultaneously, Mike Milken introduced the junk bond concept, which allowed raiders or "investment bankers" to raise capital for purchases at low cost and with low risks. Suddenly, any company might be vulnerable, and managers defended their firms by taking on debt, divesting assets, and focusing on short-term profitability. As a result, businesses with solid gold names, from every sector of the economy, have disappeared into bankruptcy.

CUSTOMER SERVICE

Since actions to improve quality, reduce costs for increased productivity, and restructure for profitability were insufficient to ensure competitive advantage, American managers turned their attention outward to the customer. A milestone book, *In Search of Excellence*,[1] was the source of many compelling slogans in this arena. The message was to "get close to the customer," and it struck a responsive cord because many of the book's entertaining examples involved U.S. companies. Readers were advised to "manage by wandering around" talking to the customers and the employees to find out what they wanted.

The success of the book helped make coauthor Tom Peters a global guru and spawned a movement that decreed "the customer should be first" and firms should be "market driven." Techniques such as focus groups became popular, and managers sat behind one-way mirrors watching customers or potential customers describe what they liked and didn't like. Customer surveys of all types proliferated. Thus began the "service crusade" that preaches only "service-driven" companies will become winners. Company after company advertises with that theme, offers guarantees, and provides "hot lines to senior executives"—all designed to demonstrate that the firms really want to please customers and meet their expectations.

But, in the words of the old song "Will you still love me tomorrow?" will these firms live up to their advertising slogans? Or will they drift away when bewitched by the next seductive management fad? The recent history of fickleness is not encouraging.

STRATEGIC LEADERSHIP VERSUS SLOGAN MANAGEMENT

American business in the 1980s was dominated by people who focused on the short-term optimization of finances rather than the long-term development of assets. A few individuals, however, did not get caught up in the "greed" mentality, and we will meet them in later chapters of this book. For now, in general terms of objectives and goals, we can define the difference between these individuals—strategic leaders—and the slogan managers:

- Slogan managers care primarily for the financials and the numbers; they dedicate themselves to enhancing shareholder value at the expense of other stakeholders, including their own employees. Strategic leaders concentrate on the long-term prosperity of their companies.

- Slogan managers are simplistic and shallow; they seek the quick fix that will solve all their problems. They blithely follow the current trend or management fad, reciting its merits without thinking critically about its effective implementation. Strategic leaders build on their own insights and intuition. They seek to differentiate their companies on known skills they can apply effectively.

- Slogan managers change for the sake of change, moving from one theme to another, sometimes with no real conviction. They tend to reorganize and restaff frequently. Strategic leaders are flexible, but they understand the value of continuity and loyalty. They empower their people because they know it is good management, not because it is the publicized business "truth" of the moment. Strategic leaders are credible, dedicated, and proud of their identity. At times, they can be predictable to a fault, but they succeed because their actions and words are consistent over the long haul.

- Slogan managers are constantly seeking "new challenges" and might be CEOs of several companies during their careers. If they are lucky, they move rapidly enough so that their short-term decisions don't catch up with them. If anything, strategic leaders are inclined to stay too long in a particular position—past their "season," as I pointed out in the introduction. Their staying power, however, provides important continuity of management.

The main difficulty with strategic leadership is matching an individual leader's abilities with the developmental stage of the company or business unit. The next chapter will address this issue directly. Indeed, the seasonal quality of strategic leadership will be the unifying theme of the entire book.

2

Leaders Are Not All the Same

We have just seen that strategic leaders are not the same as managers. Examining the terms "strategy" and "leadership" will help to define just what they are.

A company's strategy must answer four questions:

1. *What is our current business definition, and what should it be in the future?* This entails determining what the company sells and/ or what services it provides—and to whom. In other words, what are our products, customers, and markets? For instance, a company might define its business currently as providing products, systems, and services that permit its customers—say, mid-size firms in the Northeast—to communicate and to transact business. Further, it might define its business for the future as providing similar products and services to mid-size firms across the nation or even around the globe. The specification of what the business does and to whom it sells today is called its *mission*. The specification of what it wants to be in the future is called its *vision*. Both should also relate what is sold in terms of what customer buys. We sell cars, which provides transportation to our customers.

2. *Where shall we focus our energy, attention, and resources?* Here the company is setting priorities. This is the investment element in strategy making (and can be termed *investment strategy*). It requires evaluating each individual segment of the company separately to arrive at a picture of the whole.

3. *How can we create a sustainable competitive advantage?* The answer to this question is called the *strategic driver.* Its selection is critical, because winners build on their strengths and not their limitations. Determining the strategic driver is the central task of the strategic leader because it sets the tone and can ignite the passion of the entire organization. As will be apparent throughout this book, the strategic driver must be a good fit for both the company and the abilities of the leader.

4. *How will each of our functional units contribute to the implementation of the strategy?* This element, called the *implementation strategy,* focuses on the contributions of the departments of engineering, finance, sales, manufacturing, human resources, and so on. All the key programs and functional plans must be internally consistent and reinforce each other. If one is out of sync, the total plan may fail. (I will elaborate on this concept later during the discussions of "game plans." Their implementation varies from one strategic driver to another and is influenced by timing and such externalities as the market, customers, and competition.)

A company with answers to these four questions has a strategy. If the company has someone (or ones) to set the direction and guide the company in achieving its objectives and implementing its strategy, it has a leader (or leaders). The true leader is the "soul" of the company and creates the passion that will motivate performance. Indeed, the leader generates the strategy by offering the vision, setting the priorities, and determining and implementing the strategic driver.

But that is not all. Leaders must have good timing; their style and abilities must fit the current needs of the organization. For there are many types of leaders, and the company must have the right one at the right time.

THE RIGHT LEADER AT THE RIGHT TIME

There are four types of leader. Each can be highly effective at the appropriate time in the company's history.

- *Risktakers* are (usually) the founders or creators of the institution or company. They have the passion and genius to make dreams happen that others believe beyond reach.
- Leaders of the second type are interested in and committed to moving the business or institution from the early growth stage

into a healthy maturity. They are evolutionary rather than revolutionary in outlook. I call them *caretakers*.

- When the company or institution has begun to peak, a third type of leader is required. These *surgeons* select the best parts of the institution and labor to assure they survive. At the same time, they cut away those units that are not needed or whose existence threatens the total organization.

- Finally, companies arrive at a stage when the surgeon cannot save them. They require the sort of people who are not usually thought of as leaders. Their task is to harvest, close down, or merge the enterprise with another. They are concerned with the survivors and others impacted by the death of the institution. I term these leaders *undertakers*.

Risktakers

These are the headliners, the men and women who make the covers of *Business Week, Fortune,* and *Forbes*. These are the people who are lauded in the popular business books such as *In Search of Excellence.* These leaders were the folk heroes of the 1980s.

Risktakers are undeniably important, but they are only effective in specific situations and at a certain phase of the institution's life cycle. If asked to lead when a business needs stability and cautious moves, they are a disaster. I must point out, too, that not all risktakers are leaders. Some are merely "Las Vegas gamblers or promoters" who "shoot from the hip" and have no vision, direction, or strategy.

In this book, I will describe true risktaker leaders—people who bet their wealth and personal reputations on the success of the significant changes they make in the way their organizations operate. They often create products, services, or causes that might not otherwise have existed. Individual leaders in this category include Bill Gates of Microsoft, Stephen Jobs of Apple, and Ross Perot of EDS.

Caretakers

Caretakers are often needed when the risktakers leave. Their leadership attributes are stability and a clear sense of direction for the organization. Caretakers are not bureaucrats or maintenance people. Their function is to help the company evolve in a manner that will ensure long-term growth. They don't get the headlines or the spectacular publicity of the risktakers. Normally, their recognition comes in more quiet testimonials after they have labored long to strengthen the firm and make it a success.

Indeed, caretaking leaders are often maligned in today's business press. We hear a continuing cry to replace many of the current evolutionary business leaders with entrepreneurs who will shake things up. (In the governmental arena, you hear some describe Ronald Reagan and his conservative followers as the caretakers and the liberal Democrats as the movers and shakers in domestic policy.) The fact is that caretakers are necessary. They keep businesses (and governments) sound and allow them to develop in a systematic and predictable manner. Indiscriminately trashing them is destructive. On the other hand, not all caretakers are leaders. Some are really just custodians who do not add value to the business. There comes a time when the caretaker must be replaced by the surgeon, or even the undertaker.

Surgeons

These leaders often save companies on the verge of collapse. Lee Iacocca was, for instance, the surgeon savior for Chrysler Corporation. He focused the company on automobiles and cut the non-auto pieces out of the enterprise. In doing so, he moved counter to the advice of academics, financial advisors, and portfolio managers who urged that he follow the AMC model (taking non-autos over autos). But Iacocca was an automobile man; he loved the business and was good at it. He saved Chrysler by applying the abilities he had developed during his long career at Ford. He introduced the minivan and reintroduced the convertible, ironically, two decisive actions he was not permitted to take at Ford.

Iacocca paid attention to his instincts, and his talents were a match for the requirements of his company. That made him the right leader for the right time.

Undertakers

Undertakers are important decision makers at a time when people too close to a situation, too personally involved in the history, are unable to think clearly for themselves. In business, the undertaker leader must make the right decision about the life of the divisions or products of a company in trouble—or even the company itself. In the process, undertakers must deal with the emotional attachments of the survivors. It can take a real strategic leader to close a product line or withdraw from a market. At times, the undertaker leader must close an entire business when it is too sick to recover. They might be called "mercy killers" in today's parlance, but they are leaders nonetheless. (In the realm of government, Boris Yeltsin may be in this category.)

In the next chapter, I will describe the conditions that favor each type of leader. The company's stage in the business life cycle, the type of customers served, and the nature of the competitive environment all play a part in determining the appropriate style of leadership for the moment. Also in the next chapter, I will detail how the various stakeholders in the company—financial investors, community, government, employees—influence the selection and determine the effectiveness of the leader.

CHARACTERISTICS OF ALL LEADERS

Dedication

Strategic leaders are committed to the long-term survival and prosperity of their organizations. Those are their primary objectives, and they cannot be overemphasized.

In contrast, many Americans believe that striving for a healthy "bottom line" for the company is the primary mission and purpose of the leader. They feel that unless a company makes a profit every quarter, it will be set upon by vultures and asset strippers. Some also argue that positive cash flow must constantly be maintained if the company is to be able to pay its bills and remain solvent. But this obsessive focus on the balance sheet destroys organizations, because it fosters short-range, opportunistic thinking; it creates managers, not strategic leaders.

Strategic leaders recognize the difference between the means and the end. *Profits and cash flow are means to an end, not the end itself.* Of course, the company must meet the expectations of its investors and must pay its bills. Profits are the means for a company to reinvest in its future at the lowest cost. It is also true that the investors, the shareholders, are the owners and deserve their fair returns. Strategic leaders must, however, look beyond the investor and evaluate the needs of all the key stakeholders in the business. Because leaders have a vision for the company and are committed to implementing this vision, they must balance the short-term and long-term considerations.

Passion

Leaders must love the organization and its purposes. That is, they must have the selfless desire of the lover to put the goals of the company before all else; they need passion as well as the intellectual dedication of the professional. This, too, means that leaders look toward the long term. They are concerned that the organization will grow and be prepared for the uncertainties of the future.

Unfortunately, many organizations seem to be headed by the "slogan managers" described in Chapter 1. They are focused on the short haul and always put themselves ahead of the needs of the organization and its stakeholders.

The different types of leader will display different types of passion. Risktakers focus their passion and strategic drive on creating something they believe is unique; often it is not generally accepted at the time. In business, that may mean introducing a new product, implementing a new way to sell, or working closely with customers and constituents to solve intransigent problems. In the realm of politics and government, men such as Jefferson, Franklin, and Washington were risktaking leaders with a passion for a revolutionary idea for a nation. During the American Civil War, leaders on both sides, like Lincoln and Lee, risked everything for their vision of what they considered right for their country. Throughout history, risktaking leaders in all walks of life have been characterized by passionate commitment, not just intellectual attachment, to their causes.

The drive of caretaker leaders is more subdued and less visible. These leaders are dedicated to the sustained growth and profitability of the company, or to the continued health and vigor of the public institution. They are oriented toward incremental rather than dramatic changes. Nonetheless, caretakers can clearly express their goals and intentions and are passionately devoted toward making them happen.

The image of the surgeon and the undertaker is of cold, calculating professionals. But they, too, are passionate leaders with drive and dedication to make the difficult changes either to renew their institutions or to keep them productive as long as possible. The surgeon is willing to cut out the sick and nonproductive segments to make the organization as a whole healthier and better able to survive longer. The undertaker is able to do what is necessary to help the organization make the best of its final time.

Credibility

Leaders must do what they say. Consistency of actions and words is essential. And so is honesty. If circumstances dictate making changes, a leader must be willing and able to explain why; if promised results are not delivered, a leader must be able to admit mistakes or shortcomings.

Many heads of corporations today fail the credibility test. They mouth encouraging words, but the actions don't match up. For example:

Words	Actions
We will be customer oriented.	Cut out service and thus the ability to meet customer needs and wants, in order to gain a short-term profit.
We will be a quality producer.	Never slow down the line or permit the capacity utilization to decline.
Our people are our most important asset.	Lay off as many as necessary to make the annual, or even quarterly, budget. Don't consider loyalty or the talents required in the future. Hire and fire!
We empower our employees to do what is right; we delegate at the lowest part of the organization.	Only accept what the boss thinks is the right answer. Don't listen, just act.
We will be competitive.	Don't take the time to monitor competitors and never do anything that will sacrifice the short-term earnings. Sell off market share and image to make the quarterly budget.

Strategic leaders do more than make speeches that tell everyone what they want to hear. Leaders are willing to be different, if that is what is right for the organization. They select one strategic driver and stick with it as long as required. (George Bush demonstrated this characteristic during the Desert Storm war. He had a vision, made a commitment, and did what he thought was right until his goals were met, regardless of criticism.)

Strategic leaders are not only credible, but predictable. They don't overpromise and create surprises or disappointments. Because they understand they are working on assumptions and must deal with uncertainties, they think through contingency plans. When changes become necessary, strategic leaders discuss them with their team. Indeed, this sort of team communication is one of the defining characteristics of strategic leaders of all types.

Unique Talent

Whether risktaker, caretaker, surgeon, or undertaker, the strategic leader must be the best at some key aspect of the business and must be able to leverage this excellence into something really distinctive. Some leaders are the best at developing and distinguishing the company's products or services, some are great at selling, and others are unique problem solvers. This special talent is the strategic driver, and it enables the leader and the firm to gain and maintain a competitive, or even unfair, advantage.

Ability to Institute a Winning Game Plan

The passion or drive is useless unless the leader has a clear, understandable, and realistic game plan that communicates to the team where the institution is headed. Normally, it is a creative product of the leader's intuition and exploits the leader's unique talents. The game plan defines each business function and outlines the expectations for all the people in design, production, sales, and so on. The game plan shows the team how to win because it specifies what each group on the team must do to succeed and explains how each fits into the total vision, direction, and strategy.

Leaders are also participants in the game. Think of them as *playing coaches*. They are part of the action and share in the risks and rewards of implementing the game plan they have created. They take responsibility for failures as well as successes. While leaders must convert their game plans into specific actions, they cannot describe every detail of the game, that is, every activity of the company or institution. They must, however, describe the key plays vital to success, as well as how and when they need to be executed. All actions critical to the implementation of the game plan, in the short and the long term, are the responsibility of the strategic leader.

Flexibility and Willingness to Relinquish Power

The strategic leader understands that since nothing works forever, the business must anticipate and respond rapidly and decisively to changes. Therefore, the game plan and strategic driver must also evolve over time.

In sports, a good coach adapts to different playing conditions, different competitors, different players' skills and abilities, and different rules by altering the game plan to fit changing conditions. The same holds true in business and with other institutions. Leaders must be flexible to remain successful. And the biggest challenge to a leader's flexibility of vision and action is knowing when to give up leadership to a successor and being able to do so.

The risktaker's game plan is quite often based on the personality of the leader. Sales-oriented leaders develop and implement sales-driven game plans, for instance. Product creators have game plans geared in that direction, and so on. This tendency is both a strength and a limitation. It assures continuity of implementation and commitment to the strategic driver, but the good fit may mean inflexibility and unhealthy longevity for the leader and the plan.

Caretakers often take over from risktakers and institute significant changes right away as part of their mandates. A common transition is from a product-driven to a market-driven business. A successful caretaker will then develop policies and procedures to permit the organization to grow and prosper. Over time, however, caretakers can become fixated on their achievements and thus hesitant or even unwilling to make the changes needed to move to the next stage of business development. Caretakers who are effective leaders, however, understand when it is time to bow out and let another type of leader take their place, or, at a minimum, supplement their skills.

The major asset of surgeons is their ability to change. Typically, they are the "professional portfolio managers," who are skilled both at selecting and concentrating on those pieces of the business that have the greatest potential and at selling off or harvesting those units that don't fit. Their game plans are geared to survival and flexibility. They try to base each decision on objective, often financial, criteria. A unit that does not meet such a criterion, or "hurdle rate," is ready for restructuring. Nothing from the past can be held sacred.

As with other types of strategic leaders, the surgeons' abilities constitute both pluses and minuses. On the plus side, they can make tough decisions with limited emotional involvement. The downside is that others may perceive that "everything is for sale." This atmosphere may inhibit the team from making a long-term commitment and may establish a destructive, Darwinian "survival of the fittest" climate.

Ability to Build and Maintain the Right Team

Team building is a too frequently neglected aspect of leadership. Without a team, the leader can't lead; without the *right team*, a leader can't lead effectively. The right team consists of people who complement the leader's talents, share or can pick up on the leader's passion, and can implement the leader's game plan. Leaders must be able to recruit, motivate, and retain key players who meet those criteria.

Recruiting comes first. Leaders must be able to identify the different types of people they need to implement the game plan over the long haul and avoid the temptation to recruit only players who are readily available, or whom they like, or who resemble themselves. The needs of the strategic driver should specify the talents required. For instance, the applications, or problem-solving, leader will require a technical and sales team that can work closely with clients over an extended period to solve difficult problems. Team members must be able to build lasting relationships and not just "get the order and run."

Once the team is in place, the leader must be able to motivate appropriately. Rewards and measures of achievement should fit the game plan and increase commitment to the strategic driver. Some teams will require instant gratification and rewards, some will need security, others will respond to having full control over what they do and how they do it. The appropriate team rewards may not appeal to the leader personally, but providing them may be critical to success.

Retention is often the most difficult aspect of team building. The leader must be able to keep key personnel for the required length of time. During risktaker and caretaker regimes, that may mean holding on to people for the long haul. On the other hand, surgeons and undertakers might be seeking only a short commitment from certain team members. Constant turnover of important players is the most disruptive and counterproductive force on a team. *In fact, continuity of a dedicated team most often means the difference between success and failure for an enterprise.*

Continuity involves preparing for the future with strong succession planning for all the key players, including the strategic leader. I have observed during my 35-year career that many leaders lack the capacity to prepare for their own retirement, voluntary or otherwise. Because they hold on to authority too long without grooming a successor, the company does not survive for long without them. Entrenched leaders begin to believe they are infallible and omnipotent. They attribute the organization's success to their own genius and discount the contributions of the team. Thus they come to view members of the team as commodities or interchangeable parts that are easy to replace and can be used or abused at will.

That attitude is a prescription for failure. Team members will become disenchanted and even openly hostile. Destruction and chaos follow. A leader who is applauded as a savior, declared a creative genius, or simply made "businessperson of the year" should immediately start planning retirement or a move to a new career.

Once again, the world of politics and government provides an excellent case in point. Soviet leader Gorbachev, and his troubled nation, might have been better off had he stepped aside voluntarily before events dictated his forced retirement.

Characteristics of Different Team/Leader Types.   Members of the risktaker's team resemble the risktaker. They are likely to be highly aggressive, unstructured people who are willing to put their own careers and even their own financial resources on the line. They are motivated by the chance to make something new and different happen (often countercultural) and to be part of the innovative team. However, they are also likely to want a piece of the action. And when the action slows down and things get less exciting, these players tend to become bored and want to move on. Leaders must be alert to this development and prepared to find replacements. However, with the change in environment, the new team members are apt to be quite different from the risktaker and so hard for the risktaker to recruit, motivate, and retain—signaling, perhaps, that it is time for the risktaker to go.

On the caretaker's team, superstars who are more interested in "grandstanding" and the instant gratification of applause and accolades will be less important or phased out entirely. Team players will be in demand. The caretaker will need to provide structure and incremental gains and rewards. As the structure grows, layers of management and paperwork will increase, the flexible procedures that characterized the risktaker's regime will disappear. The business will become more stable, more predictable, and less exciting. As long as the business can continue to grow and prosper, this approach is justified. The challenge for leadership is to recognize when the time has arrived for downsizing, when the surgeon or undertaker must assume command of the team.

The surgeon's or undertaker's team will be small and tightly focused on survival. Members will be motivated by the opportunity to make the company healthy again. Here "lean and mean" is appropriate. The team must be willing to question all activities and cut wherever necessary. As mentioned earlier, the nothing-is-sacred mentality prevails. History and the core businesses and products may be discarded for something new.

The Role of the Strategic Driver.   The characteristics of the team will depend on how the leader wishes to distinguish the company. Not only must the team fit the leadership style, it must relate well to the leader's strategic driver. If members are not in harmony with the driver, that is, with what the leader considers to be the firm's competitive advantage, they must be reeducated or removed. The caretaker needs team players not applause-seeking virtuosos; the surgeon can't have people on board whose memories of fatter times make them uncomfortable with the demands of being "lean and mean."

Similarly, a sales-driven team will require skills and attitudes different from a team that is driven by product innovation. And these will differ even more from the applications or problem-solving team and those that are interested in production.

Steadfastness and Courage

The great leaders of history are distinguished by their ability to be true to their visions. John F. Kennedy told the world that the United States would put a man on the moon by the end of the decade, and then he took the actions that would make it happen. Martin Luther King, Jr., articulated a dream and was willing to sacrifice his life to hasten the day when it would come true. Harry Truman knew that dropping the first atomic bomb on Japan might provoke severe criticism, but he took the risk (and the heat) and did it anyway.

In contrast to these individuals who could offer a vision and then march resolutely toward it, many of today's politicians and business managers fail to display convictions and courage. They are much more likely to respond to whichever way the popular wind blows. Strategic leaders of all types, on the other hand, evidence both the vision and the will to act. Perhaps risktakers are closest in spirit to the attitude exemplified by Kennedy, King, and Truman. Indeed, John Kennedy's book, *Profiles in Courage*, could be described as a collection of case histories of risktaking leaders.

Caretakers may not have books written about their courage, but they must have the fortitude to accept their nonglamorous roles without apology. They have to withstand being called "dull," or "organization people," or "bean counters." They don't give self-aggrandizing speeches about the virtues of entrepreneurship. Instead, they back up their style with consistent action, because they are convinced that is what is needed to make their organizations grow and prosper over the long run. They have the will to stay their course and not get carried away with fads or slogans.

Surgeons and undertakers must also be willing to take the heat for such potentially unpopular actions as closing plants, selling off product lines, restructuring, and restaffing. But they must tell the truth about their intentions, and they must be able to defend their actions rather than hide from them. They cannot, for instance, promise not to close a plant in the hope of buying a little public or employee good will and then turn around and close it soon after. Credibility is crucial.

Alert to Proper Timing

Leaders can have the passion to create or survive or fix; they can develop the most consistent game plan, hire and motivate the best team, and still fail—because of poor timing. History tells of many individuals who had great ideas, at the wrong time. Businesses with good products and services have gone under because they arrived before a market could be made ready for them. Some say that's just a matter of luck. While luck can make or break a program or a product, leaders mix something else into the formula. Timing and a sense of how long it is necessary to stick with an idea or project are part of getting desired results.

Strategic leaders learn to appreciate how difficult it is to make changes or even to move a company along a steady and consistent course. Risktakers with a passion to offer the world a new product or service must understand that it will not have instant acceptance. Customers must be converted through missionary-style selling. They must be taught to recognize a need they didn't realize existed. Thus, risktakers must not overpromise or undercapitalize their business or they will not reap the rewards of their creation.

The problem for caretakers is to recognize the need for change and to prepare. Otherwise, they may inadvertently harvest the business. The corporate graveyard is full of firms that refused to acknowledge and respond to changes in the market, competition, and technology. Of course, they must not move too fast, permit the competition to gain position, and thus bring about their own demise. So even caretakers must be sensitive to timing.

Surgeons also need to recognize the difficulty and time required to save the company and restructure it properly. Like a patient under intensive care, the ailing firm must be given time as well as support to regain its health. If surgeons try too much too soon, they may destroy the entire company.

Finally, the undertaker must be careful not to assume prematurely that the institution has died. The goal is to prolong the harvest as much as possible. That may require being "last out of a dying market," a course not always popular with outside experts. However, once the decision is made to close down the business, it must be carried out in a timely and efficient manner.

In summary, strategic leaders must be:

1. Dedicated to their organization's survival and prosperity.
2. Able to build on their own strengths to install their organization in its best, distinctive competitive position.

3. Able to convert their passion and the strategic driver into a realistic, viable game plan that provides specific direction to the team and permits each of the key players to work for the greater good of the organization.

4. Able to recruit, motivate, and retain the people who best fit the personality of the team and meet the needs of the organization.

5. Flexible enough to know when to change and to prepare for change, but courageous enough to be true to their vision.

6. Alert to proper timing, including when to get out of the way.

Subsequent chapters will discuss how different types of leaders employ different strategic drivers. No one leader, however, possesses all these attributes in perfect measure. All leaders have certain weaknesses. Some may not be able to form the right team, some may lack the will to change when required, others may fail to articulate the game plan clearly. Yet, each is a leader deserving of recognition. And each has something to teach us.

3

A Leader for All Seasons: Is This Possible?

Saint Thomas More, whose life was depicted in the play *A Man for All Seasons*, lived centuries ago in England. There are people today who argue, or perhaps merely hope, that we can have a *leader* for all seasons—and for all situations. Unfortunately, this possibility is extremely unlikely. No one leader is best for every situation or stage of an organization's life cycle. Over the course of its existence, a company will require too diverse a mix of talents and personality traits to be met by one person.

As described in the previous chapter, each type of leader needs a variety of talents. That such individuals exist is not just a matter of luck or chance. Leadership skills can be developed; people can increase their range and aptitudes. This does not mean, however, that any particular leader can grow into every situation. *Leaders must understand when their talents and abilities fit the situation; and when they don't fit, leaders must be smart enough to move on to situations that do fit them.*

To help in this process of "fit," I have identified five criteria that can be analyzed for each organization.

1. *Business and Leadership Life Cycles.* The age and maturity of the business or institution, as well as the overall market or environment in which it operates are critical factors. Each stage of the business life cycle requires a different leadership type; I will discuss this criterion in detail later in this chapter.

2. *Customer Types.* It is important to determine the type and dynamics of the customers, clients, or constituents—adventurous, cautious, and so on—who are making the purchasing decisions, because that will affect how they assess the leader's style, time horizon, and approach to the market.

3. *Competition Types.* Some leaders welcome combat, while others would rather not compete at all. Therefore, the aggressiveness of the competitors is a factor in determining the appropriate style of leadership. So, too, are such other competitor personality characteristics as complacency or arrogance.

4. *Stakeholder Needs.* The attitudes and expectations of key stakeholders—investors, employees, and the community/government—will vary; some will want security, others will seek excitement or high return on their input. The style of the leader obviously will be a factor in keeping the stakeholders happy.

5. *The Dynamics of Technology.* A change in the dominant technology of an industry or business often signals the need for a change in leadership style. The organization will be evolving with the technology substitution, and the old leader may not fit the new situation. Technology can also be a leadership tool.

In evaluating all these factors, we are assessing degrees of change. Thus, timing, more than luck, is critical. Timing makes the difference between winners and losers. Timing is knowing when one leadership style must give way to another. Analyzing these five criteria is an ongoing process for the organization's leaders and decision makers; they must be alert to the proper time to make a change. The process will become clearer as we examine each factor in more depth.

BUSINESS AND LEADERSHIP LIFE CYCLES

Age is a major determinant and decision-making consideration in any situation, whether it involves an individual, an institution, a business, or a nation. What is appropriate for an infant organization or person may not be suitable for declining years. In terms of assessing business and leadership, the life cycle chart is the best place to start.

Figure 3.1 matches leadership styles with what is considered to be the normal life cycle of a business, product, or institution. The requirements of a new business correlate well with the characteristics of the risktaker leader. An infant organization needs individuals who are flexible and dynamic; it needs leadership that can function well with

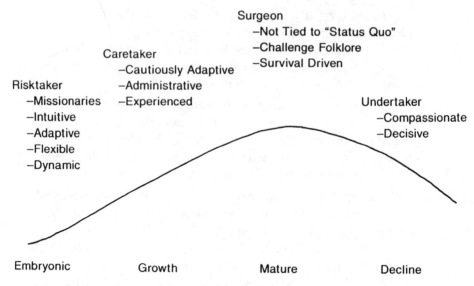

Figure 3.1 Business and the leadership life cycle.

a loose structure and with inexperienced employees. At this stage, highly intuitive and adaptive leaders who depend on their feelings and insights can be successful.

As the business grows more slowly, leaders must become more structured and more predictable. They are still adaptive, but with great caution, and they do not make changes easily. They must blend strong administrative talents with the ability to move the organization. Intuition is tempered by experience. In short, the slowly growing company is the domain of the caretaker leader.

As the company moves from slow growth to maturity, leaders must be more willing to change and less tied to the status quo. They must be able to challenge the folklore and traditions of the company, because even the long-revered may have to be cut for the good of the institution. Surgeons must leave behind the caretaker's concern for stability. In a sense, they are more like risktakers, but their focus is on immediate survival rather than growth. Undertaker leaders become appropriate during the declining stage of the company's cycle, when decline must be managed to its ultimate conclusion, they are compassionate but decisive. This may require the closing and termination of the business or merging the business with another (in which the organization loses its identity).

Embryonic and Rapid Growth Risktaker

In the beginning, the leader and his team must be willing to stake their careers and reputations on something that is newly born, or even just a gleam in the parents' eyes. They must possess both a vision of the future and the dedication to see it become reality. They are really missionaries, committed to converting others to their invention or cause.

Not all will succeed. Some might fail because, no matter how energetic and skilled the leadership, the new product or service is just too far ahead of its time. For example, the facsimile machine that is revolutionizing communications and information transmissions today was invented in the late 1890s. The inventors may have had the vision and desire to make their machine a success, but the facsimile was premature. The technology was not reliable, and the telephone system it needed was too immature to support the innovation. However deserving of acclaim the risktaking innovators might be, their reward was a small and obscure place in history.

As the company enters its rapid growth phase, it continues to prosper with risktaker leaders who can "wing it" and "make it up as they go along." Growth hides many organizational flaws, and healthy sales make the leadership look good. However, really smart risktakers who are truly committed to their company's continuing prosperity begin to consider a transition plan at this juncture. The plan should include identifying a successor to take over when the business reaches a certain size and maturity and a leader in the caretaker mode becomes the best fit.

Unfortunately, most risktaker successes begin to believe their press releases and the wonderful stories written about them. They begin to believe they can hold power forever. History tells many such sad stories. Consider Ferdinand Marcos. He was the youngest president ever of the Philippines. In the beginning, he was a strong leader who instituted democratic reforms. But he clung to power too long and became an ineffectual caretaker, perhaps even a premature undertaker of a nation that still needed dynamic leadership. Eventually, he was overthrown and died a broken man in exile.

It happens to corporate leaders, too. Henry Ford was the prototype for the American risktaking innovator. Stubbornly, he continued to lead the great company he had founded a long time beyond his ability to contribute, in fact, almost to the point of destroying his creation. His grandson, Henry Ford II, eventually took over and performed well as a surgeon leader, restoring the firm to a strong number two position in the automobile industry. But he also was unable to relinquish power when his time came and nearly duplicated the fate of his grandfather. The problem seems inherent in private and family businesses dominated by "legends in their own mind."

And even when the patriarch realizes the need to plan for a transition of authority, failures are possible. The successor may not be up to the job. Consider the story of Howard Johnson, a name once synonymous with family restaurants and lodging. Howard Johnson, Sr., turned over a profitable, growing organization to his son Howard, Jr. Young Howard could not keep the business flourishing, however. He prematurely harvested units and sold off assets to others. He was an undertaker. Today, the orange-roofed restaurants that once dotted the landscape are hard to find. And when located, customers discover that each unit is individually owned and may or may not offer the moderately priced, convenience food that once characterized Howard Johnson's.

A similar story involves An and Fred Wang. The elder Mr. Wang started a small calculator company and made it an innovative force in word processing and office automation. His company carved out a unique niche and prospered. An Wang wanted to keep the company a family business and so was unwilling to appoint an outsider to run things after he stepped aside. Therefore, instead of seeking the best leadership, he appointed his son Fred as his replacement. Unfortunately, Fred proved an ineffective leader, and An had to retake control. By then things had so deteriorated that An Wang sought an outsider to restructure the firm and try to avoid bankruptcy. Thus, the company missed a step in the evolution of leadership and business, going right from rapid growth with the risktaker to decline with the surgeon and possibly the undertaker.

Digital Equipment Corporation (DEC) also seems to be in the same position. Its leader, Kenneth Olsen, has been very successful in creating the mid-range computer and moving the company into a worldwide leadership position. Its minicomputer segment has grown at the expense of the mainframe and become very competitive against IBM and other computer giants. Olsen accomplished what others had tried and failed. Today, however, the minicomputer and the mainframe are not clearly segmented; in fact, they overlap. Thus, the business needs a new direction. It appears Olsen could use a caretaker successor and reluctantly turned over his company to Robert B. Palmer, the company's vice president of manufacturing.[1]

At this time, a number of risktaker entrepreneurs are still in control of their firms. Bill Gates of Microsoft, Ted Turner of Turner Broadcasting, and Frederick Smith of Federal Express will have to handle the transition to new leaders who are best suited for the next stage of corporate development. Each of these men has created a new business, in some cases a new industry. If and when they turn over the product of all their personal, professional, and financial investments, how will their creations fare? The answer will depend in part on the nature and timing of the transition.

Slowing Growth—Caretaker

When the business begins to move from double digit growth to more realistic levels, it will require a more systematic and disciplined leadership. The time for the caretaker grower has arrived. I insert "grower" here to emphasize that the caretaker is not expected to put the company on hold. The goal is still growth, but a consistent, conservative growth as befitting a slowing-growth business. A caretaker is not out to harvest what the risktaker has sown.

At this stage, if the risktaker is still in charge, he is likely either so bored or overwhelmed with the task of establishing systems and procedures that he cannot lead. He might prefer to hire a professional manager to operate the business while he moves on to other innovations. However, often since he really doesn't want to give up control, he hires a manager he can dominate and not a true leader.

But that is what is really needed, a caretaker leader who can build on what has been developed. *That hoped-for progress will not happen unless the risktaker is willing to get out of the way.* Unless the risktaker gives up control, there will be conflict and likely failure. Smart risktakers recognize their limitations and separate themselves from the business. They "cash out" or move out to some technological or innovative outpost. Sometimes when the risktaker is too attached to his creation, the investors or employees forcibly remove him for the good of the organization.

Two famous instances from business history are illustrative. The Morgan Bank played a major role in the transition of General Electric from Thomas Edison, the risktaker and creator, to his successor, Charles Coffin and, later, Gerard Swope. Similarly, the Morgan and the Dupont families handled the transition of General Motors from its innovative creator William Durant, to Alfred Sloan, the marketing and organizational genius, who made it the leading auto company in the world.

In more recent days, the story of Steven Jobs and Stephen Wozniak is revealing. With one product, and against overwhelming odds, they created a multibillion dollar personal computer market. Jobs and Wozniak invented a small computer in their garage and founded Apple in 1976. They had to find customers who were interested in personal or small business computers and who were willing to spend thousands of dollars on equipment and software. They then had to create a distribution and dealer network while simultaneously taking on IBM and other computer giants.

It was a classic risktaker operation. When that stage of the business life cycle passed, Wozniak took his money and assumed a less public role. Jobs continued to lead the company, but he recognized his limitations. He came to appreciate that Apple needed a strong marketing orientation and a professional manager. He hired John Scully, a marketing leader from Pepsi, with the apparent understanding that Scully would help the existing Apple grow and establish a solid position in the marketplace, while Jobs developed new products for the future.

Unfortunately, the union was not harmonious for long because the styles of the two leaders conflicted. Scully appeared to be more interested in current products that in new risky projects. To the surprise of everyone, including Jobs, Scully led a revolt and forced the young founder out of the company.

Jobs took his handsome payout and his entrepreneurial drive and started Next, Inc. This new venture targets the higher education market with what is reported to be an innovative computer system. It will be interesting to see how Jobs the risktaker fairs in his second attempt at company building—and how the transition to the next life cycle stage proceeds there as well. For the story of life is the story of transitions made well or poorly.

Maturity and Decline—Surgeons and Undertakers

As the stable, evolutionary, but still-growing company moves into the mature, and eventually, old-age stage of life, where growth first levels off and then declines, the caretaker leader may no longer be compatible with the needs of the business. Another type of leader may be required.

Once again, the established leader might be reluctant to leave. Chances are he has fallen in love with the core business he has nurtured to achieve significant size and success, even though it is now not very healthy or important in the larger scheme of things. He may have clung to the axiom, "If it ain't broke, don't fix it," and so allowed the business to decline and become vulnerable. This caretaker leader is like the aging athlete unable to admit he can no longer run five miles a day or play his accustomed three hours of tennis.

Over the years, I have witnessed several companies continue to invest in products in decline. They needed surgeon-style leadership—individuals who could look objectively at the company and prune away those parts that were adversely affecting the health of the whole. The surgery takes the form of reducing the number of products, amount of capacity, or number of people. Surgeons may even sell off or close the old core business or product to invest in the new. They may also inject a few new risktakers into the old organization in hopes that they will create something new and exciting.

Companies in every industry have failed to make the transition from caretaker to undertaker, and they have been taken over and their assets stripped away. Corporations with such familiar names as Singer, American Can, RCA, and Continental Can are either a fraction of their former size, submerged into other companies, or gone completely from the scene.

The Singer Company produced some of the best, innovative, consumer products in America. At one time, almost every American woman (especially in rural areas) learned to sew—and learned to sew on a Singer. Singer sewing machines sold across the country and around the world. Over the years, however, the role of women and the nature of families changed, and people were able to purchase ready-made clothing of good quality at a reasonable price. Fewer households needed or wanted a sewing machine. Singer was forced to deemphasize its core business and to diversify into aerospace and industrial products. But it moved slowly, and its leader, Flavin, died before the transition could be completed. The company was taken over by an "asset stripper" and split apart. The original Singer Sewing Machine Company is now called Bicoastal and is a fraction of its former size. The surgery was less than a success, and the patient almost died.

Just 15 years ago, the metal container industry was dominated by two giants: Continental Can and American Can were the industry leaders in technology, innovation, and market share. As both matured, they diversified in hopes of continuing to grow. They both acquired financial services companies and both moved into other forms of packaging, including plastics and paper. Unfortunately, both were victimized by asset strippers and by ineffective management, and neither exists in the same form as before.

American Can was taken over by Jerry Tsai, who changed the name to Primeria, sold off the core business, and concentrated on financial services and specialty retail. The company purchased Smith Barney. The financial services strategy was not successful, however, and that business was bought by Commercial Credit, headed by Sanford Weill, former president of American Express. Weill has continued the surgery of the portfolio, selling Musicland to investors and Triangle to CJI Industries. He has continued to focus on financial services, adding the A. L. Williams life insurance firm to the mix. The future will tell whether Weill has made the right moves at the right times to succeed.

The issue facing leaders of organizations in the maturity and declining phase is whether they take the necessary steps to become surgeons or undertakers themselves or wait until others do it for them. If they wait too long, they may find the company listed in the obituary section of the business news or they may find themselves forced to retire, like Robert Stemple found out in November 1992. If they are willing to take effective action themselves, however, by diverting their resources to new areas of promise and focusing on the long-term winners, they may continue to survive and prosper.

General Electric has done an excellent job of transitioning the company over the past 30 years. *It has been able to blend together effectively risktakers, caretakers, surgeons, and undertakers.* Leaders at the GE business unit level have focused on markets and businesses that were consistent with their abilities and discarded others that did not fit. Today, GE's sales and earnings receive a greater contribution from plastics, aerospace, broadcasting, and financial services than from the company's traditional electrical, lighting, and consumer products. In fact, GE has become a major worldwide player in financial services. At the same time, the company enjoys evolutionary growth in such mature markets as lighting, power generation, materials, and major appliances. The surgeon's knife has been drawn to cut consumer electronics, housewares, mining, and other areas from the corporation. Finally, undertaker-style leadership has been employed to close down businesses that were not profitable or marketplace viable. We will return to GE throughout the book as a case study of transitional and multiple leadership styles.

After a surgeon separates the unproductive units from the mix, the company may need a strong risktaker to make the discarded pieces work. This is a dilemma created during many leveraged buyouts when, as is often the case, the core or unwanted pieces are taken over by the current management. Since in a leveraged buyout the new management puts up very little equity, with the vast majority funded by debt, a company may have 90 percent debt and very little equity. As a consequence, the new leaders must watch cash flow very closely and reduce the debt as quickly as possible. Thus, they are often unable to invest in new products, services, equipment, or other critical resources for the future. They become caretaker defenders because they can't afford to be risktaker growers. This wrong form of leadership is fatal. The company is forced to live day by day, merely delaying the inevitable decline and death.

The medical analogy is to a patient who can live only with the help of a respirator or kidney machine. In the later half of 1989, a number of highly leveraged retailers, banks, food companies, and insurance firms that depended on junk bond financing and the constant generation of cash flow entered into the respirator stage. Several of them were not able to recover and had to be liquidated. They had reached the end of their seasonal cycles.

CUSTOMER TYPES

The second factor to consider in determining the most appropriate type of strategic leader is the nature of the customer. The chemistry between buyer and seller is critical. In simple terms, the risktaker must be able to find customers or users who will share the risk by trying unproven products or systems. Selling to conservative users, on the other hand, will take more time and resources than the risktaker probably has to spend. Similarly, conservative caretaker leaders mix well with conservative customers. The leader's task is keeping the customer satisfied with the status quo because a disenchanted customer may go looking for new ideas and approaches. Interestingly, the surgeon also needs risktaker customers, who are willing to chance that restructuring will not do away with the unit that serves them, at least not until their needs have been met. The undertaker requires customers that can get their needs met by others or are willing to purchase from the merged organization.

Risktaker Leaders Need Risktaker Customers

Many major inventions of a hundred years ago succeeded because of business users, distributors, and consumers who were willing to take a chance and try something new. The people, who bought an early automobile or installed one of the first telephones or electric lamps were risktakers in their own right. Perhaps they enjoyed being different or perceived as trendsetters; often they were just enamored of the new technology. Today they might be called autophiles or telephonphiles or electrophiles. Perhaps these consumers shared the innovators' vision of the potential of the product or service.

Risktaker innovators must find such customers willing to experiment. This may be easier with consumer products than those with business or industrial applications. Consumer products are not only less expensive, the customers are not betting the future of their company with the purchase. In the early days, if the automobile wasn't up to expectations, consumers could junk it and go back to the horse and buggy or public transportation. They may have lost a little money and heard a bit of laughter from friends and neighbors, but they suffered no serious hurt. The same was true for electric lights and telephones in the good old days—and with personal computers, CD players, and new menu items at a favorite restaurant today. The excitement and adventure easily justify the slight risk. Thus, the consumer markets are more conducive to experimentation. And there is also the law of averages: More purchases mean more market "tests"; and the more tests there are, the more likely the risktaker will succeed.

The industrial, business, governmental, or health care risktaker faces a greater challenge. These professional consumers are normally more conservative and deliberate in their purchases because they have more at stake. The process of adopting and switching to a new product or service is costly and complex. Converting from a manual to a computerized accounting system or from a manual to a computerized manufacturing system may have an immediate impact on the cost of doing business. If the buyer guesses wrong and the innovation doesn't work, the business could fail. Using new drugs or medical equipment, obviously, represents major risks. That is why a long process of multiple approvals is required in the health care industry. However, this process delays the use of the product, which means the innovator accrues costs but no revenue from sales.

One way around the difficulty of finding enough risktaking customers is for the innovator to reduce the risks. Consider the strategy of Thomas Watson, Jr., former leader of IBM. Watson recognized the difficulty of convincing companies to convert to IBM computers. Because his firm was cash rich, Watson was able to offer potential customers attractive guarantees as well as the option to lease machines rather than buy them. Once the IBMs were installed, the customers usually came to appreciate the great value of the computers to their businesses. Or in many cases, they had invested so much time and had made their operations so dependent on the machines, they were not willing (or able) to switch back to the previous system.

The leasing strategy erected a major barrier to entry for other computer companies and gave IBM a significant competitive advantage. For a long time, leasing was IBM's strategic driver. A common business axiom held that "no MIS [management information systems] manager ever got fired for selecting IBM equipment," but the managers knew they were vulnerable if they went with another vendor. The force of that dictum has faded with declining costs and the advent of micro- and minicomputers, but IBM continues to capitalize on the fear factor to maintain a dominant position in the market. Ironically, this dominance created by an innovative marketing strategy has inhibited the growth of many risktaking innovators in the mainframe and supercomputer business.

But the innovators are out there nonetheless. In the United States, hundreds, perhaps thousands, of new products are created every year. Contrary to popular rumor, the number of American innovators continues to grow. (In the early 1900s, it was suggested that the U.S. Patent Office should close down because everything possible had already been invented.) The problem for the risktaking leader is not with insufficient innovators, but rather with locating sufficient risktaking consumers in the marketplace—and finding them rapidly enough to prevent the innovator's business from failing.

Conservatives Love Conservatives

The caretaker leader seeks customers willing to pay for performance and service and not just for something different. Caretakers excel when their products have been tested and accepted and when their company is known for reliability. History tells of many cases where caretakers took over the risktakers and increased the size and profitability of the company. In the early 1920s, for example, most of the major companies were headed by professional caretaker leaders skilled in building institutions and teams that attracted individuals interested in a long-term career with the firm. These leaders concentrated on developing products that customers could count on and markets that were stable. General Motors, General Electric, AT&T, U.S. Steel, and the other Dow Jones companies were known for reliable, quality products. Customers had confidence because they knew they were dealing with established firms that would correct any problems in the products or systems they provided. Customers were also aware of the firm's extensive financial and human resource investment in research and development, which produced a continuing stream of new products and features. The mature companies provided a complete package of products, services, financing if needed, and long-term warranties that constituted a total solution to the customer's needs.

The operative word here is "predictability." It is what we prized in the earlier great U.S. companies, and it is what we applaud in Japanese firms today. The Japanese learned their lessons from those U.S. companies. The leaders were anonymous, because caretakers are content to have the company's name recognized and don't seek personal acclaim. Japanese and European leaders are, with a few exceptions, like that today. Most of us have never heard these names: Tadahiro Sekimoto of Nippon Electric Corporation (NEC), Kentaro Aikawa of Mitsubishi Heavy Industries, Ryuzabouro Kaku of Canon, or Katsushige Mita of Hitachi. We know the names and reputations of the companies, but not their caretaker leaders.

Caretakers prosper when customers accept what they offer without demanding significant changes. However, caretakers have problems when customers begin looking primarily for new features or applications. Caretakers also have a hard time when the market is too mature and what they have for sale has become a commodity.

Surgeons and Undertakers Want Customers Who "Believe"

Surgeon and undertaker leaders need to find customers who are, like themselves, calculated risktakers. They need people who are willing to bet on the surgeon's ability to cut out the right products and services. That is, they are able to believe the leader will meet the company's contractual commitments in the short run—and, they hope, for the long run as well.

The strength of this belief is highly dependent on how important the product or service is to the customer. A stable source of supply is an absolutely critical component, even if that means producing the component yourself, even though it's more economical to purchase from someone else. In this situation, surgeon leaders must be able to prove that they can do the job and at a competitive price and response time. That's a hard sell.

If, however, the component, product, or service is not critical to the customer, then the surgeon leader might be able to persuade the customer to believe the company can do the job, particularly if there is an alternative, backup source of supply. Again, the surgeon must make sure the company can be competitive on price and delivery. This situation is difficult because the customer is in control. The surgeon has no choice, however, but to seek out customers willing to take the risk and hope they will be together for a long time.

Exceptions, There Are Always Exceptions

We have seen that the leader and the customer are often of similar type: risktakers sell to risktakers, caretakers to other conservatives, surgeons to customers who also are willing to, or have to, take calculated risks. There are some exceptions, however.

A conservative customer might buy a new product or service from a risktaking producer if the offering is not critical to them. Such a situation might arise, for example, in the substitution of new materials in certain consumer products. The purchaser of a portable radio may not care whether the radio is made out of a certain type of material as long as the radio plays well enough, is easy to carry, and doesn't cost too much. Thus, the manufacturer of the new material may be in a risktaking mode but the end user of the product is not.

A change in the industry, marketplace, or regulatory environment can force consumers of any type to make a purchase regardless of style of leader in charge of the vendor of the moment. The regulatory prohibition of asbestos in construction materials has forced many companies to purchase a substitute, in some cases one they don't know as well. Environmental concerns have also forced electrical utilities to experiment with new sources of energy when traditional fossil fuel and nuclear generation units are outlawed, as they are in some parts of the world.

Ultimately, the lesson for an astute leader is to understand the nature and motivations of the customers to determine where they are on the risk curve. Leaders should seek out customers who are most receptive to their products and services, avoiding mismatched styles, except in a few special cases. The success of the business is at stake.

COMPETITION TYPES

The nature and type of the competition can be significant in the selection of the right kind of leader. In contrast to the customer factor where likes attract, opposites flourish in the ideal competitive situation.

Risktakers: Anybody But Another Risktaker

Risktakers are more successful when they compete against caretakers, surgeons who make the wrong cuts, or undertakers who act prematurely. They are more likely to run into trouble when in direct, hand-to-hand combat with other high-rolling risktakers.

During Steve Jobs's early days at Apple Computer, the company's innovative offering was dismissed by the dominant vendor in the industry, IBM, as a fad or a toy. IBM was managed by conservative caretaker leaders who were content with their firm's growth and profitability. These competent managers understood quite well that IBM made its money from large mainframe computers sold to large, information-intensive, global companies, governments, and institutions. They were less interested in the uncertain profits of mini- and microcomputers. Consequently, leadership at IBM watched with only slight concern, and slight amusement, as Jobs introduced his personal computer (PC). Jobs took advantage of the casual response of his competitors to build a multimillion-dollar industry.

In time, IBM established a position in the market. How? The giant, conservative company selected one of its own, Philip D. Estridge, a risktaker leader to head the PC division. On the assumption that this was a distinct business that would not affect other IBM lines, the "internal risktaker" was given the freedom necessary to make IBM competitive in PCs. Estridge moved his organization to Florida, away from the bureaucracy of IBM corporate headquarters in Armonk, New York. He assembled a dynamic, entrepreneurial team of risktakers, and they developed a product good enough to move IBM into the top position in the PC market in just a few years. The internal risktaker succeeded because he had drive and a willingness to work in nontraditional ways. For instance, he "sourced" many of the machine's components outside the company, thus making IBM more of a systems integrator than it had been in the past.

IBM is not alone; many large companies harbor risktaker leaders. These internal risktakers labor just as precariously as independents, but without the recognition and the glory. They stake their careers on the conviction they can succeed by operating counter to the corporate culture. Estridge was so successful in growing PC's market share that the PC started to eat into the more profitable IBM mainframe business. IBM took steps to curtail this success. They promoted him to corporate staff and replaced him with a more traditional IBM manager. It is interesting to note that in 1992 IBM has again created a PC business unit with the license to compete and win in this market, even if it hurts the other IBM businesses.

Another famous example of risktakers prospering when they compete against caretakers occurred in the auto industry. The Japanese successfully entered the market because the "Big Two" (Chrysler was not a real force) were not concerned with small cars. General Motors and Ford viewed small cars as small-profit items useful only in filling out their lines. Thus, they permitted the new risktakers, Toyota and Nissan, to gain a beachhead. As we all know now, that was a damaging mistake.

Toyota and Nissan were risktakers in much the same way IBM was, that is, outside their traditional markets. Both Nissan and Toyota had caretaker leaders in their home country. The venture into the American market was risky because the Japanese government (MITI) did not support the auto industry in its export push. Further, the companies had tried once before to penetrate the U.S. market and failed. Initially, Japanese cars were low priced and low quality, and they sold very poorly. The second time around, Toyota and Nissan would not risk their excellent reputations at home with anything but top-quality offerings abroad. They reasoned that even a small share of the enormous American market was a prize, and the U.S. manufacturers were practically giving that away. But what started as a 5 percent share has grown to 30 percent. Moreover, the Japanese firms have begun to move into the more profitable mid-size and luxury cars. The risktakers have established such a strong position that they threaten all segments of the market.

And still another outsider has gotten into the picture. Honda Motors defied the Japanese government order to stick to motorcycles and made inroads in the U.S. auto market against both American and Japanese companies. Honda was also a risktaker when it became the first Japanese automakers to build a plant in the United States. This strategic decision, which other Japanese firms thought made poor economic sense, permitted Honda to get a lasting foothold in the United States, where it has become the third largest auto company.

Another good illustration of how risktakers love to compete against caretakers can be found in the office equipment field. Xerox, led by Joseph C. Wilson, was able to take on and defeat the incumbent suppliers of copiers. The caretaker managements at A.B. Dick (the mimeograph technology leader) and at Kodak (the wet-copy leader) were not impressed with the dry-copy technology Xerox was pioneering. In fact, they joined other major firms in declining to purchase and develop the Battelle patents on xerography. Even the usually innovative 3M Company, the leader in thermographic copier technology, was unable to respond and did not recognize the threat posed by Xerox until too late. Typically, market leaders ignore or underestimate the potential of innovative offerings in their fields; they are disinclined to give up an established strong position.

Ironically, Xerox followed the same path years later when it was the entrenched leader and proved unprepared to repel the advances made by the Japanese in the small, portable copier market. As at GM and IBM, Xerox's second generation caretaker leadership was not interested in cannibalizing what had always been a profitable line and so permitted a competitor to gain a foothold on the lower end of the market. Interestingly, Xerox also dropped the ball with personal computers. They had the early lead in printers and had plans for a machine much like what eventually became the Macintosh personal computer.

The story is repeated throughout the history of a variety of industries. Alfred Land created and dominated the billion-dollar market of instant photography when Kodak ignored his innovative camera and film development process. Wal-Mart and KMart, innovators in volume discount retail sales, were underestimated by the established industry giants, to their sorrow. Now the "marts" are the leaders, and even Sears is trying to compete as a discounter.

The pattern is always the same. The incumbent caretaker leaders become complacent. They are so enamored with managing by the numbers and optimizing margins that they fail to recognize that a risktaker innovator may have a better product or service. Thus underestimated, the risktaker can gain a beachhead in a market segment the caretaker considers to be trivial. Once given entry, however, the risktaker takes advantage by moving into the middle and higher profitability segments. Sometimes, the risktaker displaces the caretaker and repeats the same errors. This cycle is further proof that leaders must either change with changing conditions, or be replaced.

Of course, not every risktaker wins. The story of Preston Tucker versus the Big Three automakers (Chrysler *was* big way back then) is a case in point. Tucker developed an innovative car that had front-wheel drive, four-wheel steering, high-performance engines, and such safety features as air bags, seat belts, and impact-resistant frames. The car was too good for its own good. Tucker got the attention of the entrenched car companies, they counterattacked, and he went out of business. Henry Kaiser also developed innovative and economical autos after World War II, but he, too, was unable to compete against the power of the Big Three and went under.

Tucker made a large mistake that has ramifications for all risktakers trying to invade a mature market. Tucker publicly attacked the large automakers, asserting that they were not interested in safety and should be indicted for negligence. The Big Three were forced to respond; they hauled Tucker into court and eventually beat him down. Had he followed the Japanese strategy of not antagonizing the giants, there might be Tucker cars on the road today. The moral of the story is that the risktaker should not make the venture even more risky by angering the industry leaders or making them feel threatened. Let sleeping caretakers lie.

Caretaker Leaders Must Exploit the Timing Advantage

If risktakers compete best against caretakers, then when do caretakers win? Caretakers win when they go up against any of three types of adversaries, each of whom lacks the leadership attribute of timing. Specifically,

1. *Caretakers can be victorious against premature harvesters.* These managers concentrate on short-term growth rates. They become so dedicated to "making the numbers" they lose sight of the reality behind the numbers. They are portfolio managers geared only to attracting investors and interested only in investment analysis. They push for continuing compounding of earnings per share and other measures that are supposed to maximize the stock price. They espouse shareholder value rather than a balance of the many stakeholder values. Indeed, the employee and customer shareholders are often left out of their calculations. Ultimately, the company declines and must be harvested prematurely.

   In contrast, caretaker leaders avoid this one-sided managing and invest in the future of the business through a strategy of evolutionary growth. In the long run, they will win the battle against harvesting managers.

2. *Caretaker leaders prevail over risktakers who try to do too much, too soon.* Simple miscalculations can be the source of the risktaker's trouble, so can letting your words run ahead of your ability to

act. Preston Tucker suffered from both of these handicaps. His innovative car had so many new features that it was difficult and costly to make. Thus, he had trouble delivering on what he promised. Further, many of these features were ahead of their time, that is, in advance of most consumer's needs and expectations. Tucker might have been a winner in the 1980s and 1990s; but in the 1940s, car owners were satisfied with what Detroit was offering.

3. *Caretaker leaders defeat the impatient asset stripper.* The surgeon/undertaker who acts prematurely creates a confused and demoralized organization. The caretaker leader can take advantage and make major gains in the marketplace at this competitor's expense. In the capital goods industry, for example, American companies headed by impatient asset strippers have disappeared, and their positions have been taken over by European and Japanese firms headed by caretaker leaders.

However, caretakers are not always interested in driving out competitors and gaining market share simply for the sake of gaining share. Caretakers who understand the nature of the market are *not greedy* may *encourage other competitors* to participate and *share the wealth* of the growth. Giant companies often prefer to have segment or niche-focused competitors and may even refrain from entering those areas provided the nichers stay put and the niches do not grow too large. Should either of these conditions change, however, the caretaker leader must act decisively to drive the competitor out of business or back into its niche. That is the threat IBM and GM either failed to recognize or chose to ignore when Apple and Toyota/Nissan moved into the small computer/auto market niches of their respective industries. We know now that the risktaking aggressors were able to use those small niches to establish major competitive positions.

As a strategist at General Electric, I was able to demonstrate that GE business units were most successful when competing against other large electrical companies such as Westinghouse, Siemens, Hitachi, Toshiba, and General Electronic Corporation (UK). Each of these giants followed the same course of action as GE, diversifying into consumer products, consumer electronics, defense systems, computers, and other natural extensions of their core technologies. In fact, these products were often developed inside the company were spin-offs from the core. At GE, for example, aircraft engines were a deviation from gas turbines, silicones and plastics came from insulating materials, and the credit company was created to finance GE consumer products. GE combined these internal developments with selective, complementary acquisitions. The rare attempt at diversification solely through acquisition normally failed to meet financial or strategic expectations (for example, GE's purchase of Utah International). This link between the internal and the external makes GE and others "agglomerates" rather than "conglomerates," the label that attaches to International Telephone and Telegraph (ITT) and Litton.

All the major competitors in the electrical industry were managed by professionally trained caretaker leaders. The companies engaged in "womb to tomb" employee development; they hired people right out of college, trained them, evaluated them carefully, and rotated them among business units (and sometimes functions) throughout their careers. The top people were groomed for leadership in a disciplined and structured manner; they were taught to balance revenue and earnings growth and to take only calculated risks. Thus, the industry continued to be stable and predictable. Each company respected the others and tried to sell on the basis of service, quality, features, and technology, but never price.

However, this era of good feeling could not last forever. The markets grew less profitable and became less attractive when the incumbents decided to seek share more aggressively. GE and others also had a difficult time competing against small specialists led by skilled, focused, and innovative risktakers. Lincoln Electric was such a competitor who seemed to play be different rules and continually beat GE. Lincoln's edge was the innovative way leadership treated and rewarded employees; it provided profit-sharing that transformed employees at all levels from hired hands to partners. Lincoln Electronic was so tough a competitor it was able to get GE to withdraw from the business of making electric welding equipment, and this before the "portfolio theory" of jettisoning unproductive units made such retreats acceptable. Lincoln is still dominant in these markets and still considered a risktaking innovator in its motivation and rewards of employees at all levels.

An Exception for Computers?

Some may argue that the mainframe computer industry demonstrates that caretaker leaders can lose even when they compete against other caretaker leaders. However, I believe a closer look will reveal that the pattern holds here as well. When GE, Westinghouse, Siemens, and other electrical giants participated in the industry, they competed against the risktaking leadership of Thomas Watson, Jr., the man who "bet the company" by dramatically moving IBM from tabulation and keypunch equipment to computers and the data-processing market.

GE, Westinghouse, and their foreign look-alikes entered the computer market by building on their extensive know-how and resources (today called "core competencies" by many academics). The established electrical giants were much larger than IBM and had already developed technological applications for the military. Further, they were major computer users and even customers of IBM. Watson's company was therefore justifiably worried about facing this new and potentially formidable competition. It responded by launching a risky strategy of leasing rather than selling machines. IBM relied on its well-trained and knowledgeable sales force to push the strategy and its equally skilled service department to implement it. As I have recounted, IBM succeeded by making the choice of their computers a risk-free decision for MIS managers. The competitive advantage IBM gained with its marketing and financial strategy was one of the reasons GE and similar firms did not make an aggressive attempt to win the mainframe computer market.

The IBM case illustrates how managers and leaders are influenced by their past successes: Leasing equipment was also a critical component of IBM's growth in the keypunch and tabulation business. GE and Westinghouse, on the other hand, were uncomfortable with leasing their products; they had a long history of selling large generation, transmission, and distribution systems and subsystems to electrical utilities. Utilities were regulated, and the returns they were allowed were always related to the size of their investments. Therefore, electric utilities sought to increase their investments in equipment to increase their earnings. They were quite willing to make "progress payments" to the manufacturers even before the equipment was delivered. Further, companies like GE and Westinghouse had several other new ventures growing rapidly at the same time (nuclear power, gas turbines, and aerospace were a few), and so they were cash limited. In contrast, IBM was cash rich from its core businesses and was able to concentrate its resources on computers. Thus, it was financially and psychologically able to pursue the leasing strategy aggressively and so gain a competitive advantage.

Surgeons and Undertakers Rule the Ghost Town

The best competitive situation for surgeons and undertakers is a bit unusual, a bit more complex. In essence, they do best when there are no competitors or when those who remain to compete are focused on survival and being the "last out."

The surgeon leader in calculating the cuts he must make in his company, diagnoses the cash potential of the market and *the nature of the competition.* If the competitors are aggressive and highly committed, the surgeon will probably exit the game or focus on more favorable segments. There are two reasons. First, the expense of playing will be very high. Second, the surgeon realizes that his existing company may be able to sell its market share to an aggressive competitor at a premium price. The exception, as I have just noted, occurs when the market leader is a caretaker who wants to keep a weaker, subservient competitor in the business, perhaps to avoid antitrust litigation or the poor publicity associated with the giant killing the dwarf. In fact, the caretaker may help the surgeon stay afloat through "umbrella pricing," a practice that keeps prices high and permits less productive and efficient firms to remain profitable.

The approach can backfire, however, when it creates a market conducive to the entry attack of the risktaker. Before long, the business is inhabited by asset strippers who are more interested in reaping short-term profits than investing for the future and/or caretakers who are unwilling to be aggressive. The retail business is evolving into this type of market. Many of the large department store and discount chains have been taken over by asset strippers or harvesters. In situations where they have been forced to compete against committed risktakers such as Wal-Mart, or caretakers such as Sears, the asset strippers have, quite correctly, opted to bail out rather than fight.

STAKEHOLDER NEEDS

Selecting the style of leadership appropriate for an organization entails considering the needs and expectations of three stakeholder groups: the company's investors, its employees, and the community in which it operates, as well as the government with which it interacts.

Investors

The motivations and objectives of the various types of investors differ considerably. Venture capitalists are most interested in asset appreciation. They love risktaker innovators who offer a high probability of developing new markets or even new industries. As with risktaker leaders, they are willing to gamble to score big. Traditional bankers, on the other hand, appreciate caretaker leaders who can deliver a continuous stream of income and who pay off loans punctually with no problems. Finally, managers of retirement funds and mutual funds seek a mix of investments. They might want to blend in some steady growth with a portion of high cash flow, seasoned with a bit of risk.

Not only must the needs of the dominant type of investor shape the style of the company's leadership, but the strategic leaders must be responsive to the various needs of the different types of investors who have a financial interest in the company. Too often in the past, American firms have focused on "shareholder value" as a performance objective, a myopia that has led to short-term thinking and a shortage of risktaking leadership. In contrast, Japanese firms have had a longer term horizon, because their investors have been tradition-oriented major banks, often part of the same "keitsu" or cartel.

Japanese commercial banks have sought interest income from annuities. They have discouraged borrowing companies from paying off the principal of the loan. Indeed, the banks have been happy when the principal has increased, thus ensuring the continued flow of interest payments. The situation is analogous to consumer banks in the United States. American lending institutions have encouraged consumer credit card spending and home equity borrowing, with little concern for paying off the principal. The high interest rates make it attractive for banks to offer high credit lines and maximize use. The difference is that while U.S. institutions are promoting spending and consumer debt, Japanese commercial banks are following policies that allow Japanese companies to take the risk of making the long-term commitment necessary to gain market share.

Currently, the banks' focus on making interest payments means cash flow, not profitability, is key for Japanese firms. The situation may change, however, as Japanese companies increase their presence on the public stock exchanges in their own country and throughout the world. It will be interesting to see whether this increased dependence on stockholders will shorten the time frame for Japan's strategic leaders.

Risktakers Need Risktaking Investors

Innovations require the support of people who have long-time horizons and are willing to bet on future success. Venture capitalists have filled that role in the United States by investing in risky, start-up companies, They realize that only a percentage of their gambles will pay off. Their strategy has been to increase the capital appreciation of the investment. They hope to get in early and ride the value upward. The venture capital tradition dates back to such financial titans as J.P. Morgan, Andrew Mellon, John D. Rockefeller, Sr., and Andrew Carnegie.

Caretakers Are Good to Widows and Orphans

Caretakers require investors who are willing to take their returns incrementally, as though they were annuities. In a sense, these are the type of stockholders large companies bet on in the past. AT&T, GM, and GE were known as "widow and orphan" companies because they were ultrasafe investments for people who couldn't take any risks. Later, IBM joined the list, but recently they fell out of this category. They attract investors interested in a combination of incremental appreciation and, most importantly, continuing dividends. Managers of large funds also looked to invest in widow and orphan companies for their annuitylike returns. That was the situation in American business until the 1970s (and the same for Japanese firms during their great competitive rise, as just described). Since then, the short-term mentality focused on immediate payoff has predominated.

Surgeons and Undertakers Also Need Risktaking Investors

Investors who are willing to gamble on a company's survival will come to a firm led by a good surgeon/undertaker. These people will recognize that leadership must focus on cash flow and so will be content with getting the interest they have been promised. Leaders must then make sure the interest is paid and that it has a premium over the market. In these situations, leveraged buyouts financed by junk bonds are used. Skilled surgeons manage the portfolio to get high returns for their dispositions. If the timing of their asset sales is good, they can pay off investors with enough left over to invest in the other parts of the company. Having sufficient funds for reinvestment in the growth portions of the portfolio is critical to the survival of the company as a whole. Undertakers require investors who are willing to "cash out" and seek to invest elsewhere. However, this too must be carefully managed to maximize returns and prevent unexpected bankruptcy.

Employees

Leaders cannot succeed without the efforts of the employees who work on their teams. That seems an obvious truism, but it is ignored or given only lip service much too frequently in business. I will describe the character and functions of the teams of leaders of various styles in greater detail later in the book. Now we need to look at employees in general terms as stakeholders.

The goals and needs of employees are as varied as those of investors. Some desire a long-term relationship with the company; others are more interested in the short-term payoff. Some want security; others seek challenge and excitement. Some need a say in the business; others are content to take orders. Once again, its important for a firm to have its leadership style and employee requirements in harmony.

For instance, risktaker leaders will work better with employees motivated by the challenge and excitement of the job and the possibility of scoring a major hit. They can't be cautious or looking for short-term financial rewards. It is appropriate for members of the caretaker's team to be interested in long-term security, as long as they are willing to make sure short-term results are achieved. They must recognize, in other words, the need to manage the short term to optimize the long term. If caretaker employees can be classified as moderates, members of the surgeon's team would be pragmatists. They must understand they are in a survival mode and not get too attached to any particular part of the organization. They are more like risktakers than caretakers, but they are not geared to growth for growth's sake. Those attracted to the undertaker must be willing to either seek other opportunities or retire with the closure of the firm. Age can be vital. Those sixty years old who want to retire are often suited to this situation.

Governments and Local Communities

Some communities in the United States are totally incompatible with either the risktaker or the surgeon and undertaker styles of business. Entire industries have been destroyed or rendered ineffective because of that incompatibility. The coal industry, for instance, seems to be still fighting the battles of the 1930s. The miners, the mining communities, and the local and state governments are all locked into a caretaker mode at a time when the market, the competitive forces of the industry, and the prevailing economics all demand a change. A risktaker leader willing to transform the industry into something new and exciting may be the change. Or perhaps the change is a surgeon who can cut out the fat and the ineffective elements and concentrate on the winners. Whatever the answer, there will be a better chance of success if it can be made compatible with the communities.

Governments must also recognize that different leaders may be required for certain businesses or industries and adopt policies that fit those styles. Special legislation, regulation, or taxes might help a risktaker to get started or a surgeon to turn a company around. Flexibility and adaptability are key. Unfortunately, governments and the bureaucrats that run them are seldom flexible and adaptive. The trick, of course, is balancing the public trust, such as enforcing vital environmental regulations, with the public interest of a healthy business climate—stringent enforcement of strict regulations can destroy the risktaker or surgeon and make the caretaker a manager rather than a leader.

Ideally, community, government, and business should all be flexible, adaptive, and reasonable; that would make for a productive relationship. Not easy, to be sure. But sometimes we approach that objective, if only temporarily. The Chrysler bailout was such a short-run success.

The government was willing to make an exception to help a company survive. Iacocca was the ultimate surgeon, and his operation was successful because of the government's cooperation. In this case, the bankruptcy laws worked as they are designed to work. (Sometimes they enable the ruthless and greedy to profit. We won't have a perfect world until everybody is perfect.)

THE DYNAMICS OF TECHNOLOGY

Leadership must satisfy the specific needs defined by the life cycle of the business and the nature of the customers, the competition, and the various stakeholders. So matching the style of the leader to those factors is critical to the success of the organization. The final key characteristic to consider in determining the right type of leader is technology.

Technology will have a different importance for each leadership style. For instance, the risktaker is likely to be a technology-oriented person in a technological product-driven market. Risktakers need not be scientists, but they must have an appreciation for the capabilities and limitations of the technology of their industry. Indeed, since many of the new growth opportunities are based on technological breakthroughs or unique applications of existing technology, a risktaker who is not a technologist must have competent, down-to-earth technologists on the team or available for consultation.

Many risktakers have exploited a competitive advantage created by technology. It was the breakthroughs generated by Dr. Land's optical skills that made instant photography a success for Land Camera. Xerox developed and grew because of its application of xerography. Japanese consumer electronics firms have ridden their talents in developing the semiconductor and microprocessor technologies, which, incidentally, they licensed originally from American Telephone and Telegraph (AT&T).

The caretaker leader must understand relevant technology in detail sufficient to recognize change and anticipate threats. Caretakers need not be trained in technology, but they should be able to appreciate the implications of new technology. It is the new application, or even the breakthrough, that is potentially disruptive of the caretaker's predictable world of evolutionary, slow-change technology. Thus, they must be willing and able to monitor developments, evaluate possible threats to their position, formulate a response, and move only at the proper speed.

At the end of the business life cycle, technology is unlikely to be critical to surgeons or undertakers. The markets they serve should not be technologically intensive and should not require heavy or long-term investment. In fact, a technological change is probably one of the reasons their business is under attack or in decline. If the only solution for the business is improved technological sophistication, then a risk-taker leader should be brought in who can move the company in that direction.

A SENSE OF HISTORY

In order to lead, a leader must know where the organization has been.

All five factors have been considered, and a strategic leader has been found who fits the profile of the organization at the moment. One more item remains: He should know and understand the history and previous leadership style of the company. Leaders must be able to learn not only from their own successes and failures but from the triumphs and defeats of others associated with the company as well.

Suppose that a risktaker now heads a business that has been led by a long series of caretakers. The established corporate culture will be very different from the one the new leader must create. Decision making and daily operations will have to change from a disciplined, methodical, and systematic approach to a more flexible, spontaneous, and intuitive style. Even more extreme, what if the risktaker assumes control from a harvester, asset stripper, or premature surgeon? Team members will be very cautious and quantitative in their judgments and geared toward survival. They must be taught to think creatively and to seek ways to help the company grow.

All in all, the best situation is when the succession is to the same type of leader. The easiest transition occurs when a risktaker follows a risktaker, a caretaker follows a caretaker, and so on. Of course, much leadership succession is mandated by changing conditions, which implies a concomitant change in style. Therefore, a company needs to be alert to change to manage a smooth transition over time. An unanticipated, dramatic change is not only traumatic in itself, it usually requires quick action, which increases the chances of failure.

The central message is that timing and conditions will determine the success of the strategic leader. If the leader's style and skills are consistent with the life cycle of the business and they meet the needs of the customers, competitors, and shareholders, then the leader will be a winner—provided he has a feel for the technology of the industry and the history of the company. If his abilities are not consistent with those factors, however, then he must adapt his style to conditions, or fail. Or move on. The business environment is dynamic; either leaders change with the times, or new leadership must take control.

It is astonishing how often this logical truth is misunderstood or ignored. There is no single leader for all seasons.

THE RIGHT LEADER FOR THE RIGHT SEASON

Thus far, we have discussed the four types of strategic leader. But there is another crucial dimension to successful leadership. The strategic leader has an unfair competitive advantage in a positive sense that does not involve trickery, deceit, illegality, special favors, or inside information. The advantage comes not only from the leader's special talent, which becomes the company's strategic driver, but from an ability to move from vision to realization by means of a well-conceived game plan that the company team can effectively implement. The game plan is a combination of analysis and intuition. The team skills, interests, and motivations must fit the key characteristics of the game plan.

This book will discuss the following kinds of leaders:

- *Product Leaders.* These are innovators who revolutionize or evolve products or services. Those who invent something new or create something entirely different are in the risktaker category. Caretaker product leaders build on the innovation and keep it healthy and timely through maturity by adapting or adding as required by changing markets, competition, or technological needs. As the business declines, the surgeon salvages and reorients the product line through selectivity and pruning. At times, the undertaker might completely dismantle the offering, which may result in closing or selling the business in its entity.

- *The Problem-Solving Leaders.* These leaders are renowned for the ability to attack and solve formidable problems. These leaders are the great names in science, medicine, social welfare, and even commercial and military technologies. These are the risktakers of all risktakers. On the more conservative side, some leaders are able to apply solutions from one field to the problems of others in seemingly unrelated situations. These are the consultative caretaker leaders. Similarly, problem-solving surgeons are more focused and willing to give up some of their talents to emphasize fewer problems.

- *Missionary Sellers and Marketers.* These individuals create and evolve the marketing of products and services that other leaders provide. Their talent lies in getting people to purchase and in developing longer term relationships. These leaders are often risktakers that create entirely new ways of buying. The evolutionary caretakers who follow them continue the pattern. These talents may lie in selecting the right location, providing a new concept of selling, or even in offering the customer unique services and support.

- *System Network Builders and Production Experts.* In the current culture of the United States, these leaders are often not recognized for their genius. We take for granted the national networks and production systems that are essential to our lives. But these were once the innovative creations of visionary risktaker leaders, have been maintained and improved by caretakers, and have been key-fit by present-day surgeons.

PUTTING IT ALL TOGETHER

Each successful strategic leader is capable of going beyond the concept and vision and putting it all together with a sound consistent game plan and the right people to make it happen. The following chapters discuss in detail the key elements of successful game plans.

What Customers Are Buying

The first step in formulating the game plan (Figure 3.2) is to determine what the customers are really buying and what motivates them to buy. How the company sells can make the difference between success and failure. Thus, the leader needs to ask these six questions:

1. *What is the most effective sales force?* What skills will the sales force require to implement an intuitive and differentiated game plan? In some cases, the leader's game plan will require a unique, highly skilled, experienced staff that can solve problems and act as a consultant to the customer. In other situations, salespeople need only be "order takers" and can even be part of another (distributor or retailer) organization.

2. *What is the best way to reward the sales force?* All successful leaders recognize that the reward and measurement systems must conform to strategy and driver of the business. This will include an assessment of the risk and the complexity of the offering.

3. *How will the product be priced?* A company can be a price leader, a follower, or even unconcerned about its price levels. Prices can be

A STRATEGIC GAME PLAN
The questions that need to be addressed

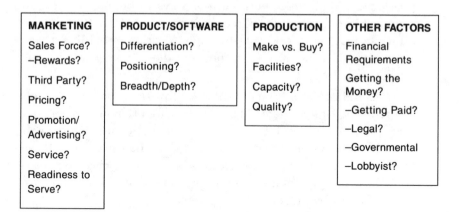

MARKETING	PRODUCT/SOFTWARE	PRODUCTION	OTHER FACTORS
Sales Force?	Differentiation?	Make vs. Buy?	Financial Requirements
–Rewards?	Positioning?	Facilities?	Getting the Money?
Third Party?	Breadth/Depth?	Capacity?	–Getting Paid?
Pricing?		Quality?	–Legal?
Promotion/ Advertising?			–Governmental
Service?			–Lobbyist?
Readiness to Serve?			

Figure 3.2   "Strategic Game Plan."

based on real or perceived value, on cost, or on some predetermined margin or profit requirements. The leader must determine whether financial terms and conditions can dictate success or failure and must realize that pricing should be appropriate to the company's customer base and competitive situation as well as consistent with its strategic differentiation.

4. *How should the product be promoted and advertised?* Leaders recognize that companies must develop and maintain customers, establish a continuing relationship with them, and remind them of available products and services. They have the insight that the message and theme need to reinforce the product being sold as well as the company's image.

5. *What services and support will assure customer satisfaction?* The leader must determine whether services should be bundled with the offering at time of sale, and, if so, for how long; whether they should be included in the initial price or cost extra, whether the company or some third-party servicer should provide the services. Applications and problem-solving leaders view continuing service as a means of maintaining the relationship, while sales-driven leaders might consider service as a separate profit center and only offer it when required.

6. *What is the "readiness to serve"?* The leader must decide how fast the company should respond to the customers' demands and must determine whether the company's degree of responsiveness will require inventory and where it will be stocked. Some drivers

require expensive and highly technical logistical systems. This has become a major differentiator for the sales leaders.

What the Company Sells

The second aspect of the game plan deals with what the company sells, namely its product and service offerings. Leaders must deal with three strategic issues to assure fit with their unique driver.

1. *How should the offering be differentiated?* Product differentiation is an integral part of all strategies but varies in importance from one leader to another. For instance, the sales leader might have products that are similar to all others but will sell them in a different way. An applications leader and a problem-solving leader may package the product differently to solve the problem. Thus, this decision is key to a successful leader.

2. *How should the product be positioned in the marketplace?* Positioning can vary from one leader to another. For the product-driven innovative leader, the product must be truly a trendsetter. In the case of the product driven caretaker, the product might be in the follower category and still be successful.

3. *What should be the breadth and depth of the product and service offering?* Most leaders must be selective in what they offer. Some applications problem solvers might need access to a very deep and broad line, whereas the product innovator should have a narrow and selective line at its early stage of development, since the product will still be in a rapid change mode. The message is the same. Leaders need to know what is critical and what makes sense for them to implement their unique competitive advantage, or driver.

How Products or Services Are Produced

The third area of consideration in developing a successful game plan focuses on how the products or services are produced. The leader must probe the following questions.

1. *What should be made and what should be sourced from others?* The systems and network leader may require more control over the entire system and therefore be required to make many of the key parts within the company. However, the applications and problem solver can be more dependent on products or components

provided by others. The leader must determine how much of the entire manufacturing cycle the company should control.

2. *Where should the production facilities be located?* Because, for some leaders, cost is the key element to success, they make or source the product from low labor cost areas, such as Malaysia. Other leaders, who require quick response and high levels of quality, make the product closer to their markets. This decision must be based on the leader's driver and not just on some trend or belief that cost is the only criterion for success.

3. *How much capacity is required?* This decision relates directly to the market and competitive situation. Leaders must be aware of the levels of capacity required to meet demand and not get trapped into adding capacity just for a safety valve.

4. *What level of quality is appropriate?* Many would argue that this is an inappropriate question. They believe that quality must always exceed the customer expectations. I have seen a number of companies suffer because they overengineered their products and gave customers more than they needed and were willing to pay for. Companies have gone out of business because they made products that lasted so long that the market disappeared. A key part of any strategy is that customer expectations must be met, and the leader must be involved in determining and even influencing those expectations.

Other Critical Issues

The leader must determine the financial requirements and strategies critical to the game plan; that is, make sure that the company gets paid for the products, can pay its bills, and always has enough cash to stay alive. We will demonstrate how these characteristics vary from one leader to another and are dependent on the leader's driver and type. Having the best lawyers and lobbyists might be vital to the success of some leaders.

Regardless of type or style, all leaders possess "unfair" competitive advantages that reside in their special talents and are manifested in the strategic drivers of their companies. Once they understand their particular edge, leaders consciously and intuitively develop the right and most viable game plan and enlist, motivate, and retain the right people to make up the teams that can implement those strategic game plans. If leaders have good timing and can sustain their efforts for the long haul, they will succeed. That is, they will fulfill their vision and assure that the company survives and prospers over time.

PART
TWO

THE PRODUCT LEADERS

Chapter 4 discusses product driven risktakers. These leaders are able to determine a need before the customer recognizes it. They are willing to bet their careers, personal wealth, and reputation on developing innovative products. Successful risktakers often create new markets and even industries. Their team and game plan focuses on the product and its uniqueness. Timing is critical to success.

Product caretakers are the focus of Chapter 5. These leaders put in place the systems and team that enable the innovative product to become a real and sustainable business. They recognize the need to invest in the future needs and wants of the customer and not be complacent. They realize the reality of competition and need to defend and keep ahead of the competitors. Though profitability is a key measure and provides funding, it is not the end in itself. They recruit and staff team players, not superstars.

In Chapter 6, the discussion of surgeons and undertakers points out that surgeon leaders are realists and must be totally objective. Their mission is to select the best of the product line and discard the rest. They are the restructurers. Many of them are outsiders, but they still have the desire to ensure the institution's survival, even if it is smaller. Undertakers must be able to take the final step in the closing of the business. This may involve closing down the company or having it taken over by others. In this case, the company loses its identity and becomes part of another company.

4

Risktakers: The Product Is the Passion

Americans, Japanese, Germans, indeed, people everywhere are fascinated with the successful inventor. A creative new product is a tangible and constant manifestation of genius.

I feel the wonder every time I use my Macintosh to write, edit, draw, calculate, and so on. I labored on my first book in 1974 without benefit of this amazing and versatile tool. I experienced the pain of writing in longhand, having the manuscript typed, having it edited, retyped, and on and on. I worked with other people for untold, and expensive, hours to arrive at something that was good enough to send to the publisher. Now, thanks to the genius of Steven Jobs, Stephen Wozniak, and Bill Gates, I have a machine and software that greatly reduce the time, expense, and support staff needed to complete the task. Their innovative products have not only improved my productivity and reduced the agony, they have changed the way I work and even the way I think.

This chapter explores the attributes of such innovative product developers. I will describe their leadership qualities, concentrating on how they formulate a game plan and how they put together a team.

First, however, I want to relate the stories of a few product innovators. A couple are famous; others are as anonymous as the inventors of the lathe, punch press, or screwdriver. *All were risktaker leaders driven to create something new and offer it to the world.* Some sought to go beyond a single product; they wanted to create entirely new systems and enable interaction between systems. These are the people who set new standards for their business or industry.

GEORGE EASTMAN PICTURES THE FUTURE

The pioneering work of George Eastman led to the development of the mass photography market. Eastman invented the dry-plate method of photography and set up his own company in 1884. Four years later, he introduced his first camera: "a small, easy to use device that sold for $25 with enough film for 100 pictures."[1] Camera owners mailed the film to the company, now Eastman Kodak, to be developed. The pictures were returned with more film. By the end of the century, Eastman had developed the Brownie camera, which turned out to be very successful. In 1923, Kodak introduced a home-movie camera, projector, and film. Under Eastman's leadership, Kodak had created a new mass market. Kodak was able to expand worldwide by licensing the technology to other companies. Kodak also invested heavily in a mass-produced camera and in improving the quality of the film. As a result, the firm made money not just on the camera, but on the film, the film processing, and the processing equipment.

STEVEN JOBS RIDES AGAIN

Three years after being forced out at Apple, Steve Jobs, a determined risktaking innovator, had started a new computer company, called Next, Inc. Jobs's second attempt at bringing a startling new product to market reportedly began with extensive funding, including an investment by H. Ross Perot, another famous risktaker. Reflecting a growing maturity, Jobs has been willing to seek, listen to, and even accept ideas from others. This approach differs from his style at Apple, where he was reputed to be impervious to staff input. Also encouraging has been Jobs's willingness to focus on a single vertical market: higher education.

However, he has not abandoned his desire to have a unique and perfect computer. In fact, some believe his new computer is the best in the world. It has a more efficient design, built around a single circuit board, which increases its speed. It also has 6 to 10 times more storage capacity. The "Next" computer offers quality sound and sharper images; it comes with a cheaper printer and is easier to program.

But a sound innovative process and a superior product still does not guarantee success. Next must overcome the resistance of some formidable competitors to establish a beachhead in the higher education market. The entrenched leaders are, ironically, Apple, with 35 percent share; IBM, with 22 percent, and Zenith (now part of Bull) at 11 percent. These firms are not likely to let Jobs penetrate the market as easily as he did with Apple many years ago. Even great risktaker leaders like Jobs do not always win, as earlier legends have known.[2]

EDWIN LAND BATS .500

Dr. Edwin Land of Polaroid was a great risktaker innovator who was not able to replicate his first successes. In 1947, after over 20 years of research and study had produced the first synthetic material for polarizing light, the company Land had formed to exploit his discovery unveiled an instant-picture camera, known as the Polaroid. By 1956, the company had sold a million of them. The introduction of color film in 1960 helped make Polaroid the second largest producer of photographic equipment, with film revenues exceeding those of the camera.[3] It was a wonderful success story.

Unfortunately, the sequel had a less happy ending. Land's motion picture version of instant photography was a market failure. Land's product had a short playing and recording time and required a second camera to project the pictures. At the same time, the Japanese competition was coming out with something better. Sony and Matsushita introduced the Beta and VHS systems, respectively, that enabled people to take motion pictures for two hours and then play them instantly on a standard television receiver. Land had been defeated. He had the wrong product at the wrong time.

SOME RISKTAKERS STAY OUT
OF THE LIMELIGHT

Not all risktakers who succeed in marketing innovative products—often working alone and with limited resources—make the headlines.

One such person you may not have heard of is Andy Hertzfeld. A key software designer for Macintosh computers, he left Apple to work for a Silicon Valley start-up company called Frox. Frox was founded in 1988 by Hartmut Esslinger, a West German, who had helped devise the striking ergonomic look of most Apple personal computers and the Next, Inc, machine. The company is building a home information center that Hertzfeld hopes will become the world's finest TV and stereo combination. The system is clever enough to read the TV listings and select and record programs. It can also edit out commercials. It catalogs and plays CDs on computer and displays the cover art and liner notes for each disk on the TV screen. The built-in computer is as powerful as an engineering workstation. Soon the machine will have the capability to monitor electronic databases for news and other information of particular interest to the owner, while at the same time it will be able to answer the telephone, watch for incoming electronic mail, and control the home appliances.[4]

And there are more wonders in store from innovative risktakers. The Media Lab of the Massachusetts Institute of Technology is organizing an American, European, and Japanese consortium of major computer, consumer electronics, and telecommunications concerns to set standards for the television of tomorrow. The ultimate goal is to integrate personal computers and televisions into one system.

Product innovations in the 1970s and 1980s, and not all of them from risktaker style leaders, have come from the fields of computers and electronics. In the 1990s, we may find significant new products and systems developed by companies dedicated to biotechnology and chemicals. Thus, the technology factor in determining leadership style, as discussed in Chapter 3, looms large in the years ahead.

THE WINNING INTUITIVE GAME PLAN FOR THE RISKTAKER INNOVATOR

Success for a company begins with the leader's vision and the strategic driver he believes will provide the competitive edge. The pattern of actions required to implement the vision and driver is the leader's game plan. Note that I have called it "intuitive." A leader of any type needs a high level of intuition to complement objective evaluation and analysis. Without intuition there is no leadership.

In subsequent chapters, I will outline and detail the functioning of the particular game plans of the various types of leaders. Here, the focus is on the intuitive game plan of the risktaker leader whose strategic driver is product innovation. The product risktaker's game plan consists of nine actions or plays:

1. Recognize a need before the customer does.
2. Protect the innovation against pirates.
3. Educate customers about the value of the innovation.
4. Be prepared for success.
5. Assure money and people are available.
6. Maintain consumer demand.
7. Maintain quality, regardless of cost.
8. Price to reinforce uniqueness, without being greedy.

9. Have the next innovation ready on the shelf, even if it makes the current offering obsolete.

Play 1. Recognize a Need before the Customer Does

The first element of the game plan is the concept of a new product or service that does not yet exist or, at least, is not well developed. The strategic innovator must then conceive a need or want that can be met before it is generally articulated by a potential set of customers. Perhaps the leader's own frustrations or desires will furnish the inspiration; that is, something that would satisfy the leader might satisfy others. This task is reflected in An Wang's business philosophy of "Find a need and fill it." The need Wang found was met by his innovative desktop calculator, which was the launching pad for further successes.

Sarnoff and Color Television.   General David Sarnoff was an innovative risktaker who created and developed the American color television broadcasting system. He was able to visualize the potential of converting from black and white to color because he realized the product would generate a demand far beyond people's expectations at the time. Sarnoff made the Radio Corporation of America (RCA) the leader in the development of broadcast equipment, in the television broadcasting network, in programming, and in television receivers. RCA created a standard that was accepted in the United States, although Europe set a higher standard for color quality and clarity.

Under Sarnoff's leadership, RCA invested heavily in broadcast equipment and consumer color receivers, that is, the system of color broadcasting. RCA's National Broadcasting Corporation (NBC) also invested heavily in the development of quality programming to stimulate the demand for color broadcasting and the subsequent displacement of the existing black and white system. Having created the demand, Sarnoff was ready with the products and the system for delivering them. By defining the industry, he was able to establish standards that have lasted for 25 years; his adversaries at GE and Westinghouse were forced to follow behind. (Incidentally, the patents and technology for color television were developed at Westinghouse labs; they were awarded to RCA, through Sarnoff's negotiation, as part of a successful antitrust suit.)

The Sony Success Story.   One of my favorite contemporary innovative product leaders is Akio Morita of Sony. Morita has made Sony the pacesetter in solid-state television sets, tape recorders, and transistor radios. Sony's radio was launched after Morita paid Western Electric $25,000 in the 1950s for technology licenses.[5] It is just one example of the company's innovative application of another's technology. In fact, Morita refers to his company as a "guinea pig," because it tries out products that have not yet been marketed. (I call that being a risktaker leader.) The giants of the industry have often let Sony experiment, while they stand aside and observe whether customers and retailers accept the products. (This "wait and see" attitude is characteristic of the caretaker leader, discussed in Chapter 5.)

Given room to innovate, Morita has led the way in VCRs (with Beta technology, since eclipsed by VHS), creating unique television screens that made Sony a preferred quality set for over a decade, and produced the Walkman, a highly portable radio and tape player (today, compact disk player). Morita's vision of innovative, high-quality, value-priced products has made Sony a winner worldwide (70 percent of sales come outside Japan). Because of the brutal competition in consumer electronics, Sony has moved into new fields, which today represent 50 percent of sales. For instance, Sony offers video systems for communications in the workplace. The user dictates memos and sends them with voice commands, to be viewed on a screen in another room. In the offing is a Walkman-size screen that would allow users to view file documents while away from the office. Sony also was the first to offer a 32-bit desktop computer, which is the heart of a complete workstation. Finally, there is interactive video that can be used for demonstrations and simulations. Such innovations are possible, in part, because Sony invests heavily in research and development, equal to 9 percent of sales.[6]

In addition to diversification, it appears that Morita is now preparing to replicate the success of Sarnoff at RCA. That is, he wants control not only of the system but the output of that system. For RCA, that meant TV equipment and TV shows; for Sony that means TV receivers and Walkmans and what is played on them. Morita learned this lesson in his attempt to lead in the videocassette market. Sony innovated the video recorder and tried to standardize the industry around Beta technology. However, Matsushita developed the rival VHS technology and was more aggressive than Sony in licensing it to other manufacturers. Thus, VHS became the industry standard and gained dominant world share of the video market. Consequently, motion picture production companies offered more films and programs in VHS than Beta, eventually rendering the old format next to useless.

Sony does not want to repeat this experience. Thus, it hopes to dominate the emerging HDTV (high definition television) market. It acquired Columbia Motion Pictures in preparation for the upcoming battle in this arena. Besides being a major player in the production and consumer equipment, Sony will have control over a significant number of programs that are critical to the success of the new technology. Morita's strategy is a replay of Sarnoff's game plan for control of color television. One indication of the soundness of Sony's approach is imitation by its competitor: Matsushita has recently purchased MCA as a source of programing.

The Need for a Total Game Plan.   In reading the biographies of these great innovators, it is often difficult to determine whether they recognized a need first and then sought a solution (as I have suggested), or whether they had a product and were looking for a market. Regardless of which came first, however, it is vital to develop other parts of the game plan. Consider the biotechnology industry: Companies such as Genentech, Neurogen, Centocor, and Chiron have been trying to use their scientific capabilities to create revolutionary cures for the treatment of major diseases and ailments. In most cases, they have the techniques and are trying to apply them to specific diseases. More information about innovators in these areas is included in Chapter 7.

Matching Need with Price.   Videoconferencing is another example of a product/service that arrived on the market ahead of demand. Rather, there was no demand at the price available. For decades, large companies and government agencies have wanted a method of holding meetings that didn't require people to travel to congregate in one place. AT&T pushed videoconferencing as the solution. However, most firms were unwilling to invest $500,000 for the equipment and facilities to set up a system or pay the $1,000 an hour it cost to transmit.

PictureTel Corp., a start-up company in Peabody, Massachusetts, has developed a system that permits a company to do away with the studio. Its system, costing as little as $34,000 a site, includes a color monitor, a two-way audio system, and a video "condec," all hooked up to a common telephone line. The condec compresses the video signal, thereby significantly reducing the cost of transmission. Another advantage is that the system is driven by software rather than hardware. The founders (Hinman and Berstein) and the investors (Kyocera, a Japanese distributor, and Accel Partners, a venture capital firm) hope not only to develop the business market, but ultimately to place the system in homes as a supplement to the telephone.[7] Already, PictureTel has formed alliances with several telephone companies. Their innovation is a product that meets a need *at the right price.*

Play 2. Protect the Innovation against Pirates

Many risktaker innovators become so excited about their innovation that they overlook or underestimate the need to protect it by legal means in as many countries as possible. They should gain strong patent positions in the United States and each developed country. That may mean filing early and as broadly as allowed, because, as *Forbes* noted in a 1991 article, broad patents granted by the U.S. Patent Office, in the name of protecting intellectual property, have held up in court. The magazine speculates that this trend is a reaction to the situation during the 1960s and 1970s when judges and juries invalidated patents for very flimsy reasons.[8]

However, unscrupulous companies deliberately violate patents and willingly run the risk of being caught and fined. They do so because they realize that (1) many small entrepreneurs are underfunded and don't have the money to fight a long legal battle, (2) the courts are so slow that even a verdict favorable to the innovator can arrive after the market has become saturated and share is hard to regain, (3) the settlements are only a fraction of the value of the innovation, and (4) some countries with no copyright or patent protection encourage their engineers to replicate innovations without regard to legal and ethical ramifications. Indeed, appropriating an innovative idea may not seem unethical to everyone; morality and ethics vary from one country to another.

Despite the uncertainties and risks lurking in the legal jungle, many cases of patent infringement are adjudicated. A noteworthy settlement was made to Polaroid against Kodak, even though Kodak was convinced it had a strong case. The terms of Polaroid's victory forced Kodak from the instant photography market. However, Polaroid had lost market share and momentum that it could never regain.

Sometimes product design is its own protection. Nintendo has learned to invent unique products that cannot be copied. The hardware system in the games contains a special "lockout" computer chip so that only licensed Nintendo software can be played on the system. This device prevents poor quality software from damaging the Nintendo name and prevents the competition from copying or using the Nintendo product as a means for selling their own highly profitable systems. Competitors, led by Atari, are filing antitrust actions against Nintendo. Ironically, Atari was once the leader in computer games but failed to protect its position.[9]

Play 3. Educate Customers
about the Value of the Innovation

A legally protected product that should meet a market need is now ready. The next element of the game plan is selling potential users on the value of the new offering. First the leader must determine whether potential customers can easily understand what the product will do for them. If so, then the selling process can be relatively straightforward, and the selling time should be short. If, however, the value is not obvious, then the process will be more complex and last longer.

The second step is to determine the best way to reach the potential customer, which entails selecting the right type of sales force and promotional scheme. Most innovations require a dedicated and direct sales force. If the product is complex or considerably different from those currently on the market, salespeople must have the ability to communicate in simple, easy-to-understand terms what the product can do. An unfamiliar product may need to be demonstrated for customers, or they may need a trial period to test it for themselves. Demonstrations, of course, can sometimes be conducted on television. Polaroid's early success has been attributed, in part, to its aggressive advertising on TV. The cameras made a splash when they took and instantly developed pictures live on Steve Allen's old *Tonight Show* in the 1950s. This campaign was targeted at those consumers with the greatest interest in this innovative product.

I have been personally involved in a number of new product introductions and can empathize with the difficulty of communicating in terms the user can understand. Innovators are so involved with their products and so convinced of their value that they have trouble putting themselves in the position of the uninformed and skeptical customer. But that very skill is needed in order to reach the customer.

Electronic home banking is one technology whose value seems beyond the appreciation of consumers. I was in many meetings in the 1970s and early 1980s in which banks tried to sell General Electric on the service in hopes that GE would become part of their system's development. Citicorp, Chemical Bank, and other large money center banks invested heavily on the assumption that most affluent people would love to use their personal computers to pay bills and make financial transactions without the bother of writing checks or visiting their local branch. The banks had a strong interest in these systems because they would reduce the costs of clearing checks and also reduce the float. Unfortunately for the banks, customers seem to have little interest in reducing the float and in paying to use the service. Further, the PC is not that user friendly for most affluent customers. And unlike the automatic teller machines at the bank, electronically linked home computers will not dispense cash on command to depositors from their accounts. Perhaps that will change in the future when home laser printers attached to the system can roll out some form of legal tender, like traveler's checks, to the depositors. Until then, electronic banking remains one innovative idea that seems good to the innovator but not to the customer.

However, other devices have attained quick popularity because people were able to appreciate their value immediately. For instance, the videotape recorder penetrated the home very rapidly. But even such an excellent educational and entertaining device had to be advertised aggressively in the beginning. In his book, *Made in Japan,* Morita describes how he had to threaten to fire the president of Sony's U.S. division to force him to put money into advertising the Betamax when it was introduced to America in 1975. Morita wrote, "In 1975, when we were ready to introduce BETAMAX, I envisioned a huge domestic advertising and promotional campaign that would be carried out regardless of the budgetary considerations. My feeling was this first use home video cassette recorder needed to be introduced to the people with a massive campaign . . . but my Sony American president was reluctant to spend the money."[10] Morita intuitively understood, even if his American associates did not, the need to think long term and make the investment to create demand.

Play 4. Be Prepared for Success

An innovator can create too much demand before the company has the ability to meet that demand. The risktaker leader must be able to estimate the cost of producing the product and determine how much can be produced and still meet the quality and reliability standards required for acceptance. Leaders miscalculate the cost and complexity of making the product when they fail to include experts and product developers in the cycle early enough. The great idea must be economically feasible, and the facilities and raw materials must be available at the right time. A product may be accepted but fail in the marketplace if consumers have to wait for it or if it doesn't work because of production miscalculations. Timing is critical. Risktakers must be able to respond to demand and avoid "stockout" (not having a product available when the user wants it).

Therefore, the game plan must specify where the product will be made, how many, and when. To arrive at those determinations, the leader estimates demand and how much can be produced or stocked in advance of demand. Innovators are usually willing to take the risk and have ample stock available; their investors, on the other hand, are often less enthusiastic and so tend to underestimate demand. Leaders must be alert to this danger. They must also be prepared for the response of current and future competitors to their new offerings. Here innovators should recognize their tendency to underestimate a competitor's ability to follow rapidly since they are convinced their unique products will overwhelm any potential competition.

I witnessed a case of the innovator's inherent pride in 1989. A large, successful Japanese company was demonstrating one of its new products, which its leadership believed to be highly innovative and protected by patents. I inquired about their competitors' products and was told that the competition did not have anything comparable. The obvious next question was: "When will they have it?" The answer: "Probably in 5 to 10 years." Whether this response was correct or not, it illustrates a potential problem. What did the Japanese company really know about the competition's ability to produce something of equal or greater value? The leaders also did not address the issue of substitution. Their innovation was designed to substitute for several current products, but it was similarly vulnerable because several other ways of attaining the same results existed in that market. In other words, what the innovating company was doing to the competition's products, the competition might be able to do to the new product, perhaps quicker and better than anticipated.

Innovations have surprised established products in all industries. Wet-copier companies were not prepared for dry copiers; Swiss watch companies were not ready for quartz watches; companies that made propeller-driven engines did not anticipate the jet engine. But these innovators must guard against being surprised in turn by unexpected competitive response. What you did to them, someone else can do to you. Alternatively, get the customer to agree to wait!

Some innovators have found unique ways to balance supply and demand. Once again, we look at Nintendo. Peter Main, vice president for Nintendo America, stimulated demand for the product through clever marketing and "rationed its availability, insuring that Nintendo games are far more desired than readily available." By design, the company does not fill its retailers' orders completely (it might ship 33 million units from a requested 45 million) and keeps half or more of its library of video cartridges inactive. Main's rationale is that retailers tend to exaggerate demand. By keeping supply tight and making the introduction of new games anticipated events, Nintendo has set records for sales.[11] IBM was a past master at getting their "mainframe" customers to wait for the next generation. Their customers had too much at stake to merely switch computer systems and IBM was able to meet, even exceed, their expectations, when they waited.

Play 5. Assure Money and People Are Available

A key part of the game plan is to have sufficient physical and financial resources to be able to attack early, stay aggressive, gain share, and prevent others from making an effective competitive response. *Financial backing is vital to the product innovation driven leader.* The company must have enough capital to invest in production capability and sufficient cash to pay for employee loyalty and to build inventory.

Horror stories abound of innovators who thought their financial backers were committed for the long term only to discover otherwise. According to *INC.*, the situation has become so serious that a New Jersey lawyer named Helen Chairman, a partner in the firm of Ross & Hardies, was compelled to put together "The Ten Commandments of Avoiding Lender Liability." Her goal was to help borrowers and lenders reach agreements free of misunderstandings. Two of the commandments are (1) The lender shalt not try to run the borrower's business, and (2) Thou shalt honor thy commitments. Ms. Chairman points out as well that it is essential to have a written agreement rather than to rely on an oral one.[12] (Often the problem is a misunderstanding.)

Long-Term Funding. The longer the product must strive for acceptance in the marketplace, the more financial resources will be needed, which means the innovator leader must seek out backers who can sustain their support. As mentioned, the Japanese have profited from long horizons because their bankers desired long-term payment schedules. In the past, American firms have also benefited from that sort of financing. I witnessed two major product launchings at GE with long-term funding commitments, where decades passed before the investments paid off.

The Need for Internal Funding. In the early 1960s, GE developed businesses in commercial jet engines and engineered plastics. Both were applications of internal R&D. Jet engine technology was an offshoot of the company's work with turbines and was based, as well, on the military jet engine developed with United Kingdom know-how and patents (obtained through project funding by the U.S. government during World War II). Gerhardt Neuman and his associates in Evendale, Ohio, were responsible for making the commercial jet engine business the success it is today. One of Neuman's allies was Jack Parker, a member of the senior management team and later a vice chairman under Reg Jones. Neuman sold GE on the potential of the jet engine and thus was able to obtain funding for the project. The actual banker was the General Electric Company, but internal selling by the product-driven team was a key factor to success.

The engineered plastics business was another electric products spinoff. Scientists at the corporate R&D research lab in Schenectady, New York, were working on a new insulating material for transformers. For a combination of reasons, including luck, they came up with a material (later named Lexan) with unique qualities. The business team, headed by Dr. Charles Reed, was also effective in selling internally and so received funding and commitment from the parent corporation. On the team was Jack Welch, current chief executive officer of GE.

These stories underscore the importance of internal selling, especially when the product innovation requires a long period to gain acceptance. The long-term commitment that can be obtained from internal selling is critical to success in many companies, and yet it is often overlooked or its worth underestimated. Internal selling and funding help prepare a business for success with an innovative product because it commits the company to a long-term struggle against competitors.

Being Prepared for Competitive Response.   Given sufficient time any innovation might be replicated by a competitor. If that firm can commit greater resources, then the original innovator may be reduced from a leader to a follower and subsequently lose in the marketplace—and perhaps the special quality of the innovation will be lost as well. The up-and-down history of People's Express Airlines illustrates this point.

Donald C. Barr's original idea was to provide no-frills air travel at a low price ($29 a ticket) to a selected number of cities. The low price was designed to fill his company's airplanes with passengers, because full utilization is critical to capital-intensive industries such as airlines. To provide the low fares, People had to keep costs down to a minimum. It did not offer advance reservations or seat assignments and did not provide free food or beverages. Employees performed more than one job: Ticket agents might load baggage, pilots might take tickets, and so on. The new kind of airline took off with the public. It was cited as a strong example of how deregulation could increase competition and provide innovative services.

However, the success was short lived, and the praise soon turned to criticism. The major airlines responded aggressively to the challenge by cutting prices to match People's low fares while still maintaining full services. His ego apparently inflated by his good publicity, Burr abandoned his strategy and lost his competitive advantage when he expanded too quickly into other markets. He acquired Frontier Airlines, which operated quite differently and thousands of miles away. Rather than hire experienced airline personnel, he depended on novice employees. Burr also began to operate like a traditional airline: taking reservations, assigning seats, and providing full services. As a result, he suffered severe financial losses and was forced to divest, selling out to his archenemy, Frank Lorenzo.[13] This illustrates the need to stick with a winning strategy and not be seduced into replicating incumbents with stronger financial resources.

Being Prepared for Success.   Boeing provides another example of a company unprepared to deal with success. In general, the airline industry has done an excellent job of creating demand. Aggressive promotion and pricing have increased the number of passengers every year (until 1991). As the early experience of People's Express demonstrated, selling seats is important to profitability. This expansion of ridership, coupled with the aging of the fleets and the new competitiveness of the industry that put a premium on efficiency and short flights through hub systems, created a demand for new planes. Boeing was the beneficiary of this surge. The company's willingness to take risks, invest in new designs, and cater to the needs of the airlines enabled it to maintain over a 60 percent market share in 1989.

However, Boeing did not anticipate the fortuitous turn of events. Orders backlogged, and the company was unable to meet demand. The result was missed schedules and broken promises. Top management has had to spend a great deal of time personally softening the anger of their best customers. Boeing was forced to "borrow" 670 skilled workers, averaging over 10 years of experience, from Lockheed's Georgia operation, paying premium salaries and generous housing allowances.[14]

Fortunately for Boeing, this turbulence has not yet inflicted any major damage. If the company is unable to manage the situation, however, competitors will take advantage. The French-based Airbus company is already gaining share in the global market. Boeing will have to hustle not to be hurt even more by its own success. Management must take some of the heat for not being ready. Most important, Boeing must not sacrifice quality for a quick fix, while it struggles to keep the customers happy.

Play 6. Maintain Consumer Demand

The next step in the game plan involves the marketing and sales strategy. I have already touched on the importance of the sales force. Salespeople must be very aware of the innovative product's pluses and minuses; they cannot undersell or oversell. When pitching a new product, direct selling is best. But if the sales force cannot reach all the customers, then the innovator leader may need to use agents, representatives, distributors, or franchisees to penetrate the market rapidly. These outside individuals and organizations must be well trained.

The danger for risktaker product innovators lies in two areas. First, though they may personally be able to sell their own product, they may not be trained in sales or marketing. Second, these leaders may love their product so much that they incorrectly assume everyone else will, and so the product will "sell itself." The temptation then will be to cut back on the sales effort too soon, or worse, improperly staff it at the beginning. Innovators often go this route when resources are scarce, as they frequently are.

Because selling new, innovative products and services can be time consuming, staff must be motivated to make the long-term efforts required to win acceptance. Thus, they must be compensated for their time with a package weighted toward base salary rather than incentives and bonuses. If too much of the compensation is based on getting orders, the new products, particularly those with complex features, will not be given sufficient effort and will fail. Customers need time to understand what they are buying. If that understanding is incomplete, their expectations will not be met, and they will not reorder or recommend the product to others. And repeat sales and word-of-mouth testimonials are often the difference between the success and failure of a new or significantly modified product or service.

Play 7. Maintain Quality, Regardless of Cost

Related to creating and maintaining demand is the ability to create and maintain a quality position. That may seem integral to other phases of the game plan, but it deserves special attention. An innovative product or service must perform to user expectations. That is my definition: *Quality is meeting customer/user expectations.*

If the product is vital to the user, and the user has taken the risk of switching to the new offering, then it is absolutely critical that the product perform as well as or even better than expected. That involves (1) not overpromising and thus creating expectations that cannot be met and (2) testing the product's capabilities extensively, both in the plant and in the field. Further, the innovator must be willing to guarantee the performance and be able to maintain quality with minimal disruption of the production process.

Hundreds, if not thousands, of innovative products did not meet these specifications for quality and failed.

Setting expectations is important, but they must be feasible expectations. Unfortunately, the innovator and his sales staff are usually so enthusiastic about their product or service that they overpromise and oversell. The result: Customers have high expectations that the product cannot satisfy. A number of prestige consumer items fall into this category. Perfumes are normally sold on perception, and so celebrities like Liz Taylor or Cher are used to give perfumes a "mystique." If the consumers feel the perfume did not deliver on the mystique, they won't buy it again and the product is finished. The entire designer fad in clothing is another illustration. The designer label creates expectations of greater sex appeal and popularity. If it offers only distinctive styling, comfort, long wear, and so on, but not the promised more fabulous social life, then it will fail to meet expectations and will fail in the marketplace.

Play 8. Price to Reinforce Uniqueness Without Being Greedy

Pricing strategy is another important part of the game plan. If the product is truly unique and provides real value to the user, then price should be based on value and not cost. Getting the highest possible margin is part of creating a mystique. If a product is priced too low at the introductory stage, then consumers might not believe it is really new and different. (The exception occurs when the mystique is "no frills," as with People Express.) Remember, it is always easier to reduce prices than increase them. The danger is excess: You can't be greedy.

One way to get premium prices for new products is to sweeten the appeal by working out leasing arrangements, possibly with the option to buy. Toyota and Nissan entered the luxury end of the car market in this manner. Lexus (Toyota) and Infinity (Nissan) were introduced with upscale prices and attractive leasing and rental contracts. The Japanese were, however, not greedy. They priced their new brands lower than Mercedes and BMW but still targeted consumers who were interested in luxury cars and willing to pay top prices.

If switching to the new product requires the customers to take personal or business risks, then the innovative leader must do something to minimize or share the risk. Various financing options might be appropriate and effective. I mentioned, in an earlier chapter, Thomas Watson, Jr.'s, leasing strategy with IBM's mainframe computers. The move made sense for cash-rich IBM and reduced risks for companies wanting the expensive new machines. In fact, leasing may offer tax advantages for both parties. As I related before, the IBM strategy was a financial and competitive success. It simultaneously broke down the barrier to entry and erected a barrier against responses by other computer firms. IBM enjoyed and exploited this major advantage for many years.

Play 9. Have the Next Innovation
Ready on the Shelf

The final part of the innovative risktaker's game plan is to prepare for the next act, the next innovation. Preparation begins with the innovator's acceptance that competitors will follow into the market with possibly even an improved version of the product. Leaders must avoid wishful thinking or the arrogant notion that their innovation will prevail forever. The successful risktaker gets the next generation in the mill and ready to be introduced *at the right time*. The right time is when a competitor has just replicated the first version of the product and announced it to the world. The innovative company will use this occasion to announce that its new, improved line is available and at the same or slightly higher price. It is critical to have this aspect of the game plan in place and ready.

Regrettably, the risktaker is often impatient. The innovator, who loves the original product and has even greater affection for the next generation, will want to display it to the world, prematurely. The poor timing can be devastating. An early announcement can cannibalize the current product by inducing the customers to purchase the new version, if it is ready, or to wait, if it is not. In either case, the original may go begging and total sales may slow down. For instance, many businesses routinely delay purchasing personal computers, copiers, and other office equipment because they have learned that new models will be available soon and that prices are likely to fall rapidly. Therefore, the leader or someone on the team less emotionally involved must make sure that product introductions are well timed and carefully placed in the line.

Many Japanese consumer electronic and camera firms have been guilty of this sort of poor timing, thus cannibalizing their own lines and reducing the size and growth of the market. Most consumers recognize that if they wait, they will not only get a product with better features, but at a fraction of the price.

The mistakes in the consumer electronics industry (which is dominated by the Japanese and other Far Eastern countries with few American and European competitors) are not apparent in the auto industry. Here, the Japanese have resisted competing on price alone. Instead, they have kept competitive focus on service, quality, and features. Indeed, they are moving into the luxury segment of the market, where those elements prevail. I've already noted how Nissan's Infinity and Toyota's Lexus are now in competition with BMW and Mercedes. Honda had already entered the upscale picture with its Acura. All have avoided head-on price competition, perhaps because they are in an industry in which American and European companies historically have been able to increase average prices on a regular basis.

It will be interesting to see if this situation changes when there is an overcapacity in world production of autos. Will the Japanese follow the path of steady and timely introduction of new models that has always defined the auto industry? Or will they resort to the cutthroat pricing and chaotic introduction of new products characteristic of the consumer electronics industry, which they dominate?

THE TEAM AND TALENTS
NEEDED FOR SUCCESS

People implement game plans. The right mix of human resources is critical for any enterprise. And as I have indicated, each style of leader requires a distinct blend of talents, organized into a team that has the proper personality to make that leader's strategy work. Of course, the risktaker leader who is focused on product innovation is the key player; he has the vision and the initial passion. He has the talent to develop the product or service by himself and the will to assume the risk of making it happen. He has the number one position because he has to come first in the formulation of the team. But the leader can't do it alone. He needs several other individuals to round out the team. Players two through six are listed somewhat in the order of when they make their distinctive contribution, with the understanding that *teamwork is a continuous interactive process.* Everyone is important, and everyone is involved.

Thus, the team members are as follows:

1. Leader.
2. Legal advisors to protect the product and the assets.
3. Missionary sellers with enough zeal and faith in the product to spread the word.
4. Production talents to convert the promise of the product into reality.
5. Product developers to look constantly for the next innovation.
6. Financial and accounting wizards to seek funding and manage the money sensibly for the long run.

Legal Advisors

As I pointed out earlier, it is important to protect the product legally so that potential competitors cannot easily replicate the innovation. The risktaker strategic leader should get the best group of legal experts possible. Specifically, they must be able to convert the innovative concept into documentation that can afford protection. This includes patent searches to see if others have already made claims that would impact the innovative features of the product. Today, the patent search must be global since we are part of a global market. When the legal staff is confident the patent can be defended, the leader can then develop a sales and marketing plan and hire the staff to implement it.

However, the legal staff must warn the leader if it is likely that the innovation will have difficulty gaining patent protection and thus be vulnerable. Preparing a legal defense and conducting a court fight might consume enough money and time to endanger the successful introduction of the product. Further, the firm's legal advisors may have to contend with unscrupulous competitors who will intentionally violate the patents and take the risk of being sued, hoping the innovative company will not have the will or resources for a protracted legal battle. Several firms have had their innovation's market advantage lost in this manner.

The risktaker innovator may rely on outside advisors for some or all of the firm's legal needs. Costs and potential risks will be determining factors—as long as the product is protected. Outside legal help might be required to defend against some international "reverse engineering" group attempting to circumvent the patents by discovering the secrets of the innovation. (Reverse engineering involves dissecting the product to identify how patents can be circumvented.) Without protection, the innovating company could be left with all the costs of development but few rewards.

Missionary Sellers

These team members are characterized by *enthusiasm* and *faith*. Not only do they understand the features and value of the new product, they love the product and believe they are offering something that is truly better than what already exists.

However strong their enthusiasm, they must be down-to-earth salespeople. They must be credible; they must be able to speak in the customer's language and present the product's attributes in terms the customer can understand and appreciate. They must not oversell or overpromise, although they should assure the customer that the entire organization stands behind the product.

Because the product is innovative, demonstrations and even trial use periods may be required to win over the customer. Thus, the sales missionaries assume the customers' risks. They assume the risk of time as well, because acceptance may come slowly. Their faith must have staying power. They are available to make sure the product meets expectations. They minister to the flock, not just make converts. If the product doesn't meet expectations, they will fix it or even take it back. If the sales missionary can't do it personally, then the company must have a group of customer servicers to provide responsive follow-up.

I am completely amazed at the lack of strong warranties for high-priced consumer and business products. Computers, camcorders, VCRs, CDs, and stereo equipment, which can cost customers hundreds, even thousands, of dollars, come with only a 90-day limited warranty. Increasingly, specialty retailers offer their own extended warranties, but for a significant fee, normally 20 percent of the retail price. These service contracts are highly profitable; however, they imply that the products may not last past the 90 days guaranteed by the manufacturer. This message is completely inconsistent with the value-priced strategy for innovative products. Customers expect quality, reliability, and producer commitment to performance when they buy innovative and highly priced merchandise.

Another issue is the size and growth of the sales force. Since dedication is required, leaders must be cautious about expanding to include third parties. Retailers, agents, value-added retailers, and distributors must be selected and/or trained to have the patience and missionary zeal of the regular sales force. If possible, it is best to rely on a small, focused group of missionaries. They must be supported with a sufficient base salary, as I indicated earlier, to sustain their efforts for the time needed to gain acceptance for the product. As the product becomes well known, incentives can replace salaries as the basis of compensation. Profit sharing and equity accumulation in the company might be used to sustain loyalty and assure continuity, qualities often overlooked in today's "quick buck" business world.

Part of selling for the long term is sustaining market demand once the product has become accepted. The team will require the talents of people skilled in developing advertising, promotion, and pricing strategies. The key is to not forget to remind consumers and industrial customers continually of the product's virtues. Nor can the team assume that everyone knows how good the product is. Think how strong McDonald's and certain packaged goods companies are in this area; their products are always in our minds. Morita of Sony was thinking of sustained demand when he forced his American president to promote and advertise the already successful Beta VCRs. However, advertising and demand creation must be tied to the product and what it does. Campaigns must be based on real, not just perceived, product differentiation.

Production Talents

The efforts of the innovator leader, the legal/patent experts, and the missionary sales force will all be in vain if the team does not include a group that can deliver the product on time and in sufficient quantity and quality to meet customer expectations. Once demand has been stimulated for an innovation, customers can't or won't wait.

If the company makes its own product, experts in manufacturing and production will be needed on the team. If the product is made by outsiders, experts in sourcing and negotiation must be on board. Normally, the innovative company should build its own; but if it is not economically feasible to make the product internally, then dependable suppliers are a must. Polaroid used other companies to produce their cameras until it introduced its SX70 in 1972.[15]

In too many cases, the ability to produce was not addressed, and the great idea failed. The old philosophy of meeting production schedules at the expense of quality and fixing the product in the field is not appropriate for the product risktaker. I continue to stress that innovative products must be reliable and of good quality. While production speed is requisite to meet demand generated by zealous missionaries, customer expectations include that the product perform when it is delivered. Orders are canceled, or not renewed, when products fail, as well as when they fail to arrive. In either case, competitors will be eager to step in with their own versions of the innovation. Introducing a new product is a fragile venture. Many things have to be done right and at the proper time.

The team's manufacturing talent must be forceful in communicating what they can and cannot do. They must have the courage to stand up to the missionaries and, especially, the innovative leader and demand that they have the proper resources to do the job. They must refuse to run with inadequate facilities and equipment, insufficient skilled workers, or inferior quality standards. The production team also needs always to be looking for innovative production paths, including backup outside suppliers if they are needed to make schedules. They must be able to take some risks in having capacity and inventory in advance of demand. They must be willing to not just go by the book. Finally, members should have the courage to stop the line if they see quality being sacrificed (as workers in Japanese auto and consumer electronic companies are noted for doing). In short, the production team must reflect the character of the risktaking, innovative leader—the "fit" is critical. GM's new Saturn project demonstrated this type of commitment.

Product Developers

Engineers and professional customer researchers make up the segment of the team charged with developing new products. *The team must be constantly probing what is next.* Members continue to evaluate customer responses to determine changing needs and wants. Even if the customer is satisfied with what is currently offered, the team must focus on improving the product's performance, making the product more user friendly, or doing whatever is necessary to maintain the competitive edge. Today, people expect a company to enhance its products often, and if consumers don't see improvements, they begin to look elsewhere. The complacent attitude of "if it ain't broke, don't fix it" no longer is valid because it allows competitors to enter the market with something better.

The best solution is to continually work on the next generation and be prepared to put it on the market when the time is right. As noted earlier, the time is right when a competitor introduces its version. But when customers make demands that the product cannot meet, it also should signal the need for something new. I will discuss timing in more detail in the next major section of this chapter.

Financial and Accounting Wizards

Once the people are in place who can innovate, protect, sell, produce, and maintain the product, another group is required to manage the finances. The company may have sought funds from venture capitalists, which is only half the battle. Venture capitalists do not invest because they are true believers; sometimes they seek big returns, sometimes quick returns. They may not be willing to wait to see if the product really works, or until the plant and equipment are in place to produce a sufficient quantity of high-quality product. Good cash flow management is necessary to keep these investors happy.

Therefore, the company also needs a "friendly banker," with whom the members of the financial team can negotiate a continuing and low-cost source of funds. The company's financial people determine the optimal degree of debt and equity, they establish realistic expectations for the investors, and they bargain for long-term commitments. Once the company has the funds, the accounting talent establishes monitoring and budgeting systems to assure that the funds are well spent. They are responsible for convincing team members that success is possible with sound financial controls and making them operate within those structures. Good financial professionals will not permit an organization to believe that it is necessary to lose money in this type of situation. *Risktaking innovators can make money early in the cycle.* Innovators are often not concerned about financials and good bookkeeping practices. It falls to the financial professionals to plan, control, and monitor the money so that the company's cash flow is sufficient to keep it in operation.

Incidentally, the innovator leader may go outside the company for accounting help, if that makes more sense than having people on permanent staff. The guidelines discussed earlier for lawyers apply here as well. The critical factor is having people available who can instill the discipline needed for the company to meet its financial obligations.

TIMING IS EVERYTHING

I've already discussed how critical timing is to the successful implementation of any strategy. *Timing is even more important for the risktaker product innovator than for any other type of leader.* The following situations illustrate why this is so.

Situation 1. A Sleeping Giant or a Greedy Leader

As I have described, a complacent, or even a greedy, market leader creates a situation ripe for exploitation by the risktaker innovator. Here, the market leader has stopped innovating or offering differentiated products. That is the telltale sign the top firm is now driven by production rather than product or marketing leadership.

This scenario played out in the auto industry. American leaders had decided to maximize profits by concentrating on large cars. They invested in massive factories to produce those cars and their power plants (engines). As the smaller Japanese and European cars began to catch on, U.S. industry leaders ignored or arrogantly disregarded the signals from American consumers and continued to invest in the same big cars they and the public had always loved. Eventually, Japanese firms took over leadership because they had high-quality products that were right for the market—and because American leaders let them into the market.

Even when the giants begin to wake up, a smart risktaker with a superior innovative product can make inroads. Soiechiro Honda has done just that. He took on several giants along the way to making Honda one of the top-selling lines of cars in the United States. First, Honda had to outmaneuver the Japanese ministry, which tried to discourage him from expanding beyond his original motorcycle business. Second, he had to compete successfully against Nissan and Toyota, the entrenched market leaders in Japan. Third, he had to battle the American leaders on their own turf against their superior financial, distribution, and large engineering resources.

Honda succeeded with a strategy that included building cars in the United States; the company has a plant in Marysville, Ohio, and plans a second in East Liberty, Ohio. More importantly, Honda offers a high-quality car that is superior even to the products of other Japanese manufacturers. For four straight years, Honda has received the highest customer satisfaction commendation. An improved dealer network and concern for the customer have also been part of Honda's strategy. But product development is the company's real strength. Building on its well-earned reputation for high-performance small cars, Honda has led the Japanese invasion into the luxury car market, competing on quality with BMW and Mercedes Benz, and offering a lower price.

The decade of the 1980s saw Honda move past Nissan and Toyota into third place in America, with 9 percent of the market (up from 4.2 percent and sixth place in 1980). The major strength of Honda is its integrated product development leadership. This company's leaders have developed a team that blurs the lines among engineering, styling, and marketing to create a car noted for quality and performance. This has been coupled with creative, continuous advertising, and with the strengthening of a loyal, committed, trained dealer network that continues the customer relationship and provides after-sales service. If the company can sustain its integrated strategy (which also includes strong advertising), then it should strengthen its position and possibly vie for second place in the American market.

Another way a sleeping giant can be attacked is with an innovative approach that changes the definition of the business. Consider the current chaos in financial services: Banks are trying to compete against the investment and stock brokers, life insurance companies are trying to offer better deals than mutual funds, and so on. Many believe the cause is deregulation. However, the changes are really the result of innovation. Merrill Lynch and other brokers invented the "money market account," a multiple investment medium with high returns. Money market accounts permit customers to manage their own money by moving funds into different types of accounts: checking, savings, CDs, and a variety of mutual funds (in stocks, commodities, precious metals, foreign currency, etc.). Customers can take as much or as little risk as they find comfortable and take advantage of the best interest rates available in the type of account they choose.

The money market innovation spawned others, even in life insurance. The insurance industry used to comprise stable, unexciting, and profitable companies. Traditional whole life insurance accounted for 70 percent of the industry's premiums. The policies were very profitable because the customer's return on premiums paid was only 4.5 percent, and the policy holder had to wait 30 years to collect. But competitive pressure from more lucrative (for the customer) investments led to the introduction of "universal life insurance." This innovative product required that the insuring company put the cash value of the policy into investments and provide the policy holder with returns higher than the money markets, often over 10 percent a year. Many insurance companies have been forced to acquire or initiate their own investment firms to be able to achieve those mandated returns.

Once again, innovation is redefining an industry. Banks have been forced to become more competitive to maintain position against these new investment options. Banks now offer their own money markets, long-range certificates of deposit, and interest-bearing checking accounts. Brokerage firms responded as well. Discount brokers made transactions at a low price, while other firms offered new funds or faster service using phone hookups to computer technology.

Situation 2. User Dissatisfaction

The right time for the risktaker is when the user is unhappy and looking for something new. Several recent cases involve communications. The facsimile found its niche in time recently when businesses became dissatisfied with the difficulty of sending correspondence quickly and reliably. Fax machine sales have boomed. A related dissatisfaction grew with the problem of getting and leaving messages. People would call and either get a busy signal or not find their party. Innovative computer voice mail systems provided the solution in companies; answering machines have satisfied many customers in the home and business markets.

People also were dissatisfied with the limitations of the phone system for another reason: they couldn't make calls while in transit. In flight, in their car or company truck, they couldn't communicate with the office or with customers. The innovative cellular phone systems have solved the problem for an increasing number of traveling executives, salespeople on the road, and tradespeople on the job. The "aerophones" are beginning to meet the needs of travelers in planes and, recently, in trains.

Finally, while banking hours have expanded, banks are still not always open when you need them, and never on Sunday. The timely innovation: automatic teller machines (ATMs), which are always open for customers who need ready cash.

Situation 3. A Second Chance

Many products and services have been literally reborn. The risktaker tried again because the initial failure was traceable either to a market that was not yet ready or to technology that was ahead of its time and not to a basic flaw in the product.

George Hatsopoulos is one individual whose patience and persistence paid off. He has formed several companies to exploit his technological innovations. In 1956, he built a thermionic converter, a pioneering device that turns heat directly into electrons, thus creating a very efficient source of electrical power. He was not able to commercialize this breakthrough at the time, but it is now the basis for the success of his current company (Thermo Electron Corp.). Thermo provides medical devices and detectors for drugs and bombs. A subsidiary, Thermo Instrument

Systems, sells instruments that analyze pollution and nuclear radiation. Thermo Process Systems, another subsidiary, provides systems that burn hazardous waste.[16] Hatsopoulos hopes to form more subsidiaries and lead a multibillion-dollar company by the end of the century.

Incorporating innovations in separately financed subsidiaries was the path to prosperity for Thomas Edison, who incorporated and financed each innovation individually. He was, of course, the epitome of the inventor, who built on others' ideas as well as his own. Edison had the perseverance necessary to proceed through sometimes long periods of trial and error and R&D until the idea finally worked.

CONSISTENCY OF "ACTIONS" AND "WORDS"

Leaders are characterized by a high degree of consistency of words and actions. What they say corresponds to what they do. Risktaker innovators can at times have difficulty fulfilling this criterion of leadership. They may become infatuated with the new product and make promises that they cannot keep. Claims concerning projected levels of growth, success in both revenue and earnings, and even product performance may go beyond objective sense. Thus, other team members must take responsibility for controlling the leader's exuberance and keeping promises within realistic bounds. But they should certainly not prevent the risktaker from leading and creating enthusiasm.

CHANGE AND FLEXIBILITY: THE SIN OF PRIDE

The risktaker may be a little too willing to change and be flexible. Consider the story of Harold Katz, who founded Nutri/System in 1981. Katz's innovation was to franchise weight-loss centers that looked like medical offices, charged customers hefty up-front fees linked to the amount of weight they wanted to lose, offered weekly group therapy sessions, and required customers to buy prepackaged, calorie-controlled entrees at highly marked-up prices. The combination was very successful, and the company stock rose precipitously. The product was unique and the timing was right.

However, Katz apparently started to believe his own press releases and lost perspective. He owned 65 percent of the company's stock and so was a wealthy man. He began to live like one, spending lavishly on himself and the trappings of the business. He also bought a slew of other companies (including the Philadelphia 76ers basketball team), some of which had nothing to do with the original business. These acquisitions caused Katz to neglect the core business, and they were a drain on earnings. The franchisees became annoyed because Katz charged them prices for the food that were too high for them to make a profit on resale to the Nutri/System customers. Finally, Katz was forced to bring in a professional manager, Donald McCulloch, to take over operations.[17]

I'll discuss McCulloch's regime in the next chapter on the caretaker innovator. The point here is that Katz was too eager to change strategy; he became more interested in making money than in helping his franchises to remain successful. His use of the core business to support new ventures and acquisitions is similar to Donald Barr's experience at People Express. Barr lost his company when he turned its unique assets into liabilities. Both Katz and Barr displayed what could be called a character flaw common to risktaker innovators: *They come to believe they can do anything.*

THE RISKTAKER HIDDEN
IN A MAJOR COMPANY

Often the real risktakers are not the entrepreneurial owners, but the hired hands. In large companies, these individuals usually head divisions or business units. They are what Gifford Pinchot III calls "intrapreneurs."[18] Two large firms justifiably renowned for their intrapreneurs are 3M and GE.

3M: Institutionalizing Innovation

Intrapreneuring is not accidental at 3M; the company has deliberately established procedures and created an atmosphere conducive to company-wide innovation. Six elements are at the heart of 3M's success.[19]

1. The company has demonstrated a tolerance for new ideas. Corporate culture (actions as well as words) is oriented toward innovation and favors the long haul over immediate payoffs.

2. People are paid and promoted according to how well they guide new ideas to commercial realization. Employees, designated as "product champions," are allowed to manage the ideas as though they were their own businesses. This sense, and fact, of ownership is critical to the success of the product. I have witnessed several cases where the innovator's idea languished when it was given to someone else to run.

3. The process is continuous and often spontaneous. 3M people are always sharing information informally in labs, meeting rooms, and hallways. The company recognizes that innovation cannot be programmed; it happens in a variety of, sometimes strange, ways.

4. The activity is a team exercise from the very beginning. The individual with the idea forms an "action team" by recruiting full-time members from management, marketing, maybe finance, and whatever technical areas are affected. The team designs the product and figures out how to make it and market it. The team also examines new uses and line extensions. All members of the team are promoted and earn raises as the project reaches each stage in the progression. The team is made responsible and given credit.

5. The product is not limited to a specific market size. Many companies go only for the big score, refusing to consider small markets or niches. They thereby allow other firms (like 3M) to develop little markets and make them grow. When employees know the company is only interested in the big hit, they tend to exaggerate a product's potential and make poor decisions. 3M knows it is impossible to judge the size of a market when the idea is in the embryonic stage. That's why they encourage innovation of any size.

6. 3M intrapreneurs are allowed to fail. The company doesn't expect all ideas to be winners. Leadership knows, however, that a steady stream of new products can only come when there is a flood of ideas from which to choose. In most companies, failure means embarrassment, demotion, or even dismissal. Of course, it is not easy to determine how long to wait for an idea to succeed. At 3M the structure is in place to make sure failure comes only after an effective effort has been made to succeed. 3M encourages creativity, but it also requires discipline in project development and a continuing evaluation of how well the project is progressing.

In my experience at GE, I saw intrapreneurs not always given a chance to win. And if they failed, they were not given a second chance. Although in this respect GE could learn from 3M, the company did, however, have many successes.

Risktaking at General Electric: Willard Sahloff

Internal risktakers are often not well known, even in their own companies. In addition, they may not get the full financial reward for their contributions. Luckily, these individuals seem to derive sufficient motivation from the success they bring their companies. Throughout the book, I will describe the achievements of several innovators at GE, some of whom never got famous or very rich. Willard Sahloff's story belongs in this chapter on product innovation.

Willard Sahloff was the leader of GE's portable appliance business (toasters, irons, skillets, clocks, etc.) in the 1950s and early 1960s. Sahloff understood the need for innovation to expand markets and stimulate demand. He was not willing just to improve existing products; he wanted to create new features and even new products. He introduced the electric blanket, the electric toothbrush, the electric clothes brush, the electric knife, the electric can opener, and so on. Obviously, GE had a strong desire for new applications of electricity that would make life easier and more convenient.

These new applications were created and built by a team of product developers. Each new offering was analyzed, and team members were encouraged to find more ways of using the product. They were also challenged by Sahloff to look ahead to the next generation. As I have mentioned, this is a very important element of product innovation leadership. Sahloff was always ready for the next step. When competitors were offering their version of the electric toothbrush, for instance, Sahloff's team could counter with the electric hair dryer or hairsetter. Constant innovation kept GE ahead and forced the competition to continue to invest just to keep up, never giving them the chance to gain a leadership position.

Pricing and distribution tactics, product quality control, and promotional campaigns were all part of the winning innovation strategy. Pricing was controlled by the manufacturers, and this gave them control over the retailers. The manufacturers established "value pricing" because that is the key to leadership in innovation. Once the product is developed, it must be distributed by people who can explain the benefits of the new features and encourage customers to pay "extra" for them. GE and its competitors had franchise retailers who sold the products. These tended to be servicing dealers who could fix the product if needed. Since prices were controlled, the dealers competed on service and know-how and not on low price. As I've stressed, an expert sales force is vital to this distribution approach.

In the 1950s and 1960s, value pricing was synonymous with "fair trade pricing," and it constituted a major advantage to product innovators in consumer markets. Fair trade referred to the legal right of producers to keep retail prices high and control distribution to protect their investments in their new products. When Sahloff started his product innovation strategy, he did not have to contend with large chain discounters. (Later on, he was forced to sell to discounters by the courts.) Small appliances were sometimes discounted, however, but only with the cooperation of the manufacturer. They were called "traffic appliances" because they were used by retailers and department stores to generate traffic. Indeed, small appliance manufacturers developed products that would encourage people to come into the retail stores. A variation of this tactic is applied today in the use of "loss leaders." These are items often sold below cost to attract customers to the store in hopes that they will buy other merchandise sold at a higher margin.

GE practiced quality control and low-cost manufacturing by establishing plants dedicated to specific product lines. These decentralized units invested heavily in automation and were able to maintain cost parity or superiority and ensure quality. Assured performance is vital to the success of the differentiated product or service leader. (McDonald's, for example, exemplifies this proposition.) GE Housewares pioneered innovation in all aspects of the production development process, which includes the manufacturing and delivery systems, such as warehousing and logistics.

Finally, leaders must create and meet demand. GE, and its housewares division, was adept in advertising and promotion. The General Electric Corporation's famous slogan was "Progress is our most important product." (Its spokesperson was Ronald Reagan, then an actor in "B" movies.) The advertising reinforced and was consistent with the company's policies and performance in one of the most profitable eras of its history. But advertising and promotions are useless if you cannot deliver the product. To avoid stockouts was and is key. GE invested in inventory, taking the risk of having too much on the shelf rather than disappoint the customers by not having enough to meet demand.

That last point about meeting demand deserves elaboration. In many industries today, the time competitors require to replicate innovation is declining. In the 1950s, consumer products companies may have needed years to follow the leader. In the 1990s, they may only need months. The time frame has tightened because there are now several alternative sources for products. Since following is easier and quicker, it makes even less sense to go to the trouble of developing and advertising a new product and not have enough on the shelf. For example, in 1990 Black and Decker (B&D) brought out a new electric screwdriver and advertised it heavily. However, many people could not find it at their local stores. Within months, Skill and other manufacturers had competitive products on the market and capitalized on the demand Black and Decker had created. Thus, B&D may have failed to earn all it deserved for being the leader.

In summary, it is apparent that product differentiation and innovation can be a rewarding leadership driver. It takes a strongly integrated team and implementation strategy backed by the knowledge and commitment of the entire organization. The designers must have input from the sales force and the marketplace; they must be willing to challenge the current designs; and they must look for ways to improve them. However, the designs must be producible and the manufacturing organization must be part of the early design and not be informed when it is too late. If suppliers must be involved, they too must be involved early and not late. Once the product has been developed, it is necessary to promote it and price it to maximize its acceptance. This will involve having appropriate sales, distribution, and commitment to the inventory and response levels that will optimize the acceptance and sales. Overall, this tough team approach requires a high integration of the organization and its rewards. When GE used this leadership driver in its product lines, it decentralized and built organizations around the products called *product departments*. They had their own integrated engineering, manufacturing, sales, and finance. The team was rewarded as a whole. If the product was successful and achieved its objectives and goals, all benefited. If it failed, all were punished or held accountable. There was a minimum of "finger pointing," since it was a team development and not just one functional organization. This is a major difference from the highly functionalized organizations that are prevalent in many companies today.

Of course the key was the leadership. Sahloff was a powerful merchandiser. He spent his early career in Montgomery Ward (when Ward's was a merchandising leader), and so he was informed about retailers and their needs and expectations. However, because he was also committed to the product development process, he recognized that it would take risk and that all products would not be successful. He looked longer range—in fact, several years ahead—and he funded for the longer term. He understood the need to protect pricing, and he fought hard to maintain fair trade. He was unwilling to sell to the discounters of the time and only acquiesced when required to do so by court order. In addition, he protected his brand name. GE would not sell to others for re-labeling. All the pieces fit together and he was a winner.

POST MORTEM

It is interesting to note that the GE housewares business is now part of Black and Decker and that B&D management appears to be following the strategy and driver used by Willard Sahloff 30 years ago. However, different business conditions may not permit B&D to have the same level of success enjoyed by GE. Companies now have more difficulty controlling the entire cycle. They must rely on the mass merchant to sell their products, which limits their ability to practice value pricing and to maintain high inventory levels.

Since discounting has come into vogue, the margins established by "fair trade pricing" have deteriorated rapidly, and the nature of the seller has changed as well. Instead of knowledgeable salespeople who could explain innovative product features, customers are confronted with order takers or, worse, people who don't know anything about the product. Thus, any product change that is not obvious must be communicated to users by advertising. Discounters also cannot service or repair the equipment; they must refer customers with problems to the manufacturer. Finally, since the discounter competes purely on price, when prices decline and costs increase, there is little money left over from sales for manufacturers to use for innovations. Manufacturers are thus pushed into a strategy driven by concerns for low-cost production. This focus has resulted in the movement of plants offshore, the consolidation of component construction in centralized areas, the substitution of cheaper materials such as plastics, and, most importantly, the loss of the innovative edge. Therefore, fewer firms make such common consumer items as small appliances, and not many of them are American.

The lesson is that competitive strategies must be adapted to the changing environment. But the environment is not the same everywhere. Japanese and European firms have been more successful in repeating past American innovative strategies because they have their own version of fair trade and distribution control. The same products command higher prices in Japan than they do in the United States because there are no discounters. High domestic margins generate the funds to innovate and to compete aggressively in the United States. Thus, consumer product innovation strategies work best in some consumer lines and in some parts of the world, especially where fair trade and distribution control still exist (where the innovator sells direct and controls pricing to the end user).

PRODUCT STANDARDIZATION AND AFTERMARKET LEADERSHIP

Another important strategy might be considered a hybrid containing elements of the risktaker and caretaker leadership styles. It applies to the situation in which risktaker activity develops an innovative product that becomes the industry standard and then caretaker leadership reaps the reward by selling the highly profitable aftermarket.

This approach is affectionately called the "sharing the wealth strategy." The concept is simple but very difficult to achieve. Here is how it works. A company comes up with an innovative product or service. However, instead of trying to produce and sell it exclusively, the company takes a bold step and licenses others to offer the same product. In this way, the innovating company creates competition but standardizes the offerings around its design. The licensing fees are also a source of income in the short run. In the long run, the firm sets itself up to sell a variety of related products. Once the industry standardizes around its design, the firm is in position to make profits selling consumables, parts, or key components.

Many have followed this approach. For instance, Kodak created camera designs, licenses them around the world, and then concentrates on dominating the film and processing business. Kodak made enormous profits on the aftermarket and not on its original innovation. A number of industrial and high-tech firms employ the sharing strategy. For instance, chemical companies license others to produce their chemicals and then supply some of the major catalysts or reaction agents to make the process work correctly and efficiently.

Four special conditions must be met to make the "sharing the wealth" strategy work:

- The innovation must be unique and not easy to replicate. If alternatives that perform the same task and meet the same need are within easy reach, competitors have little motivation to accept a licensing agreement that would place the innovator in a commanding position.

    This first condition rarely occurs, as testified by the recent failures of several firms to employ the razor blade strategy. Sony was unable to get the VCR business to standardize around its Beta technology; instead, Matsushita's VHS technology won out. In the field of nuclear energy, the battle was between GE's boiling water reactor (BWR) and Westinghouse's pressure water reactor (PWR), adapted from the U.S. Navy Nuclear Submarine Program. Westinghouse has had more success, and the PWR standard is more prevalent. In computers, IBM was unable to replicate its mainframe success in PCs. The giant became a giant, in part, because it created the dominant standard for the large computers, but in the small computer arena, several standards vie for supremacy.

- The competitors must be able to succeed without being in a leadership position. In other words, everyone has to be able to win with one industry standard. A single standard allows the market to grow faster and generates more confidence because users don't need to worry about constant changes. In the mainframe computer market, for instance, customers can invest in applications and operating software without concern that what they bought today will be obsolete tomorrow. In the video recorder field, film companies were hesitant to offer programs until they could see which technology would become standard. Now that VHS has taken control, more and more programs are available.

- Companies must have opportunities to make money in the aftermarket for parts or consumables. Clearly, Kodak found it profitable to concentrate on film and processing equipment. However, Polaroid was in a similar position and didn't adopt a similar strategy. Why not? Because Polaroid was not the provider of film for the instant camera until the mid-1960s. Polaroid focused on the camera business and permitted Kodak to produce the film. When Polaroid finally decided to make its own film, Kodak became interested in the instant camera business. Polaroid prevailed, but the company's exclusivity restricted the growth of the market. Thus, the company has not become as big as it might have grown if it had followed the standardization strategy.

- The innovative product must have global potential. Some products are restricted by national barriers. For instance, different parts of the world have different electrical standards. Thus, electrical products made to U.S. standards cannot be used in Europe, which has different voltage requirements, without adaptation or modification. Similarly, the same television receivers cannot be used in both the United States and Europe because of differing standards and transmission requirements. The different standards were created intentionally to protect national suppliers. There will be greater opportunities in the future only if nations cooperate to establish international standards. Unfortunately, this hoped-for situation is unlikely. Two or more standards will continue to be the norm for most markets.

In this chapter, I have described in detail the characteristics of risk-taking product innovators. In the next chapter, I will turn to those who improve existing products rather than create new ones. These are the evolutionary, rather than revolutionary, leaders.

5

Caretakers: Evolutionaries Ensuring the Future

Many companies survive and prosper because of the caretaker leaders who follow the risktakers. The risktakers may get the headlines, and the companies may bear their names, but their successors are the ones who really make the difference over the long haul. Many of the great business leaders of the post-World War II era have been "caretaker innovators." They built on the achievements of the earlier risktaker innovators and made their companies more stable and more profitable. Caretaker leadership increased the confidence of investors, stockholders, and employees, which resulted in sustained commitment by those stakeholders to the futures of their companies. Evolutionary growth naturally followed revolutionary creation.

Donald Petersen of Ford, Reginald Jones of General Electric, John Scully of Apple, and many of the heads of major Japanese and European firms are in this evolutionary leadership category.

Under the leadership of Donald Petersen, Ford Motor Company was able to spring back and regain much of the image and position lost under the management of Henry Ford II. Ford's share of the market had declined in part because its cars were generally considered unexciting and poorly made. Petersen introduced a family series of high-performance new cars that were stylish and aerodynamic. Taurus and Sable moved Ford back into the position of industry leadership, and while General Motors was losing ground to the Japanese, Ford was gaining market share (23 percent share in 1989, its largest in 10 years). Further, this recouping of share was accomplished profitably.

Reginald Jones was the strategic leader of GE for nearly all of the 1970s. During his tenure, GE generated earnings consistently and predictably, something it had lost the ability to do early in the previous decade. As a result, GE was again in favor with the investment community, and the company was able to manage solid growth of its asset base. Reg Jones created the proper corporate climate and systems, and he assembled the management team that balanced growth, repositioning, and divestiture simultaneously. Jones's leadership was responsible for the firm's internal acceptance of change, and his strategic planning system smoothed the way for the major shifts instituted by his successor, Jack Welch. Under Jones, GE became a strong portfolio company. Jones committed GE to long-term investments in plastics, aircraft engines, and financial services; he also withdrew from or deemphasized businesses that were not in the company's long-term best interests.

Historically, GE has been able to select the right leaders at the right time, just as Reg Jones picked Jack Welch from an array of risktakers and caretakers. Normally, the CEO at General Electric reigns for 8 to 10 years, long enough to develop and implement the required strategic changes but not long enough to engender dependence. All that changed with Jack Welch, who took over at age 45 and has already served 10 years at the helm, with potentially another 10 to go. I believe this extralong term of leadership could dramatically affect the company—beneficially, if a successor is firmly in place before Welch retires.

Although John Scully of Apple is often depicted as a marketing entrepreneur and risktaker, I believe he better fits my concept of the caretaker innovator. As I pointed out earlier, Scully was hired by risktaker-founder Steve Jobs to provide more management stability for the company. Scully built demand for Jobs's Macintosh and won for it a position as a major personal computer. Under his leadership, Apple continues to prosper and even gain share with more aggressive pricing and lower-end products. He has personally taken charge of product development, and Apple has introduced a more powerful and competitive operating system. He has also taken the unusual step of forming an alliance with IBM, the company's traditional archrival. Whether Scully's leadership will enable Apple to maintain its unique product and systems position only time will tell.

THE EVOLUTIONARY INTUITIVE GAME
PLAN FOR THE CARETAKER INNOVATOR

Caretaker product leaders are more interested in improving on existing products than creating something completely new. They add features, enhance the quality, make products more useful, and may even increase the number of applications. To accomplish these strategic objectives, they need a game plan consisting of eight actions or plays:

1. Assess objectively, and invest in, the current product line's assets and abilities.
2. Create strong advertising and promotions to spur demand.
3. Be prepared to meet customer demands.
4. Employ competitive, periodically aggressive pricing to maintain position.
5. Maintain a strong "relative total cost" position to ensure a continuing and long-term cost advantage.
6. Have the next innovation ready in advance of need.
7. Know where and how the company can make money.
8. Continue to meet the user's expectations, especially with quality and reliable products.

Play 1. Assess Objectively, and Invest in, the Current Product Line's Assets and Abilities

Caretakers are interested in increasing company revenues and profits by expanding the sales volume for and extending the life of existing products. They do so by evolving changes on current designs. In the past two decades, Japanese camera companies have exemplified this type of innovation. They have added "built-in" flash, automatic focusing, and light control; they have made the units smaller and provided faster film. They have introduced these features systematically in an attempt to force obsolescence and compel users to replace their old cameras with newer models. Their strategy was based on consumer research and creative engineering. The changes were evolutionary because they came one at a time (deliberately) rather than all on one model.

Recently, the Japanese have repeated this approach of incremental improvements in the videocassette recorder market, continually making the units more automatic, smaller, and easier to use. Historically, this strategy has been the foundation of the American and Japanese automobile and consumer electronics industries. Each year, a new model was introduced for each car line, with enough new features or "improvements" to make it more attractive to the customer. Now, for instance, we are seeing the addition of computerized systems to control fuel and monitor engine functions. Radios, televisions, and audio components are also being improved bit by bit as part of the methodical game plans of caretaker leaders in the consumer electronics industry.

Another success story concerns Harley Davidson motorcycles. Over a decade ago, Harley, once the market leader in large motorcycles, was on the verge of collapse. Harley Davidson was part of a struggling conglomerate when it was acquired by its management in a leveraged buyout. Harley has been able to regain its previous position and much of its repute as a world leader in its selected segment because of the leadership of Vaughn L. Beals. The new CEO personally talked to his customers to determine what they really wanted. The company was able to respond by systematically enhancing the motorcycles to meet the customers' expressed needs. As a result, the glory days are here again for Harley Davidson.

In contrast, Honda's motorcycle division tried to "hit a home run" with innovative new machines. Unfortunately, they didn't click with the customers, and Honda's market share dropped from 58.5 percent in 1985 to 28.9 percent in 1989. Meanwhile, Harley rose from 16 percent in 1985 to 25 percent share in 1987 and again dominated the upper end of the market. The Harley case proves that no one has a strategy that will last forever; leadership must continually assess products and listen to the signals from the market place.[1]

Play 2. Create Strong Advertising and Promotions

Communicating the value of the product is less difficult for the evolutionary leader than it was for the original risktaker innovator because customers are familiar with how the product functions and know its assets and liabilities. However, customers may not have a complete understanding of the full potential of the product. The caretaker innovator must then build customer need for new product features.

This task is often accomplished by continuing, intensive advertising and promotion. The product evolutionary leader might illustrate the new features and buttress their appeal with testimonials from sports and entertainment figures. For instance, prestige, upscale products are often promoted by famous people who are perceived by the public to be both wealthy and smart. The strategy of associating new consumer products with convenience and the good life has been practiced successfully for decades.

It was been responsible for the development of today's sophisticated packaged goods industry. Procter & Gamble, Coca-Cola, General Foods, and Nabisco have led the way in increasing demand through advertising and promotion. But in the consumer sector of the economy, McDonald's heads them all. The restaurant chain continually adds menu items and promotes them with the largest advertising budget in the world.

Many industrial product companies are also successful in adding new features and creating "real differences." Features that increase flexibility, speed, ease of use, and reliability have been winners. Sophisticated controls and measurement devices enable operators to monitor their machines and to learn their jobs faster. Promotions for these improvements are usually made directly via seminars, trade shows, special publications, demonstrations, and testimonials and speeches by experts and users. The key selling point is that the differences between products must indeed be "real," rather than perceived or contrived.

Play 3. Be Prepared to Meet Customer Demands

Performing this task is even more critical for the caretaker innovator than it is for the risktaker. Because the risktaker innovator has, by definition, a truly unique product that can be protected by patents, the company may have more time to defend that product against offerings from competitors. In contrast, the caretaker is likely to be dealing with slight, easy-to-replicate differences or improvements that competitors can rapidly equal or surpass. Thus, if the innovative improvement is not available when the customers want it, they will be able to switch quickly to the competitive brand. Avoiding stockouts becomes critical to success.

To perform this strategic task, the caretaker leader must assume a calculated risk; he must believe and act on his forecasts. This faith is not as natural to the caretaker as it is to the risktaker. It flies in the face of the "just in time" inventory reduction kick. The caretaker is profit oriented and so is inclined to keep both finished and in-process inventories to a minimum. The results are stockouts and missed opportunities. Sales may even be increasing, but not as fast as the growth of the market would allow. A caretaker not alert to the inventory problem or fettered by conservative leanings will permit the competition to take advantage of the company's inaction and gain market share. Sales relative to those of the competition are important; caretakers frequently fail to recognize that they are losing competitive position until it is too late.

In late 1990, Apple introduced several new, competitively priced Macs, but the company was not able to meet the expectations of the marketplace. Apple not only failed to capitalize on demand for its products, it irritated dealers, who were counting on sales, and customers, who wanted to purchase the computers in time for Christmas. The same thing happened to Saturn, GM's new brand when it was first introduced. The Saturn division rolled out its autos systematically and was able to build strong public interest. However, it couldn't roll out enough of them to satisfy its new dedicated dealers, who were then forced to disappoint customers waiting for delivery. Irritated and disappointed customers buy someone else's products. Caretaker innovators must believe in and be responsive to their own forecasts.

Play 4. Employ Competitive, Periodically Aggressive Pricing to Maintain Position

Premium pricing is as vital to the caretaker innovator as it is to the risktaker innovator. The new featured product line must be priced higher than the standard product. However, the caretaker's window of opportunity does not open as much or remain open as long as the risktaker's. The caretaker innovator who holds the prices too high for too long creates a protective umbrella for a competitor. The aggressive competitor keeps prices lower and gains market share at the expense of the "overpriced" market leader. It is both easy and common for the caretaker to move from value pricing to umbrella pricing, and to do so unawares.

Innovator caretakers should assume that their product's new feature will be replicated and offered at a lower price. They must be prepared to bring the price down to match the competition's or even to preempt the expected replications by reducing the product's price before competition can enter the market. "Preemptive pricing" is a legal term. I use it here in a competitive sense. I am not saying the leader should violate the law and price below cost. However, I do assert that the leader should invest in making the product cheaper and achieve a cost position that permits aggressive responsive pricing when necessary.

Competitive and responsive pricing is often a problem for caretaker leaders. They are likely to want to continue the premium pricing that generates high margins as long as possible; in fact, they are reluctant to reduce the product's price even after the competition enters the market. They cling to the belief that because they were first, they are superior and will be so recognized and appreciated by the customer. As a result, they wait too long, practice umbrella pricing, and allow a competitor to gain a beachhead from which it can only be dislodged, if at all, with great difficulty.

Several very visible cases illustrate the dangers of passive pricing. Xerox waited too long to respond to the Japanese low-priced penetration of the portable copier segment, and it lost share that it has not completely regained. Kodak permitted lower priced competition to gain a foothold in the film market, and today Fuji is a major player. Zenith is the only remaining U.S. maker of televisions, and it is on very shaky ground. Pricing and cost positioning account in part for the demise of

American TV manufacturers. During the 1960s and early 1970s, bottom line/margin-obsessed managers at RCA, Zenith, and General Electric were more concerned about maintaining profit margins than market position. They literally sold off market share and permitted the competition to use a combination of low prices and new features to penetrate the market. Many of these managers were unaware of the dangers of such short-term thinking, but the Japanese recognized their strategic advantage and made substantial long-term gains that could never be recovered.

In some cases, American TV makers could offer innovative features beyond the Japanese competition. They were not willing, however, to reduce prices to stop the competition from obtaining a beachhead. Part of the problem was the inability of the caretakers to reduce costs in advance of the need to reduce prices. Some chose to keep prices high and reap short-run profits; others erroneously assumed they were the cost leaders and so were invulnerable to competitors. Whether a failure of perception or will, however, the result was the same: near extinction.

Play 5. Maintain a Strong "Relative Total Cost" Position

Even though most caretaker leaders are disciplined and strong managers, many do not know their true product and system costs.

The Boston Consulting Group made a major contribution to contemporary management thinking by restoring emphasis on "learning curves" (also called "experience curves"). The plotting and analyzing of these curves forced many companies to reevaluate the costs of their materials and labor. Many were shocked to discover that they were not only not cost effective, but at a cost disadvantage, even in highly creative and innovative product lines. Unfortunately, too many managers demonstrated lack of leadership by refusing to accept the truth until their competition had made inroads into their markets. For instance, all the U.S. automobile and consumer electronics companies once believed that the Japanese did not have the cost advantage and succeeded only by "dumping" products below costs on the American market. U.S. business executives lost control of the markets before they discovered that the Japanese, and later the Taiwanese and Koreans, had earned their cost advantage by investing in total cost reduction programs.

Caretaker product innovators must initiate a system for evaluating and monitoring their company's total cost position, must accept the reality of their findings, and take action to make their firm cost competitive. That does not necessarily mean the company is the lowest cost producer. After all, the leader is attempting to differentiate the product with innovative features, which might preclude rock-bottom costs. However, the innovating company must restrain costs sufficiently to be able to respond to a competitor's attack on its position.

To obtain this pricing flexibility, leadership must continue to invest in modern, efficient, highly productive systems in all phases of the business, including the factory and logistical support. Leaders should also assess the need for multiple modes of distribution and selling. Certainly, all the major manufacturers today have made these investments and have improved their cost position in *absolute* terms. However, the real key is *relative costs*. Caretaker leaders must constantly and objectively probe for the answer to the critical question of how well they compare with the competition, now and in the future.

Play 6. Have the Next Innovation Ready in Advance of Need

I have already pointed out that the risktaker must be prepared for the day when the competition will catch up. Preparation means having the next generation, or several generations, on the shelf ready to introduce to the market at the proper time. Timing and rapid response are even more critical to caretaker innovators. They also should be planning as far ahead as possible. The cost and risk of development is less when a company is so positioned that it does not need to rush a response to competitive action. If a company is prepared, it may be able to use the improved features or combine features to maintain value prices and higher margins.

Many believe American firms have been guilty of failing to prepare for their competition's response. I have witnessed a number of Japanese and European companies making the same error. I have already related the story of a Japanese office products and systems company that had too little regard for the ability of its competitors to replicate its innovative products. In addition, this firm seemed to ignore the other products and technologies that could perform the same functions for the users.

You can follow the strategy of maintaining prices and competing on the basis of new features only if you are prepared with the next two generations on the drawing board. The personal computer market offers a good illustration. Compaq was able to maintain its leadership position in lap-top computers for several years by having new features available before the competition. IBM, Hewlett Packard, and Apple were unable to take away market share, even though Compaq retained high prices and high margins. Once the product lagged and innovations were not continually introduced, however, Compaq lost the edge and was forced to adopt a pricing strategy. The ensuing conflict within the company resulted in the removal of president Joseph Canion by board chairman Ben Rosen.

Many other companies have lost share when they lost their lead in innovations. Consider the case of Formica, a household name for many years. It dropped to second place in the laminated products market (with a 32 percent share) behind a comparatively unknown company, Ralph Wilson Plastics, of Temple, Texas, which assumed market leadership (with a 45 percent share). Wilson's products used a simplified, though more expensive, group of resins that drastically cut production time. Thus, if a distributor were out of stock, Wilson could respond in 10 days, much faster than Formica's 25 days. Wilson's speed advantage demonstrates how to differentiate a product in a way that cannot be easily or rapidly emulated by a competitor.[2]

Play 7. Know Where and How the Company Can Make Money

While making money is not the sole goal of business (despite what many American managers seem to believe), profitability is certainly important for the business's long-term growth and survival. Therefore, the caretaker leader must know where and how to make money. That entails determining whether profits are highest when the company focuses on making and selling the product or when it concentrates on the related consumables, parts, or services. Many companies could literally give away or break even on the equipment and product and make their profits on the aftermarket parts, consumables, and add-on options, accessories, and service.

As I discussed in the previous chapter, the aftermarket may be more profitable than the market for the primary product. Recall, for instance, that Gillette did better focusing on the blades rather than the basic razor. Today, it makes three times as much on cartridge refills (the contemporary form of blades) than it does on the disposable razor. However, Gillette has not ignored the popularity of the disposable razor (spearheaded by Bic), which in 1989 accounted for over 40 percent of the razor market. Gillette has continued to invest in improving the replacement blade/cartridge as part of a strategy of convincing users of disposable razors to switch back to the old method of keeping the razor and throwing away the used blades. Because that strategy required a superior blade and razor, Gillette put over $200 million into the Sensormatic shaving system, which was successfully introduced in 1990.[3]

Gillette's leaders also illustrate many other key actions required of the caretaker evolutionary product leader. Gillette recognized that its heavy investment mandated heavy security to keep the product a secret, surprise being a key strategic element when introducing an innovation. The company built a large fence around its Boston facility, swore staff to silence, and implemented tight controls. Gillette managed to create a compelling design in secret and launch the product when it wanted. However, the company was not prepared for the demand it had created. Gillette had expected to sell 18 million Sensor razors in 1990; 24 million were shipped. Gillette planned on shipping 200 million blade cartridges; it shipped over 350 million.[4]

The Sensor strategy followed in the tradition established by the company founder, King Gillette, who considered the "greatest feature of the business" to be "the endless chain of blade consumption." Gillette articulated a willingness to invest in a long-term relationship with his customers by meeting or exceeding their expectations. The company believes it continues to accomplish that mission by *consistently* producing a superior product at a competitive price. That attitude reflects caretaker style leadership that has learned where and how the company makes money.

The Eastman Kodak Company learned this lesson a long time ago. Kodak was willing to license the competitors to build their camera innovations at low prices. They were not greedy about the licensing fees and recognized that it was better to have the market standardized around their designs than to have competing standards and designs. The reason was not altruistic, it was highly profit oriented. Kodak realized that they made more money on the film and the processing equipment than on the camera. The leadership of Kodak recognized that they would sell more film and supplies if the entire world standardized their cameras around their technology and so they set out license major camera companies in all parts of the world to use their technology to build cameras but not the film and supplies. Further, they understood the need to advertise, and so they invested heavily in making the "little yellow film box" an easily recognized symbol of film quality and excellence.

Kodak's film-based innovation strategy worked even when Dr. Land's Instant camera was introduced. At first, Polaroid developed the camera but not the film. Kodak provided the film and was content to let Polaroid make the camera, along as they had the dominant position in film. However, Polaroid changed the rules and Kodak was forced to respond with a camera of their own. This was the trigger that caused Kodak to offer its own instant camera design. Unfortunately, because Kodak was not prepared for the Polaroid change, the leadership had to take some shortcuts that resulted in a violation of the antitrust laws and ultimately into the loss of trial and large penalties.

Kodak also seems to have misjudged the popularity of the 35-mm camera and allowed the leadership and development of this camera technology to be taken by the Japanese. This has permitted Fuji film to take a more aggressive role and to penetrate the world, even U.S. markets at the expense of Kodak. If Kodak had led or quickly followed with the 35-mm technology and had used its traditional strategy, Fuji would likely have not been able to gain a beachhead in the U.S. market. Even Polaroid has learned that the aftermarket can be a more significant profit contributor than the hardware and thus has joined the pursuit by developing a standard film.

Xerox also learned that the aftermarket game could be played for sustained profits. In its risktaker phase it had developed innovative copiers and gained a dominant world position. Later in the product life cycle, Xerox allowed others to license the technology, while it continued to produce innovative features for plain paper copiers. By leasing equipment and continuing to innovative, Xerox was able to make many demands on its customers. The company required that its units use Xerox fluids, power, and even paper. Service costs were incorporated into the lease agreements. The profits from the aftermarket service and consumables were highly attractive.

This arrangement allowed Xerox to maintain good relationships with its customers and to constantly upgrade and innovate on the larger equipment. However, the approach caused Xerox to ignore the less profitable and "for sale" lines of copiers, thus permitting the Japanese to gain a toehold in the market and ultimately a major share. No strategy can last for long without adaptation to changing conditions.

Play 8. Continue to Meet the User's Expectations

Innovative caretaker leaders must be able to provide their customers with products that are reliable and consistently of high quality. That is, leaders must back up the lip service given to "quality" (one of the management slogans identified in Chapter 1) with features that meet the customers' expectations from the first day. The new features must work completely, not partially. Thus, real innovative leaders implement quality right from the start.

The process begins with market research to discover consumer wants and needs. For instance, if the customer is happy with the product and not interested in new features, the leader must adjust the game plan. Customers resistant to change increase the complexity of selling and the time needed to gain profitable sales volume for the innovative new features. Illustrative of this situation is the current attempt by the electrical utility industry to persuade customers to replace their current energy-consuming appliances with more efficient but more expensive ones.

Most people are unlikely to scrap functioning and attractive kitchen appliances just because they are consuming too much electricity. Energy-efficient equipment must be in use for 8 to 10 years before it "pays back" the extra purchase price. Selling these appliances will require a long-term effort as well, perhaps more time consuming and expensive than getting people to use electrical appliances in the first place.

The second step in establishing quality control is to meet and even slightly exceed the customer expectations you have created. Innovator leaders can become so enamored of their improved product or new feature that they tend to promise more than it can possible deliver. This tendency is not as destructive as at the risktaker stage but still causes problems. The law remains: *Do not overpromise!*

Third, invest in the quality systems required to ensure that products reach the customer in good working condition. That means producing to standards and shipping without damage. It also means basic things such as providing clear, concise instruction manuals, making sure all the parts are in the box, and having in place a follow-up system to solve problems. The more complex the product, the more important is attention to these details and the more vital is the commitment to a quality perspective.

THE EVOLUTIONARY TEAM

In contrast to the risktaker phase, the evolutionary caretaker stage of the business functions best when characterized by total team play rather than when dominated by the exceptional performance of one or two superstars (although risktakers still operate in a team setting). Thus, the entire team, and not just a few, must be motivated and rewarded for success. Further, the measures and rewards must be appropriate to the life cycle of the product innovation. Initially, the team should be driven to gain a major share of the market, even at the cost of sacrificing some profit or of incurring some loss. As the market grows, the leader should increase the pressure on the team to make a profit while continuing to emphasize that loss of share is unacceptable. Finally, as the product matures, the leader should reward the team for profits and display less concern for market share.

Although developing and implementing a team reward system is not easy, it can make the difference between winning and losing. The key is for the leader to understand what each part of the team must contribute and when. That understanding begins with the nature of the leader. Caretakers, themselves, are not usually the innovators. Instead, they rely on others in the organization to do the job.

Engineers and Product Developers

The first and most important team members are those individuals charged with improving the product. To do this, they must constantly examine competitive products and determine how they compare with their own. This process may involve "value engineering," in which the competing product is taken apart and each component examined. The total piece of equipment is analyzed for cost, quality, reliability, and performance. The task must be approached with objectivity and the results accepted with humility (if unfavorable), because the analysis is worthless if not done honestly.

The critical question is how much does it cost the *competitor* to make and sell the product. Many companies make the mistake of asking how much it would cost *them* to make the product in *their* factories and sell it with *their* sales force, which may be quite different from the competitor's. Asking the wrong question is why many American firms failed to understand that it was the Japanese superior cost structure that allowed them to sell quality products for less.

But properly applied, value analysis, an approach that has been in use for over 50 years, provides important insights into the competition. Well-informed leaders have been able to anticipate the competition's next moves and out maneuver them. By understanding the competitor's total costs, the caretaker's team can reduce its own costs and offer a strong competitive response that can prevent the opposition from gaining market share.

The product developers on the caretaker innovator's team must also recognize that it is the user of the product who really matters. Empathy for the perspective of the customer will help them focus on features that customers need rather than on those that appeal to product engineers. This requires a talent for listening carefully to the customers/users to appreciate their degree of satisfaction with current products and features as well as their desire for improvements. The goal is to develop unique products that will be readily accepted by the marketplace.

Product Introduction Managers

Since a significant part of the caretaker innovation strategy is evolution and planned change, the team must have people who can skillfully manage the process of introducing the improved product. They must sense when a new line can be introduced without cannibalizing the existing line and, at the same time, without losing position to the competition. Cannibalization or premature displacement is a major threat for the evolutionary caretaker leader. Good timing requires sensitivity to the market and an intuitive feeling for when the competition may strike. Those "feelings," of course, are grounded on solid and up-to-date information from a monitoring system that offers a clear assessment of product positioning.

The leader must be willing to discard some of the line to remain competitive and avoid excessive duplication or overlap. These decisions entail a combination of science and art. The scientific aspect involves tracking sales and customer needs. In today's world, the leader may need strong computer modeling skills. The computer model should include a pricing element, because the leader will have to determine when to reduce prices on the old products and how to position the new line in the market. The artistic element is the leader's intuitive sense for introducing the line at the right time.

Salespeople

The sales force must be informed, credible, and enthusiastic—though not, at this stage, with the zeal of the missionary. While the task of the risktaker's salespeople was to convert individuals into product users, the job of the caretaker's sales force is to explain the differences in the product and how it is better than anything else currently on the market. Salespeople thus need to be up on the competition's products as well as their own. Once again, they must avoid overpromising and thereby creating unattainable expectations that will threaten long-term customer relationships.

At this evolutionary stage, the leader may have to supplement the company's own direct sales force with third-party distribution or sales representatives. They will be needed in locations where the company's sales force is weak or where the economics do not warrant having direct salespeople on staff. These supplemental agents must always be as well trained and knowledgeable as the company's own sales force.

The reward and measurement system should be geared toward gaining and maintaining market share and building long-term customer relationships and loyalty. What works best is a combination of salary and commission that takes into consideration the time required with the customer to explain the improvements in the product and also encourages the effective use of time to make a significant number of sales.

Advertising and Promotion Talents

To maintain demand, the team will require people with strong advertising and promotional skills. Advertising and promotion should communicate the products' special features and sustain consumer interest. Its role is to support but not oversell the product. A blend of team insiders and outside experts is appropriate here, with the emphasis on the outsiders. The team will need to establish a long-term relationship with a strong, committed advertising firm or with individual professionals. These people must know enough about the product to understand what it does but not be so immersed that they fall in love with it. They must remain realistic and objective and so help the inside staff avoid overselling.

Production Experts

The skills of this part of the strategic team include a firm understanding of the complexity and timing involved in the production of innovative features. These experts should be consulted early, during the design stage. Too often the production team is brought into the cycle too late and asked to perform the impossible. However, Gillette avoided this mistake with the Sensormatic innovation. The new-feature razor required mounting blades on small springs that would cling to the contour of each individual's face as he shaved. Development of the system demanded a creative integration of materials and processing that would have been unachievable without the up-front involvement of Gillette's production experts.[5]

Good timing for the production team also means delivering the product when it is needed, in sufficient numbers, and ready and able to perform up to specifications. The same criteria must be met with each introduction of improved versions. Sustained, consistent results are the hallmark of an effective evolutionary team.

Inventory Managers

Logistics is another often overlooked but vital element of success. The team can respond to the created demand for the product and avoid stockouts by establishing an efficient inventory control system linked to market needs. As I have stressed earlier, the key is to strike a balance between too much stock on hand (which will be rendered obsolete when new versions of the product are introduced) and too little. In the evolutionary phase, inventory control of vital components and consumables will be of particular importance to the servicing of the aftermarket. Important components will probably be produced internally, but the more common commodity parts may be purchased from outside manufacturers. Thus, inventory/logistics managers must develop strong relationships with these outside vendors to ensure timely deliveries.

CONSISTENCY (SAYING MUST EQUAL DOING)

More so than for the risktaker, consistency is a critical element of the caretaker's leadership style. The caretaker strives to build long-term credibility and avoid overpromising or underpromising. This credibility is an effective defense against an aggressively promoted entry into the caretaker's market. Trust and market share are acquired over time.

CHANGE AND FLEXIBILITY

The ability to adapt to change distinguishes the caretaker leader from the manager. Most caretakers are conservative and thus inclined to hold on too long to drain the last drops of profitability from a product. The leader must be alert to and guard against this tendency.

When, as is so often the case, caretakers follow risktakers, they need to make the changes that will allow the company to prosper over the long haul. Just such a situation developed with Nutri/System (see Chapter 4). By 1984, the once vigorous company was struggling; revenues had fallen in one year from $167 million to $101 million, and profits had declined to $1.8 million. Under pressure, founder Harold Katz hired Donald McCulloch.

McCulloch was an experienced businessperson. He knew nothing about the diet business, but he did know how to add innovative products and how to turn companies around. McCulloch mollified the franchisees and the sales force, and added more franchises. He introduced several innovative products, including caffeine-free iced tea and cheese with a long shelf life. He integrated sales with product and increased incentives, paying bonuses to employees who signed up customers. McCulloch beefed up advertising on the radio. A successful sales promotion put more than one thousand disk jockeys around the country on Nutri/System programs. Their testimonials were very effective, although those who could not maintain the discipline, and the weight loss, had a negative impact. McCulloch continued Katz's value-pricing strategy; he enhanced the company's image by citing the studies of the National Health Sciences Advisory Board and employing its members as advisors.

Revenues have increased fourfold under McCulloch's leadership, and he was able to take the company private. He has used inspired advertising (the disk jockeys) and improvements on an already strong product to construct his success. The sale of Nutri/System food has exploited the consumables aftermarket and has been a major profit maker for the business. McCulloch has resisted the temptations that Katz could not, declining to diversify the business or increase costs with the trappings of success. He has remained focused on his mission to make money for himself and his franchises and to share the wealth with the employees. Nutri/System customers still appear to be happy, and they continue to support the program and spread the word to others.[6]

TIMING

Just as for the risktaker, timing is everything for the caretaker leader. Specifically, the leader should be aware of five situations that require strategic action.

Situation 1. The Mature Market

When the market or product has matured to the point that it is difficult to tell one product from another, the caretaker leader should consider differentiating the company's offerings. One common approach when all the products look alike is to stand out by cutting prices. That's good for the customers in the short run, but competing firms lose financially, and many are forced out of the market. Those that remain have a hard time making a decent return. This is the situation in today's consumer electronics markets, especially for television receivers.

A better solution for the caretaker innovator is to create a true product difference that will allow the company to value price rather than compete directly on the basis of costs. Systematically introducing product improvements has been the fundamental strategy of the auto industry since Alfred Sloan institutionalized market segmentation at General Motors decades ago. Before that, Henry Ford's least cost strategy was threatening to turn cars into commodities ("the customer can have any color of car he wants, provided it is black"). If Ford's approach had prevailed, automobiles would be just another dull means of transportation (and only Ralph Nader would be happy). Instead, we have a dynamic marketplace with an enormous variety of cars from which to choose, and new models come out every year.

Situation 2. Lower than Expected Saturation Rates

Suppose the innovative caretaker leader has done research and concluded that the company's product should achieve 30 percent market penetration by the end of the year. Instead, it only achieves 15 percent. The time has come to create new designs and features to stimulate demand and usage. The lesson of the women's clothing industry applies.

Each year the industry changes styles—and with a flourish—to make people dissatisfied with what's in their closets. We discard the old and purchase the new, for the most part, just to keep up with fashion. Women in particular are targeted by the industry. Hemlines are moved up and down from year to year to increase sales; one season, women are encouraged to wear pants, the next, they are persuaded to wear skirts. The same concept has been used with almost all high-saturation consumer products. The lesson: Innovate to stimulate the market.

Situation 3. Competitors Closing the Gap

Market leaders continually monitor the competition to make sure their share is not being eroded. Meanwhile, they are working of Play 6 of the evolutionary game plan, which calls for having the next generation of the product ready. The caretaker leader waits until the competition is able to catch up and introduce its "me too" product that replicates the company's current offering. The leader then introduces the next product generation with new, innovative features that reestablish the firm's leadership and neutralize the competition. The strategy is effective, but the timing is delicate. New features must not be introduced too early and so reduce sales of the current product, or too late and allow the competition to gain market share that will be hard to retake.

Situation 4. Technology Now Available

Sometimes established technologies become available for new applications, and the alert leader will seize on the opportunity to add innovative features to the company's products.

For instance, long-life batteries were developed originally to support the U.S. aerospace and military programs. Only later were they applied to numerous consumer and industrial products. These batteries now provide backup power for computers and other microprocessor equipment so that unexpected power interruptions will not damage the software. As a result, some computers and video equipment have become truly portable. Technological developments in such diverse things as plastics, energy sources, and microminiaturization that originated in space and defense research have made possible many other consumer and industrial innovations.

Long-lasting batteries will also play a major role in the development and extended use of the electric automobile. Electric vehicles have been around since the first decade of the century. For a variety of reasons, internal combustion became the dominant technology for car engines. Now, however, environmental and energy concerns have renewed interest in electric cars. General Motors has announced it will produce electric cars in the 1990s. Long-life battery technology offers hope to the industry, although we cannot know yet whether the batteries will be able to meet customer expectations. Another problem is electricity; many utilities are reducing rather than increasing capacity, and they may not be able to meet additional demand generated by electric cars. Those factors will no doubt influence the timing of the product innovation. The development of the electric car may take the combination of risktaking and caretaking leaders.

Situation 5. Geographic Dispersion

Over time, conditions change, and existing products from one geographic region can be rolled out into new areas. Consider the global history of small, efficient cars.

In the 1970s, Japan did not have the massive highway system that crisscrossed the United States. Gasoline was very expensive, parking was impossible, and most homes were without garages. Thus, Japanese car buyers rejected the huge gas guzzlers offered by U.S. companies and opted for the small, fuel-efficient, durable cars produced by their home manufacturers. In Europe, drivers bought European high-precision cars that offered the smooth ride and firm handling required on highways with no speed limits. Neither of these car types had a big market in the United States of 20 years ago.

The gas crisis in the United States changed all that. The Japanese and German car makers were positioned to provide small, high-performance, fuel-efficient cars Americans suddenly wanted. The Big Three U.S. automakers, on the other hand, were either unprepared or reluctant to displace their high-profit large cars with small cars of their own. The invaders from abroad capitalized on their fortunate timing. They had the right products ready, and the Americans couldn't or wouldn't respond—until it was too late.

Windows of opportunity close fast. The innovative leader, caretaker or risktaker (or, as we shall see in the next chapter, the surgeon or undertaker), steps through the opening and seizes the competitive advantage when it is available.

6

Surgeons and Undertakers: Rethinking Priorities and Viability

The role of the surgeon leader is both similar to and different from those of the risktaker and the caretaker leaders. It is similar because innovation and creativity are just as important when a business requires rethinking and restructuring as when it is growing rapidly or maturing. The primary mission of the surgeon is to determine how to save the company. The solution may entail changing the product mix, weeding out those products without a future, and supporting the real winners. At times, the surgeon may need to make an innovation in a product or service to change it into a winner.

The surgeon's role is different because it requires selectivity and a focus on what needs to be discarded as well as what might be added. However, surgeons are risktakers who gamble the very existence of a company on their intuition and judgment. The margin for error is very small. Asserting that, as with the medical surgeon, a slip of the scalpel can be deadly would push the analogy to dramatic extremes. Nonetheless, every decision of the surgeon may be critical to the health of the business, more so than for other leaders.

In the life cycle of the company, a surgeon would normally follow a caretaker who had become complacent and unresponsive to change or a risktaker who had gotten too ambitious and had tried to grow or diversify too quickly. The latter case occurred at Nutri/System. A surgeon leader was called in to trim the excesses added by the overly aggressive and profligate Harold Katz (founder-risktaker), before the company was

116

turned over to the steady, innovative McCulloch (caretaker). The extraneous and failing ventures needed to be cut away from the company before the core business could be nurtured back to vigorous health.

Many companies have needed the talents of the surgeon leader. Some have succeeded; others have failed. Lee Iacocca's surgical skills saved Chrysler, but not just by cutting. The company was restored to health by the infusion of Iacocca's missionary zeal and with the introduction of his new line of K cars. Years later, it appears that Iacocca may have to perform his surgical role once again to reinvigorate the company. It will be interesting to see if he can do the job twice or whether it will take a more aggressive risktaker to launch Chrysler to its previous levels.

The story of a competitor also entails a complicated mix of leadership styles. Roger Smith was a member of a complacent and overconfident General Motors management team. They assumed the auto industry would condense into a few global players by 1985. In line with that thinking, GM changed from a product-innovation and market-driven strategy to a production-based strategy. GM began to make medium- to low-quality autos that all looked alike. Leadership badly underestimated the market share potential of the Japanese (they assumed 5 percent was the top). As a result, when Roger Smith took over, the company was in a poor competitive position.

While it may be an exaggeration to say that Smith had to *save* GM, his actions constituted necessary surgery. Smith restructured the company and diversified by acquiring Hughes *Aerospace and Defense Systems* and getting into information systems services and management with EDS. To regain a strong competitive position, he closed many plants and made alliances with other companies. He changed the way GM built cars, even entering into a joint venture with Toyota. Since 1985, GM has redesigned over 84 percent of its cars. In 1990, the company introduced its fuel-efficient Geo line. The new Saturn, also fuel efficient and expected to rival the Japanese offerings for quality and performance, began to arrive a year later. These moves should position GM well for the future. Investments in product innovations, like the ones made by Roger Smith, are part of the function of the surgeon leader.

James Cotting took the scalpel to International Harvester. He restructured the company by selling its construction business to Dresser Industries and its agricultural equipment business (the original core) to Tenneco. In fact, Cotting was not only willing to sell its foundation product, but its brand name as well. In 1986, International Harvester became Navistar, essentially a truck company. It redesigned 85 percent of its line in 1987 and, in 1989, introduced 27 new models. Innovations included a nine-speed transmission (developed jointly with Dana) and a smokeless diesel engine.[1] Thus, Cotting has demonstrated how a combination of product innovation and selective pruning can be a powerful prescription for survival.

Most of the time, the surgeon is an outsider who is brought in deliberately to make the tough decisions necessary to save the company. The task requires a person who can be analytical, financially skilled, objective, and decisive. While avoiding emotional involvement in the situation, the surgeon cannot be too hard-hearted, or cutthroat or she will be unable to motivate employees and gain the cooperation needed for a successful turnaround. Remember, the successful surgeon is a healer, not an asset stripper. The asset stripper sells the vital organs to the highest bidder, without regard for the patient. Time and commitment are integral parts of this game plan.

THE SURGEON INTUITIVE GAME PLAN

The surgical strategy may seem simple, but it isn't. Like risktakers and caretakers, these innovative product leaders must be able to perform a number of plays to obtain their objectives.

1. Analyze the company's vital signs and make a quick diagnosis.
2. Evaluate the reasons for past successes and failures.
3. Assess the competitive arena.
4. Build customer, employee, and supplier confidence.
5. Balance inside and outside personnel.
6. Employ responsive pricing to balance short-term and long-term needs.
7. Establish the ability to meet demands over the long haul.

Play 1. Analyze the Company's Vital Signs and Make a Quick Diagnosis

The surgeon game plan starts with a careful financial and market assessment of the business. The leader is seeking answers to these basic questions:

1. What is the financial and market health of the products and services we provide?
2. Is our competitive position deteriorating? If so, why?
3. What is the cost and profitability situation? Is everybody in the industry losing money, or is it just us?

4. How competitive are our products and what can they survive in the long term?

This traditional portfolio assessment identifies the company's "cash cows," "stars," and "dogs." (These are the apt and useful terms coined by the Boston Consulting Group to describe the profitability and potential of a firm's offerings.) During my association with GE, we classified many products, and those deemed not fit for the future were sold or harvested to reap their cash potential.

In Chapter 4, I described how GE housewares grew under the risk-taking leadership of Willard Sahloff, a true product innovator. Sahloff retired in the early 1960s, and by the early 1970s his old business was in a crisis. The loss of fair trade pricing increased pressures on costs and restricted innovation (see Chapter 4). A series of surgeon leaders took over. One of the first decisions was to reduce the offerings (e.g., the vacuum cleaner business was sold) and focus on fewer products. Part of the strategy, however, was to introduce new, innovative products to replace the discontinued lines. For example, security devices such as smoke alarms and motion detectors were added. Unfortunately, the strategy failed and the housewares business was sold to Black and Decker.

Thus, GE housewares demonstrated the full range of risktaker, caretaker, surgeon, and undertaker leaders in less than two decades. The business life cycle progressed rapidly, and so did the turnover in leadership.

Play 2. Evaluate the Reasons for Past Successes and Failures

Current vital signs may not tell the whole story. Some products may be ailing from mismanagement, underfunding, or poor marketing and could still be viable. Therefore, the surgeon must be more than a bean counter or number cruncher. He must talk to the firm's customers and employees to gain their perspectives on the product. Failure to "get out in the field" in this way would be analogous to the medical doctor who only reads Xrays and blood test results and never examines the patient.

Unfortunately, in many businesses that is what happens. The accountants look at the numbers and declare the business dying or dead! The leader must discover the customer's feelings about the product and determine the impact on the customer should the product not be available. (This is particularly important in the industrial and commercial sectors.) The leader may discover that the product is vital to the customer's business. In fact, customers may be willing to pay a higher price and so turn that red ink to black.

Play 3. Assess the Competitive Arena

The surgeon must seek to understand the competition's products and leadership. Besides performing a product value analysis, the leader evaluates opposing senior management's motivations and strategies and looks for answers to such questions as: What are the competitors trying to do? How committed are they to this specific business or product line? Do they care whether we stay in the business or get out? What will they do if we do get out?

Conventional wisdom has it that every company would be glad to have the competition drop out of the market. But often the opposite is true. Companies welcome a competitor that complements them by offering a product they do not want to provide. In this case, the poor performing competitor is an asset. Its presence in the field might deflect the perception that the dominant firm is greedy or violating antitrust laws. The surgeon leader might also discover that the competition would be willing to join parts of the two lines into a new company.

The real value of the firm's assets and product line may be measured by standards other than performance in the marketplace. Some company might want them even if it is not interested in participating in the business. The situation is analogous to the antique dealer, who recognizes that collectors purchase things that other people consider to be junk. Dealers pick up castaways and resell them at a high profit. The surgeon must investigate this possibility before cutting a product adrift.

Play 4. Build Customer, Employee, and Supplier Confidence

One of the most difficult tasks for the surgeon during a turbulent period for the company is maintaining the morale of employees and the trust of suppliers and customers.

The leader's first job is to determine how critical the product is to current major customers. If the company is providing a component or service that is vital to the customers' business, profitability, or way of life, the leader must labor to assure them that the product or service will be available. If the customers do not have confidence in the leader, they will seek out alternative sources of supply; they may even be forced to develop their own capabilities and become competitors. The second confidence factor is price. A customer buying something expensive will want the supplier around long enough to back up a warranty, service the product, and/or provide parts. The third element is complexity. The more complex the product, the greater the risk for the customers, and the greater the need for the leader to instill customer confidence. *And the only way to build confidence is for the leader to make a personal guarantee, perhaps with a written agreement, and then meet those commitments.* The leader who fails to deliver may never get a second chance.

Employees, too, must have enough confidence in the leadership to give their best efforts for the time needed to obtain the desired results. The leader must expend the time and effort to communicate the game plan.

Norman P. Blake, Jr., Chief Executive Officer, USF&G, illustrates how communications with employees is critical to the successful surgery leader. Norm took over the company in 1990 when it was in very poor condition. He immediately performed significant surgery. He sold off $1.2 billion in weak investments, dismissed 31 percent of the employees and cut ties with nearly 800 underperforming independent agents. These actions permitted the company to move into the black and position it to regain some of the market share it lost.

Even with all of these dynamic changes, Mr. Blake was able to install a winning culture and make his employees feel as though it can be a success. He made strong efforts to open lines of communications. This included open meeting and visits to employees as well as answering letters from employees agents and customers. He instituted bonus programs that more equitably spread money around. Profit sharing, previously the domain of senior executives, is now available to all.[2]

Norm clearly instituted the changes required and restored stability to the company, while positioning it to take risks in the future. For instance he is moving the company more aggressively into personal lines as home and auto policies which are being exited by other insurance companies. This demonstrates that a surgeon must do more than cut out, he must be willing to reinstitute both stability and calculated risktaking.

Once the employees understand what is going on and the risks they will be taking, they must be properly rewarded. This way they will be true partners, just as though the old, struggling business were a new venture.

The company's suppliers must receive this same type of consideration. They must understand the situation and be willing to take the risk. They, too, must be thought of as partners; an adversarial relationship could be fatal. Those that supply key components especially should get a lot of attention.

The lesson is to be honest with all the stakeholders. Surgeons must be credible to succeed. They themselves must recognize, and must convince customers, employees, and suppliers, that only win/win relationships will work. Further, when a company survives and later prospers, the leader must not forget the partnerships that made it possible. Of course, win/win relationships are important for risktakers and caretakers also. I stress them here because in the desperate struggle for survival, the surgeon leader is more tempted to take shortcuts that will only get her lost in the woods later.

Play 5. Balance Inside and Outside Personnel

Often the path to success for the surgeon is to have the least cost position and generate enough cash from volume sales to keep debtors and other key stakeholders content. Cash flow is vital to pay investors and suppliers and keep the company out of bankruptcy.

Costs can be reduced by having as few employees as possible in all areas, but especially in sales. This need conflicts with the desired approach of a dedicated, aggressive sales force. A company in trouble, however, must rely on distributors, wholesalers, retailers, agents, and representatives to supplement the sales staff. The challenge for leadership is to gain the loyalty of these third-party sales agents so that they will perform as though they were part of the team. They need to feel they are partners in a long-term relationship. They must be assured that the company will deliver its product and will keep its promises; otherwise they know they will be left alone facing dissatisfied or irate customers.

The leader must evaluate carefully the use of third-party suppliers for accounting, personnel, warehousing, and other support functions. In desperate situations, being totally "lean and mean" may be the only way to survive. When the enterprise recovers, however, the leader must be prepared to take on board certain key professionals. The decision to staff internally or from outside is ongoing.

Play 6. Employ Responsive Pricing to Balance Short-Term and Long-Term Needs

I stressed in the previous two chapters that the risktaker inventor and the caretaker innovator should attempt value pricing in the early stages and be prepared to meet the competition as it appears. The surgeon has a different problem: generating enough cash to survive while meeting or beating the prices of the competition. To do so, the leader must assess the competitors' intentions and degree of aggressiveness. The competition may want the leader's company in the market and may be willing to subsidize its survival with artificially high umbrella pricing. This solution cannot be counted on for the long haul, however. The surgeon must eventually establish and maintain a cost position, regardless of the pricing strategies of competitors.

Surgeons do a good job when survival is at stake. But when things improve and the pressure is relaxed, they often add expense and drift into another financial crisis.

Play 7. Establish the Ability to Meet Demands over the Long Haul

While taking some short-term measures to help the company survive, the surgeon must also invest in product development and production capability to increase the company's marketing and sales capabilities. These investments in the long term need to be made gradually as the company increases its ability to pay the bills and meet the expected returns.

When Lee Iacocca was brought over from Ford, his first step was to evaluate Chrysler's portfolio. He sold off selected assets for the cash to invest in new products. Next, he moved aggressively to get the federal government to support his survival plan and to guarantee his loans. Iacocca had to overcome considerable opposition to this unprecedented action; many people believed the government should not be financing a private company, especially one on the verge of collapse. He essentially sold the strategy to the stakeholders, which now included the American public, with a missionary zeal.

Once Iacocca had the confidence of the customers and investors, he built a new line of attractive and competitively priced cars that sold well enough to move Chrysler into third place in market share. I remember amazing myself by buying a new Chrysler; before Iacocca I wouldn't have considered even entering a Chrysler showroom, let alone purchasing one of Chrysler's cars. And I was not alone. In time, sales increased, profits improved, and a major portion of the debt was repaid. Chrysler's surgeon had pulled it off.

However, between 1989 and 1992, Chrysler's share has declined from 12 percent to 9 percent. The cars were no longer innovative nor as attractive to the public, but leadership seemed unwilling to invest in improvements to the line. Increasingly, Chrysler was forced to compete on price and to reduce margins. As a result, Chrysler dealers were pushed out of business and into bankruptcy. Another consumer crisis of confidence looms. No one wants to buy a car not supported by a strong dealer network that can provide parts and service.

Chrysler's situation illustrates why the game plan must include arrangements for orderly leadership succession from the surgeon to the risktaker who can facilitate the company's growth. Iacocca's shortcomings in this regard have produced what *USA Today* has called a "brain drain at Chrysler." The newspaper reported in late 1991 that not only had Chrysler lost executives, engineers, and computer experts, it lacked the key people needed to develop a new luxury car.[3] The Chrysler board of directors selected Robert J. Eaton of General Motors to succeed Iacocca in early 1992. Eaton, a 29-year career veteran of General Motors, was depicted as a risktaker. He was able to turn around the GM European operation and opened plants in Poland and Hungary. He was depicted as a "product" guy, an engineer who thoroughly knows and loves cars. It will be interesting to see whether this outsider risktaker can provide the impetus to rebuild Chrysler and whether Iacocca can resist the temptation to stay involved.[4]

THE SURGEON'S PRODUCT-DRIVEN TEAM

The surgeon's team has some of the characteristics of the risktaker's team. With both, personality is at least as important as personnel, and both must have a unique combination of skills.

First, the leader needs true believers, in all parts of the company, who are dedicated to the company's survival. And the number one true believer must be the leader himself. Once again, Lee Iacocca is a prime example. He approached his task with missionary zeal, putting himself on the line to guarantee the quality of his cars. Chrysler became, in effect, Iacocca Motors. Iacocca backed up his promises with the then innovative 5-year, 50,000-mile warranties that have since become the industry standard. The dealers and distributors of Chrysler cars demonstrated their commitment as well by building facilities and generating customer confidence that they were in business to stay.

The second characteristic of surgical teams is that every member is a gambler willing to bet on the turnaround. All feel they can be winners and make the game plan succeed. Their compensation may have to be based almost entirely on sales and job performance, with little or nothing guaranteed. And because the organization must be kept lean, every team member will have to work harder and for longer hours.

Third, team members must be willing to work under pressure with limited resources. They will not have large inventories to draw upon; they will deal with vendors concerned about getting paid; they will labor under the scrutiny of financiers who will track their every move. Thus, the team must project the appearance of solvency while operating with insufficient inventory or limited product scope and depth. However, despite conditions, team members must be honest people, not hustlers. They are gamblers, not opportunists playing a confidence game.

TIMING

When is the season of the surgeon? When drastic measures are required to save the patient, but reason still exists for hope. Here are four situations when the time is right for surgery—and one when it is time for the undertaker.

Situation 1. The Company Has Real Assets to Build on, but Those Assets Have Been Mismanaged or Prematurely "Milked"

Suppose the company has been led by a non-leader "caretaker" who cashed in on the company's products without reinvesting in new ones. Or perhaps poor timing or some unusual problems have put the firm into trouble. For instance, a unique product may have been introduced when the economy was struggling and customers were postponing purchase decisions. I have witnessed two such situations.

The first involves electric utility companies. Over the past 10 years, many American companies have been unwilling to take the risk of building new power-generation plants for a variety of reasons: the slow growth in electrical usage, the difficulty of building power plants, the environmental movement, the concern about both nuclear power safety and the ability to activate plants when they are ready to go on line. As a result, many electric utilities have followed the more cautious path of letting others build the plants and then purchasing power. Private investors or industrial companies build plants for themselves and sell the excess to the utility. These are called cogenerational plants. Laws require utilities to purchase the excess power at rates comparable to what it would cost them to supply power from their own facilities.

The noninvestment trend has had an extremely negative impact on General Electric, Westinghouse, Siemens, Hitachi, and other producers of turbine generators, transformers, and electrical apparatus. A number of electrical equipment companies are losing money, and the shake-out of producers has been dramatic in the past decade. For instance, GE has exited the market for transformers and other distribution and transmission products. Companies that make large turbine generators have had to survive without an order for over a decade. They have focused their efforts on improving the spare parts business and repair and maintenance services, while upgrading existing plants. Such surgical actions have enabled the companies to survive the downturn and be prepared for the upsurge that is likely to happen in the next few years when electrical utilities must begin replacing their aging and inefficient equipment.

A second, similar surgical situation has occurred in the financial services industry. Many banks, savings and loans, and other financial institutions have been forced to sell off their best assets in order to survive. In addition, the federal government has taken over many sick or terminally ill financial institutions and is packaging and remarketing the best assets to others, while retaining the unproductive liabilities. In some cases, the government is offering guarantees against loss to the acquirer. As a result, surgeon leaders in the industry have excellent opportunities to pick up valuable assets and combine them with their own to create a successful operation.

Situation 2. The "Be All Things to All People" Strategy Is No Longer Working

Over the years, many companies grow top-heavy. They offer too many products and too many models for too many markets. Earnings suffer. This situation is made for the surgeon leader who can assess the entire portfolio, make the hard decisions, and select those segments that are attractive for the company or in which it has some unique advantage. General Electric has made these surgical selections in many of its businesses. For instance, it has focused on power generation and discontinued its participation in power transmission and distribution.

Situation 3. The Competition Really Needs You

There have been several cases in which strong competitors have not been anxious to let second or third tier companies exit the market. I have already touched on three reasons for this desire: (1) the dominant firm is afraid of antitrust laws, (2) the dominant leader is concerned it will look greedy, and (3) the struggling company makes products for a segment of the market that does not interest the stronger firms.

In this last situation, strong competitors fear that outsiders will enter the market on the low end and eventually emerge as formidable competitors. For this reason, market leaders are also concerned that the failing company not be acquired by a robust outsider. That was why Ford and GM felt it would be better for Iacocca to succeed than to have the Chrysler brands and plants acquired by a Japanese or European company, which would have then offered tougher competition.

Situation 4. The Customer Really Needs You

I have alluded to situations in which the customers absolutely must have the product and so work with the ailing company to keep it from going under. The company might provide a unique component, part, or service that the customers do not want to make or cannot afford to make internally. This situation has been very prevalent in the transportation and logistics markets. Carriers are critical to receiving and shipping operations, and so companies are often willing to put together mutually beneficial deals or invest or loan money to keep a carrier rolling.

Situation 5. There Is a Chance to Be the Last Out

Someone once said that 80 percent of success is just showing up. Sometimes success is being the last one to leave. Over three decades ago, integrated circuits (semi-conductors) began to replace the power tubes in radio and television sets. Many of the industry leaders decided that power tubes were a dog product, and so they got out of the business as fast as they could. Some companies, however, decided to stay in the game and harvest the product, and they did so for over two decades. The lesson is that surgeons need not follow prevailing thinking. They can wait and see if they might be the lucky survivors who seize the opportunity to invest a little and gain the rewards of the past.

THE UNDERTAKER LEADER

Sometimes a business unit cannot be saved. It may not even have any market value and thus cannot be sold. The undertaker will then assess each of the unit's products as though it were a business in itself. Some may be critical to another part of the corporation and should be transferred before the skills and abilities associated with the product are lost. Some of the equipment might be moved and some of the people might also have the chance to transfer to other segments of the company. The undertaker must be able to wind down operations without panic and damage to people and other valuable assets.

The term "undertaker" bothers a lot of people. Is an undertaker really a leader and how does an undertaker differ from a surgeon? Undertaker leaders recognize that it is inevitable for the company or institution to cease to exist. Normally, this happens after the work of a surgeon who prunes and deduces the line and the scope of the business. The undertaker takes the final step.

A recent example of a CEO who was considering becoming an undertaker leader was William A. Anders, the leader of General Dynamics (GD). In November 1992, GD, faced with the declining orders of the military sectors, declared that it was considering selling the company in pieces to others in their industry. Anders had already sold off "nondefense" related parts of the company in 1991. His divestitures included selling the data systems division to Computer Sciences, the Cessna business-aircraft unit to Textron, Missiles business to Hughes, and Electronics division to Carlyle Group.

Anders believed that GD should focus only on defense-related businesses and that it was critical to gain and maintain *critical mass*. If this was not viable then he was considering the option of selling the core business (Military Aircraft, Electric Boat, Space Systems, Land

Systems, Aircraft Parts Maker Convair) and sharing the returns with his stockholders.

His strategy is not close businesses down where necessary, but rather to get rid of them. "I have objected to the use of the term 'liquidate' to describe our program," he said in a speech. "I use the term 'monetize' instead." Anders appears to be an excellent example of a leader who would fit the undertaker category, provided he has compassion for the key stakeholders, other than the shareholders.[5]

Craig B. Parr is the general manager of GMs Pontiac-West assembly plant. His mission is to close the Pontiac-West plant in 1994 and consolidate it with another GM plant. Parr summarizes his leadership principles in this way.[6]

- *Communicate.* Give notice as far in advance as possible. Be thorough and repetitious. The workers may not be able to absorb everything the first time.

- *Be Visible.* Take personal responsibility for guiding the people through the change.

- *Be Honest.* Be blunt about the plant closing.

- *Be Positive.* Reward top performers and implement workers' ideas for improvement.

- *Demand More.* Remind workers that improving skills will help the plant today and make them more marketable later.

- *Keep Plant Looking Good.* Don't let the equipment deteriorate. Morale is iffy already.

Thus, you can see Craig Parr is exhibiting true leadership characteristics. He is not running away and hiding, he is active and vital. He depicts a positive attitude. Further, the role of the undertaker is to provide comfort for the survivors and also in this situation to protect the best people so that they can be used in other plants or businesses. Undertakers know how to wind down slowly and not have an abrupt ending.

I have known many leaders of this type in my career. Closing plants and business units was a way of life in the 1970s and 1980s. These general managers were very skilled at helping to ease the pain while maintaining a positive attitude. It is similar to being a general on the losing side who must surrender with dignity.

In Part Two, I have described how product innovation can create a competitive advantage for every type of leader, given a complete game plan, the right team, and good timing. In the next section, I will examine a range of leaders who are successful because they can solve the seemingly insolvable problems.

PART
THREE

THE PROBLEM SOLVER LEADERS

Chapter 7 discusses the characteristics of leaders who knowingly seek to solve problems that are considered to be unsolvable. These problem solver leaders are dedicated to the cause and are not motivated by just money or power. Their team is also committed for the long term. Open-mindedness, optimism, and willingness to admit mistakes and start over are key attributes.

Consultative leaders and their team are truly customer driven. They clearly understand that their role is to meet the needs and solve the problems of the customer. Chapter 8 explores the ability of these leaders to listen, analyze, and respond in a timely manner. Timing and responsiveness are vital since customers want the solution when they want it and not just when it is convenient. Further, consultative leaders are able to take what they have learned and apply it to other situations and clients.

7

Solving the Insoluble: Leading the Possible Dream

In Part Two, I described various styles of leaders dealing with products and businesses that were at different phases of the life cycle. These leaders shared a strategic mission to create competitive advantages for their companies through product innovation. All the leaders *loved* their products, but none more so than the risktaker innovators. For them, especially, the products were the focus of everything; these innovations could almost be described as solutions in search of problems (or market needs).

In this chapter, I will depict the risktaker leaders who begin *with the problem and not the solution*. Such risktakers are willing to sacrifice short-term profits and personal honors to solve complex and often socially significant problems. They are not scientists cloistered in workshops, isolated from the demands of the world. Rather, they are founders and heads of organizations that are structured to work for solutions beyond the tenure of the leader. These leaders recognize the demands of the financials as necessary means to an end and not the end itself. They are not opposed to making money, but their goal is finding the solution to the problem that drives them. I call them risktaker problem solvers; they are out to make "possible dreams" come true.

What are those dreams? Finding long-term solutions to society's major problems. We need a way to diagnose, treat, and cure AIDS. We need to make quality, affordable health care available to everyone, everywhere. We need school systems that provide a good education for all students at a manageable cost. We need to reduce pollution and save our environment without severely damaging our economy. We need to provide equal rights for all our citizens.

Does that sound like a campaign speech? That's because these problems have significant social and economic impacts and thus have become the domain of public servants and politicians. But since I am not running for office, I am not going to concern myself here with public policy and leadership issues; instead, I will focus on leaders in the private, nonprofit sectors who are just as dedicated to solving major problems.

A FEW EXAMPLES

AIDS has become the plague of our times. We are spending four billion dollars a year to diagnose and treat the disease, and that figure is sure to climb. Numerous start-up companies and global pharmaceutical giants are working on various aspects of the medical problem. Some are seeking vaccines to prevent the disease with vaccines (Chiron, Genelabs, Immune Response), some are identifying the most appropriate targets for drugs (Agouron, Cephalon, Vertex), and others are focusing on diagnosis (Cambridge Bioscience, Dupont/Repigen, Abbot Labs).[1]

Many of these names are relatively unknown outside the industry. Companies such as Biogen, Microgenesys, Chiron, and Genentech were started by entrepreneurial risktakers to combat serious diseases through the application of biotechnology skills. These individuals were motivated by both the chance to solve problems and to make money. This dual purpose is consistent with the history of the pharmaceutical industry, where companies such as Abbott, Squibb, Hoffman-LaRoche, and others have been able to develop needed drugs while making sufficient profits to warrant the financial gamble.

Another problem area in health care is cost. The United States spends over 12 percent of its GNP on health services. Further, several factors combine to push health care beyond the reach of many citizens: the aging population; the greater number of homeless; persistent drug users; and increasing costs of equipment, systems, and malpractice insurance. Resources are not well distributed: Hospitals are overcrowded in poor areas and underutilized in affluent ones. How do we provide high-quality, affordable health services to everyone who needs them?

An increasing number of risktaker leaders have taken up this problem, including one of the oldest organizations in the health care field: Blue Cross/Blue Shield. BCBS is a nonprofit association that has worked with hospitals, doctors, and patients since the 1920s to assure quality and affordable health care.[2] Another dedicated organization is the Hospital Corporation of America, founded in Nashville, Tennessee, by inventor and drugstore owner Jack Massey and Dr. Thomas Frist. Together, they have built a major "for profit" hospital chain that has been able to provide quality, reliable, and responsive health care.[3] Other such organizations are involved in this task as well.

Risktaker leaders are addressing education issues, too, although with mixed results. William Norris, founder and CEO of Control Data, invested hundreds of millions of dollars in PLATO, a super-computer-based educational system. He envisioned students in schools everywhere learning and researching through a massive computerized information system. Unfortunately, Norris's dream is not financially viable at present, and his company has had to discontinue its investment, but the idea may still bear fruit in some way not yet discovered. Certainly, computers are becoming an increasingly important learning aid. Other entrepreneurial types are establishing private schools; some have even expressed a willingness to take over public school systems and operate them as a business.

Risktaker leaders are working for solutions to a wide range of societal problem areas. What links these diverse efforts is the dual goal of arriving at answers that are both effective and economical. As with any other leader, the risktaker problem solver will need a well-devised game plan and a properly assembled team in order to succeed.

THE RISKTAKER PROBLEM SOLVER'S INTUITIVE GAME PLAN

The game plan for this special risktaker consists of nine elements or plays.

1. Probe to understand the real problem.
2. Obtain long-term commitment and sponsorship.
3. Create and then meet realistic expectations.
4. Avoid the "not invented here" mentality.
5. Be flexible, adapt to client needs, admit mistakes, and try again.
6. Protect the solutions and use the know-how to solve other problems.
7. Leverage the results to get maximum coverage.
8. Prepare for the next issue.
9. Prepare for resistance and unexpected side effects.

Play 1. Probe to Understand the Real Problem

The risktaker and every member of the risktaker's team must listen, probe, understand, and then specify the real problem before jumping to solutions. This approach reverses the method of the product innovator, who begins with a product that is assumed to be the solution (to a market need). Problem solvers must also concentrate on the primary problem and not be distracted by subproblems.

Many aerospace companies have failed to perform this task and so have failed to transfer their technologies to more earthbound ventures. In the 1960s, for instance, General Electric's aerospace division decided to provide low-cost housing with factory-built modular homes. GE believed it could apply what it had learned from space vehicles to the construction of housing units. And, in fact, GE did produce, in a factory, homes in four sections (modules), each with plumbing and wiring installed and ready to be connected. Each home had real plaster walls, not wall board, was sufficiently insulated, and was constructed using attractive, low-maintenance exterior materials. They should have helped solve the problem of inadequate affordable housing.

But the solution missed the target. GE did not listen to experts in housing and local markets and so failed to understand that the real problem was not just providing quality buildings at low costs, it was gaining acceptance from local zoning boards and trade unions. Because GE did not probe to discover what was needed to please local zoning authorities or persuade trade unions to cooperate and support the new designs, the modular homes did not meet local building codes and were boycotted by local tradespeople, including the plumbers and electricians. As a result, the homes failed in the U.S. market; equipment and patents were sold to Japanese companies for use in Japan.

Play 2. Obtain Long-Term
Commitment and Sponsorship

Financial backing is even more critical for problem-solving risktakers than for product-innovators. Solving major problems can take years, decades, or even lifetimes. Of course, some problems are never solved. Therefore, the leader must locate a sponsor who will have continuing faith in the project. Commitment must be long term, not subject to annual renewal.

Charities have special advantages of course, but they do demonstrate how to sustain commitment. A classic example was President Franklin D. Roosevelt's very public support during the 1940s for the campaign to cure poliomyelitis (infantile paralysis), the disease that had confined him to a wheelchair. In more contemporary times, United Way has been able to gain the ongoing support of major employers in each geographic region. The annual fund drive is often spearheaded by community leaders and senior executives from the private sector. Companies assist by providing facilities, allowing employees to participate on company time, and permitting payroll deductions for those who wish to contribute. The 1992 disclosures of extravagant use of United Way funds and even personal gain by the National Director may place this historical relationship in jeopardy. National and local business leaders might withdraw their personal endorsements and refuse to allow payroll deductions.

Some problems are so large and require so much funding that only the federal government can support them. Major health and education problems and defense and space projects fall into this category. Now, in some cases, the initial phases of certain projects might be funded by private or charitable organizations. Once the project is set in motion, however, private funding is inadequate to solve the entire problem.

But aside from treating society's major ills or ridding it of disease, private sources might appropriately finance other, more finite, good works. The risktaker problem solver must assure the investor—an investment banker, for instance, or an executive from inside the risktaker's organization, who might be a mentor or an advocate—that the project is solid and will be a long-term winner. The best case, of course, has the company CEO in the role of risktaker, especially if the CEO anticipates a future with the organization that is sufficiently long and secure to see the project through the unprofitable phases.

Selecting the "best" sponsor means understanding who the real decision makers are and how funding decisions get made within the organization. If the decision maker is not truly committed, then the risktaker leader will have to factor that element into the strategic plan and contingency alert systems. The leader must also understand the prospective sponsor's idiosyncrasies, personal biases, and susceptibility to office politics. I will have more to say later on the need for flexibility and for being prepared to respond to change.

For now, consider how the American public's support for *funding* public education has waffled. At one time, we would support education regardless of costs, and funding grew year by year. Schools were constructed, teachers's salaries were increased, and expensive equipment was purchased. Today, while there is still support for the *concept* of education, we find the public less enthused about the necessary funding. An aging population is less personally involved in education, and many older Americans must get by on fixed incomes. Schools have, some studies have shown, failed to perform up to our expectations. Hard times have crunched first federal, then state, then local budgets as government funding for services has declined from the top down (the poisonous side of the "trickle-down effect").

In the private sector, sponsors can be equally fickle. Many of the innovative companies I described earlier that were addressing the AIDS problem have been the favorites of Wall Street investors and institutions. In particular, the biotechnology companies such as Genentech, Amgen, Biogen, and Cetus have had high price/earnings multiples. In fact, these multiples are infinite, since the companies have made little or no profits over the course of their history. For instance, Genentech was trading 34 times earnings in November 1991 despite having made only marginal earnings since start-up. Cetus always lost money and merged with Chiron in 1991. Amgen was in the black in November 1991, but at a 61 PE (price/earnings). Why? Because investors have been betting that these companies will grow in the future. However, even the optimists have become a bit disenchanted, and the stock values are highly volatile. Some have risen dramatically only to fall in the same dramatic fashion because expectations were not met.

These days, companies with long-term commitments are rare. One such favored firm is the Engineered Plastics division of General Electric. GE started the business in the early 1960s in Pittsfield, Massachusetts, to develop applications for the polymers invented in its R&D labs in Schenectady, New York. It began as a technology without a market. But the division's resident genius, Dr. Charles Reed, decided to use the technology to solve problems, not just to produce chemicals and plastics in commodity volumes. Reed's team developed extensive problem-solving capabilities and facilities to help customers succeed with their material substitution and improvement projects. Reed also excelled at getting the investment dollars required to keep the business alive until it became profitable. His winning a long-term commitment from his internal sponsor at GE was just as important as his decision to make Engineered Plastics a problem-solving business.

In an earlier chapter, I talked about Thermo Electron, an innovative company led by George N. Hatsopoulos. Hatsopoulos's strategy is to acquire and develop companies using "innovative technologies to attack potentially huge markets in socially important areas like the environment."[4] Among other things, Hatsopoulos hopes to provide instruments that analyze pollution and nuclear radiation, systems that burn hazardous waste, and devices that detect drugs and bombs. His focus has been and will be on helping customers use these products to solve major social and environmental problems. Hatsopoulos also has a creative approach (adapted from Thomas Edison) to sponsorship and funding. Since 1983, he has set up pieces of his company as separate businesses and sold from 10 to 40 percent of the shares to institutional investors and the public at large. This decentralized structure permits Thermo Electron to spread funding risks and at the same time allows investors to back selected segments rather than the whole corporation. Further, the strategy permits Hatsopoulos to offer stock options to senior management from whichever segments of the company they choose, which is an effective tool for attracting talent and motivating employees.

Play 3. Create and Then Meet Realistic Expectations

Risktaker problem solvers suffer the same crisis of overconfidence exhibited by risktaker product innovators. They overpromise, not out of deceit, but because they are so dedicated to their cause and so convinced that problems can be solved that they underestimate the complexity of the task. Often, they do not clearly understand all the ramifications and aspects of the problem, such as the political and human interactions required to succeed.

The key to creating and meeting realistic expectations is to establish clear, reasonable milestones and goals that can demonstrate progress when reached. Most sponsors are more willing to stick with the game plan when they see tangible results, even if they are more qualitative than quantitative. Solving problems is not as easy as making and marketing a stand-alone innovative product. The product's success can be measured in revenue dollars and growth, and progress can be observed without difficulty. In contrast, selling solutions takes a long time, and sales growth can be very slow.

The leader must keep the sponsor informed and avoid surprises. If sponsors are continually surprised and disappointed, they will rethink their commitment and support. The risktaker is better off setting low expectations and continually exceeding them; *these* surprises are good for morale. If delay and failure do occur, however, the leader must swiftly inform sponsors and admit the problem—but in such a manner that continues to inspire confidence.

This dictum is violated routinely in the public sector. Politicians have decided that the best way to get elected is to promise the world and then explain later why they couldn't deliver. George Bush made this classic error in his now infamous "read my lips" promise not to raise taxes. Unfortunately, circumstances forced him to back down, and he paid a price in lost popularity. Of course, he exceeded expectations in his handling of the Iraqi war, which caused his polls to soar. The roller coaster swooped down again a year later when the recession was worse than he led the country to expect. The 1992 presidential election was a continuation of the "overpromising" by both presidential candidates. Unfortunately voters turn off their sensors and don't believe anyone. This is a clear violation of the requirement that leaders must try and do what they say, even if they fail.

Leaders of nonprofit and business enterprises, with all the best intentions, also create unrealistic expectations. Academics have promised a level of education for the country's youth that has not been attained. "Give us more funding . . . more people . . . more facilities . . . more equipment," they argue, "and we will improve the educational process and raise the test scores." We have given, but they have not delivered. The same is true in company research laboratories. Scientists ask for additional resources from the company and promise results they cannot achieve. As a result, they lose credibility and any hope of continuing commitment to their R&D projects.

Play 4. Avoid the "Not Invented Here" Mentality

Thomas Edison is one of my favorite problem solvers. He is often incorrectly viewed as a genius who invented things for the sake of invention. In fact, Edison was very disciplined and selective in his projects. He established one of the first industrial laboratories and hired a staff of technical experts and assistants, who were required to document all their activities. Edison built on the experiences and achievements of others. He did not make the first incandescent lamp, but he was able to produce the bulb that made the first practical one. He improved on the work of Alexander Bell and helped make the telephone a reality. He may not have always been the original inventor, but he was often the chief problem solver, and as such he has greatly influenced the way we live and work. The lesson, which many organizations stubbornly resist, is that we can use an idea/method/product even if it was "not invented here." Borrow from the best that is available.

Because today's problems are so vast and complex, alliances between companies and between the public and private sectors are increasingly necessary to generate practical solutions. The U.S. space program is one example of teamwork involving different types of expertise from a variety of sources. The Japanese have been leading the way in forming cooperative ventures with American and Japanese universities to solve major social problems. The Massachusetts Institute of Technology (MIT) is one of the Japanese firms' favorite partners. They have funded research into materials, fiber-optics, and diagnostic instruments to improve living standards and create commercial opportunities. Kokusai Densin Denwa is funding media laboratory research; Kyocera, Toyota, and TDK are supporting material sciences projects.[5] Slowly, American companies are receiving government permission to establish consortiums for research into such promising areas as electronics and biotechnologies. Many have opened R&D labs in Japan to learn from and build on the success of the Japanese.

Interdisciplinary and complementary teams formed with outside organizations are the wave of the future. Risktaker leaders must learn to deal with the inevitable contentions and disagreements. These can be healthy if constructively managed. Leaders must keep in mind that the goal is to find the best solution and not to appease one part of the team or let those with the loudest voices prevail. While using persuasion and seeking consensus, leaders must make the tough decisions when necessary. They should be fair, weigh all the evidence, and not be arbitrary or preemptive. The wisdom of King Solomon would be helpful as well.

Play 5. Be Flexible, Adapt to Client Needs, Admit Mistakes, and Try Again

Because no one can predict the exact path of solutions to complex problems, leaders should consider initial planning to be directional in nature. Game plans are geared to help team members know their roles and what is required of them. As leaders gain insights into the causes and implications of the problem, they should modify strategy accordingly by establishing a clear set of milestones and contingency alternatives. I call this a "contingency alert," and not an in-depth contingency plan. A contingency alert enables the leader to know when changes in the game plan are required and to have some idea of potential alternatives. I don't believe it is practical to have contingency plans in place before you know what has happened and the cause. Actions must address the cause and not the results.

For instance, suppose a pharmaceutical company's proposed new drug is not accepted rapidly by the medical profession. Before actions can be taken to stimulate acceptance, the leader must determine why the drug has not been accepted. Causes could range from poor selling and promotion to concerns about side effects and potential litigation. Obviously, such different reasons for poor performance would require quite different corrective actions. The leader needs a game plan that anticipates alternatives but does not spend too much time on details. The risktaker problem solver can then act quickly and purposefully without embarrassing delay. With contingency alternatives ready, the leader can also communicate the difficulties and responses to clients and other stakeholders and reassure sponsors that the project is under control and on course.

Making mistakes and admitting failure is part of being a successful risktaker. Nobody bats 1000. In fact, just as in baseball, a problem solver who averages .250 (solves 1 in 4) isn't bad, and one who hits .333 (1 in 3) is great. (Especially, if a few of those hits are homers.) Smart leaders recognize this truth and plan for some setbacks and changes. They will admit to their failures and try again.

Consider a headline in *Fortune,* "Great Japanese Mistakes." The article went on to describe several technological blunders made by Japanese companies. These included (1) an electric car project that cost $46 million from 1970 to 1977 and failed because the battery couldn't last long enough to drive the car; (2) a nuclear power blast furnace for steelmaking that cost $110 million from 1973 to 1980 and failed because MIT underestimated the power of the antinuclear lobby, which killed the project before it could be completed; and (3) a remote controlled undersea oil rig that cost $36 million from 1970 to 1975 and failed because it was no cheaper or easier to operate than conventional offshore rigs.[6]

Even the Japanese make mistakes in business. That's a truth companies, institutions, and governments should keep in mind when they are tempted to deny their own errors. This tendency is not only a personality problem. Organizations that don't recognize their mistakes don't learn from them and continue to back losing approaches and projects. Problem solving is an incremental approach that builds on trial and error. If error is not recognized, it becomes the foundation for the edifice, which surely will crumble in time.

In addition, leaders must see to it that those involved in the failure are not unjustly punished. In other words, avoid the temptation to look for a scapegoat. Ridiculing, removing, or demoting the project manager and associates is a commonplace and destructive behavior. It inhibits risktaking and causes people to leave for other positions, thus defeating the organization's attempts to innovate. I have witnessed this process several times in my career. For example, in 1960 the culture at GE did not tolerate failure. When a project flopped early, it would be scrapped and a majority of those involved let go even if they were not at fault.

Play 6. Protect the Solutions and Use the Know-How to Solve Other Problems

I pointed out earlier that product innovators need strong patent protection to prevent others from stealing their ideas. The need may be even more critical for the problem solver risktaker. Because the solution is both time and financially intensive, it would be a tragedy for the leader to do all the work and solve the problem and then let others use these results for free.

Patent protection can be elusive when the project is funded by the government or the public. In that case, the solution becomes part of public ownership and domain and thus accessible to everyone. Therefore, the leader must determine early in the game which skills, capabilities, and resources can, and must, be protected and how the solution can be used for the future benefit of the organization. Normally, the risktaking team gains know-how and experience that is impossible to duplicate by those not involved in the development of the solution, and that is the organization's competitive advantage. Consequently, team members who possess that knowledge and experience constitute the organization's most valuable resource. Thus, it is vital that the leader both retain key team members and train new ones, so that the organization will not be held captive by a few individuals. In addition, the organization should document the procedures and the lessons learned and protect them as though they were the crown jewels.

Documentation and protection mandate a strong front-end legal and negotiations team that can make clear who owns the rights to the solution and how it can be used in the future. Complexities increase when the leader and the legal team must deal with government agencies, tax-exempt institutions, and several partners. Further, problem solvers are generally not as interested in this part of the process; usually, they are too consumed with finding a solution to worry about what happens next. Because they are motivated by a desire to help rather than to achieve personal gain, they may be concerned about not appearing greedy or self-serving. However, the ability of the organization to survive and the investors to reap their just rewards depends on the protection process.

Consider also, that if the leader can gain ownership and future use of the results of the organization's research and problem-solving capabilities, the solutions can be applied to other areas or even used to develop unique products and services. The space program, for instance, generated a number of earthly innovations. The lightweight, atmospheric-adaptive materials needed for space flight have been used to reduce the weight of automobiles and so increase fuel efficiency. Some materials have been adapted to make heart valves and replacement limbs. Computers and integrated circuits developed by the space program have also found their way into consumer products and commercial equipment.

The knowledge and capabilities gained in the process of solving one problem can often be applied to other worthy endeavors. The risktaker leader is obligated to protect the organization's opportunity to participate in those arenas by protecting what it has learned and what it can do.

Play 7. Leverage the Results to Get Maximum Coverage

In the discussion of product-driven leaders, I described risktakers and caretakers who hoped to standardize their industries around their product innovations. In part, their goal was to make money on the aftermarket by selling repair parts, services, or consumables. Problem solvers may have to do something similar to make their solutions viable. They may have to license their capabilities and solutions to others, even competitors. Their solution may become the standard for the industry or scientific field, which means it will be used globally. Certainly, a cure for AIDS or any other infectious disease would have to be so shared; it would be unthinkable to do otherwise.

However, part of the game plan is a strategy for protecting the innovations and solutions while sharing. Risktaker leaders must exercise enough control to ensure that the solutions are being applied in the prescribed fashion. They must require that the practitioners are licensed and competent. If they fail to do so, the solution might cause new problems. For instance, a vaccine that is administered in the wrong dosages or at the wrong time may infect the patients with the disease. Further, care must be taken that the vaccine is not used restrictively for political purposes or used maliciously by unscrupulous people to injure dissident populations. This type of protection requires sound and ongoing training, as well as a system of audits and quality controls.

Play 8. Prepare for the Next Issue

Most problem solver risktakers never think about what they will do when they succeed. Therefore, the game plan should include a vision of the future: what to do once the problem is solved and the organization need no longer work on the original project.

Government agencies or public institutions that were established with a single mission often are caught short when they suddenly reach their goals. For example, the National Institute for Infantile Paralysis was created to find a cure and treatment for the disease. The organization labored for decades before a breakthrough was made by Dr. Jonas Salk. The Institute's leadership seemed surprised by the development. Quite unexpectedly, they had to reevaluate their mission and decide how their expertise could be used to attack other diseases. They also evolved into a caretaker mode, concentrating on educating the public and disseminating the treatment. Similarly, NASA, after meeting goals, has had to redefine them periodically. The agency was established originally to fulfill President Kennedy's promise to put a man on the moon.

Once that was accomplished, NASA began applying the talents of its skilled personnel to other space and nonspace projects. It is too dynamic and vital a national resource to just go out of business.

Play 9. Prepare for Resistance and Unexpected Side Effects

The risktaker problem solver must expect that a solution (1) may have unanticipated and unwanted side effects and (2) may be resisted by other groups because it conflicts with their own missions.

Many drugs and chemicals while effectively combating the problems they were developed to solve, have unexpectedly caused new problems. Chlordane was a terrific killer of termites, ants, and other insects. People overused and misapplied it, however, resulting in many cases of cancer. The chemical has been banned in the United States. Even aspirin, the all-purpose wonder drug, can cause serious problems for some patients, and so its use is now restricted more than when it first became available.

The asbestos case is better known. Although the substance was once considered an effective and economical form of insulation, inhalation of asbestos fibers was discovered to cause cancer and other respiratory illnesses. Its principal manufacturer, the one-time highly profitable and respected Johns-Manville company, was driven into bankruptcy in 1982. The firm has been forced to establish a large trust fund to pay for the treatment of asbestos victims. Manville Corporation (current name) phased out its asbestos operation and now concentrates on fiberglass and building products. It will not be allowed to pay stockholders a dividend until 1996.[7]

Side effects are one potential obstacle for the problem solver; resistance from groups with a different agenda constitutes another. Consider the use by medical science of animals for experimentation. Humans may benefit in the long run, but animals suffer in the short run. Specifically, in my home town of Norwalk, Connecticut, the U.S. Surgical Company is developing innovative surgical staples for use in operations of all kinds. The company's R&D requires experimentation to test the effectiveness and utility of the staples. Dogs are most often used for this purpose. Animal rights groups have been suing, boycotting, and picketing to stop this practice. (One activist was accused of trying to bomb corporate headquarters.) U.S. Surgical has been forced to spend money and time to defend itself.

I take no sides on this issue. I bring up the case to illustrate that risktaking problem-solving companies must anticipate and plan for resistance; they must be prepared to defend themselves or cope with the consequences. In today's litigious society, leadership has no other viable option.

Further, the threat is not just to the organization. The leader is also at risk personally. One wonders whether problem-solving risktakers such as Pasteur or Salk would have been willing to work under today's conditions. What are the hopes for the future? We probably will need special laws and regulations to reduce the vulnerability of these individuals, for the good of society. In the interim, problem solvers need skilled legal counsel on the payroll, or readily available, to guide them around or through litigation. In some cases, security personnel and systems may be required to protect leaders and team members from bodily harm.

RISKTAKER PROBLEM SOLVERS' TEAMS

The size of the team should vary during the project. Initially, the team comprises a small group of dedicated individuals. As the project progresses, the team grows, but in a highly selective and controlled manner. Total size must be constantly monitored and managed. Members must understand that the team may be reduced once the problem is solved. The team will need a different mix of talents during its history, but it should always be characterized by four distinct traits.

Character Traits

First, both leader and team should have faith in the project and total commitment with a long-term horizon. They cannot be dabblers and run from one problem to another. They need to be prepared for the disappointments that will occur and continue to work without becoming discouraged. This attitude is becoming rare in American and, increasingly, European cultures. Today's young people seem to gravitate toward jobs that require less commitment and risktaking.

Second, all members of the team must be real, proven problem solvers. They must know how to prove, listen, and study in order to understand and specify the problem before making decisions and reaching conclusions. They never jump quickly at solutions. They look for all the possible causes of the problem and determine all the potential solutions.

Third, team members must be willing to use any and all the resources available to solve the problem. They must avoid the ego trip of believing they have all the answers and can do everything themselves. Problems have become so complex that alliances and partnerships are necessary, sometimes even with competitors. These will be effective only if there is mutual and complete trust and sharing, which requires a different type of thinking and management. The allies must be willing to listen to each other and then be able to change opinions and compromise. Everyone needs to be thinking of creating win–win situations rather than establishing win–lose dominations. I have seen too many alliances that were viewed by the participants as "marriages of convenience" or "live together" arrangements. Lacking the commitment for lasting union, these relationships became destructive "one-night stands."

Finally, everyone needs to be a team player. A loose group of individual superstars or experts will not succeed. Some superstar talents may be needed, but not superstar egos that require the sort of special treatment that builds resentments. The situation is analogous to athletics. When one team member gets all the headlines and the big salary and begins to believe he is the only key element of success, the team is likely to fail.

Talents

The team leadership must be able to plan, organize, integrate, and measure. It must be flexible and adaptable to change. The problem solver leader also needs to have on board three groups of people with special skills:

- *Financial Planners.* Risktakers often overlook or underestimate the talents of budgeting and forecasting. The team needs people who can make investors feel confident that their money is being used wisely and that finances are under control. The team's financial planners and monitors must be able to persuade the rest of the staff to accept controls rather than try to force compliance autocratically. Scientists and creative people resent being told what to do or that funds are not available to finish the job. They wish to be independent of mundane money matters.

- *Legal Advisers.* The team also needs legal talent to keep abreast of current, and anticipate future, laws and regulations that can affect the implementation of the solution. The legal talent will also need to be alert to the reactions of competitors and those advocacy groups that might challenge the project (remember the animal rights groups).

- *Pricing Advisers.* Pricing skill is also important. In the early stages of the project, conservative, cost-based pricing is appropriate. But to plan for future pricing, someone on the team must be monitoring and tracking the potential value of the solution and of the other applications that might be derived.

At least one person on the team, probably the leader, will have to be good at the soft sell. She must practice the art of building strong relationships with all the stakeholders, keeping them informed and making them feel they are part of the team. She must "sell" investors and funding agents, making them aware of progress and leveling with them about problems and potential solutions. She must motivate the team day after day, not letting them become discouraged over the inevitable failures and setbacks. Above all, she must continue to sell herself on the project; the strength of her motivation will determine its success.

TIMING

When is the best time for a risktaker problem solver to succeed? The timing is favorable when any of the three following situations arises.

Situation 1. When There Is Concern, but Not a Total Crisis

Government representatives at all levels reflect the public's fickleness. They are elected every two, four, or six years, and seem to spend a lot of their time in office working to get reelected. The system teaches most politicians to be opportunistic and to shy away from long-term commitments. They tend to support only those programs that have an immediate impact. Therefore, the risktaker leader must capitalize on the opportunity when society becomes concerned about "the firm's problem" and ally the organization with individuals and groups that can maintain public concern at a level high enough to elicit financial support. However, if public concern is so high as to reach "crisis" proportions, then the government will be pressured to take shortcuts and not really solve the problem.

Consider the energy crisis of the 1970s. When OPEC reduced production and drastically increased prices, the world went into shock. Americans confronted with waiting in long lines for what was then considered expensive gasoline cried out for action. One response was to attain energy independence by using alternative forms of fuel. People installed wood-burning stoves and solar panels; pictures of windmills appeared regularly on TV and in the popular press. Politicians jumped out to lead the parade. Many companies were established to promote new forms of energy. Some are still at it.

In time, however, prices stabilized, and people got used to paying more for gasoline and heating oil. The long lines at the pump faded into memory. We slid back into easy reliance on, mostly foreign-produced, oil. During 1990–1991, the crisis rejuvenated with the Iraqi conflict but subsided again when prices returned to "normal" in 1992. No major leader in government or society seems willing to take on the role of risk-taker problem solver and drive the country to develop and implement an alternative energy policy. When the crisis occurs again, as it must, it will be too late for the leader to succeed. The timing is right, but no leader is in sight.

Situation 2. When the Technology and Know-How Are Available

Some solutions must await the right technology. Problem solvers need the proper equipment and techniques to do the research that leads to discoveries. Think how complex, high-speed computers with massive memory capacity have not only increased what scientists in all fields can do, but how fast they can complete their work. Computers allow researchers to store and analyze enormous amounts of data, to synthesize situations and test hypotheses, and to run numerous trials very quickly.

Further, advances in communications allow problem solvers to exchange information, share concepts, and relay results almost instantaneously. Enhancing the "great conversation" between researchers makes it easier for them to build on each other's work and less likely they will repeat or reinvent what has already been done.

Advances in medical technology enhance the prospects for breakthroughs in conquering cancer and other devastating diseases. Sonic and nuclear diagnostic tools provide a means of probing and studying patients without actually cutting into their bodies. Noninvasive procedures increase information while decreasing risk.

Situation 3. When Talented and Trained People Are in Supply

Problem solver leaders need quality people in the right quantity. Vital skills must be available or transferable to others. In too many situations, teams have lacked depth and sophistication and so took too long to solve problems. Problem solver leaders must have access to capable people; they cannot afford to stop and train them to do the job.

In the United States today, too few of the best and brightest have been pursuing professional careers in science and technology. Many are lured instead by the promise of quick wealth in business and law.

Fewer American students are enrolling in science and engineering programs, although foreign students are happy to take their places in American universities.

Problem-solving leaders can be found in every walk of life, not just in business and commerce. In fact, it is more difficult to focus on profitability when you are trying to solve key societal and medical problems. This is why most problem solvers in business and commerce concentrate on lesser and more easily solved problems. I call these leaders "consultative" leaders; we will discuss them in the next chapter.

8

Solving the Client's Problems: The Consultative Leader

In the preceding chapter, I analyzed risktaker leaders who attempt to provide solutions to complex, long-term social problems. Those in business have the dual goals of doing good and making, perhaps modest, profits for their firms through the competitive advantage offered by their solutions. Now, I want to focus on those, perhaps more pragmatic, business leaders who are interested in helping their customers and clients deal with more "solvable" problems. I call these individuals applications and consultative (A/C) leaders because they apply the concepts and techniques they have learned to new and different situations. In style, they are caretaker leaders.

Many companies have gained industry dominance under the leadership of A/C caretakers. The following section describes two famous leaders and a few who are less well known.

THE INFORMATION SYSTEMS A/C LEADERS: THOMAS WATSON, JR., AND JOHN AKERS

Many people think that IBM has always been a product-driven company, dedicated to the single mission of making and selling large computers. My view is quite different. I believe that IBM has been defined by former CEO Thomas Watson, Jr., as a customer service company, focused since his time on helping customers use the power of computers and information systems to solve specific business problems.

My own experience in 1955 typified the type of leadership IBM provided. I had been hired by General Electric through an accounting training program and assigned to the cost accounting organization in the Motors and Generators Division at Schenectady, New York. GE had contracted with IBM to install a new computerized system to replace the manual cost accounting and payroll systems. I was amazed and impressed with the willingness of IBM to dedicate hundreds of specialists to work with us to implement the system. They were not just selling hardware; they were helping to solve major accounting and bookkeeping problems.

Many years later, during the 1970s and early 1980s, IBM's enormous success had caused the company to become complacent. IBM's leaders believed that they were not vulnerable to competition and change and so they moved from a customer focus to a production-driven business. The shift is common for entrenched market leaders. They begin focusing on what they are selling rather than on what customers are buying. Somehow, companies get arrogant and forget the obvious truth that made them successful: make a product or perform a service that meets the customer's needs.

IBM recognized the need to reclaim its heritage when John Akers took over leadership in the early 1980s. In an article in *Fortune,* he outlined how he was moving IBM from a product-driven to an applications-consultative company. The magazine headline read: "The New IBM," but I recognized it as the old IBM I knew from 1955. I'll relate the core of Akers' operation, as he describes it in the article, and add some thoughts of my own on the transformation.[1]

Akers' first task was to decentralize the company and so put responsibility closer to the customer. The A/C leader cannot succeed when separated from the customer by layers of bureaucracy that filter out customer needs and wants. Second, Akers began teaching his executives, not just his sales force, how to listen to the customers. Third, in the fall of 1988, Akers broke tradition by inviting "several key customers to participate in the company's strategic planning conference." He created a "customer advisory council" and shared "plans for the new computer before it was introduced." Fourth, customers were invited to meet with people from IBM's Applications Solution Division, a large software business unit that Akers described as "breaking tradition" by recruiting industry experts "from stock and bond traders to CPAs, from teachers to hospital administrators." By having people on board who have worked in the customers' businesses, a company can better understand what those customers need.

"We've struggled to make sure we have all the right skills and abilities," Ned Lautenbach, the Applications Solution Division leader, was quoted. The service organization was told that when the customer asks for something, "just say, 'Yes.'"

To make sure "the troops keep priorities straight," Akers overturned the traditional sales commission system that rewarded salespeople for the number of units they rented or sold and replaced it with a system that measured reps on total revenues. This switch apparently motivated the sales force to spend more time with the customer. (People do what they get paid to do.) Salespeople reported feeling a part of their clients' teams.

In December 1991, Akers took another step to move the company closer to its customers when he established strategic business profit centers. These units were both product and applications driven. They were designed to force a closer coupling with the customers and so thwart the competition's attempts to divide and conquer IBM.

Akers' efforts clearly demonstrate a desire to return to the tradition of Thomas Watson. However, IBM has had an entrenched, noncompetitive culture that will take years or even decades to change. It is not clear that IBM has the luxury to wait that long. Perhaps the leadership of a surgeon may be required to accelerate the pace and get results faster. I believe that even though Akers is taking some of the actions of a surgeon, he and his associates are really caretakers. Further, I am not certain that all the IBM businesses need to make these changes. Some units might continue to be driven by production, some by sales, and others by product innovation. Some units may require risktakers, others caretakers, and still others surgeons. Overall, however, surgery and selectivity appear to be warranted. Applying one leadership approach to the entire company could be a mistake.

THE ELECTRICAL SYSTEM A/C LEADERS: GERARD SWOPE AND OWEN B. YOUNG

As I emphasized in Chapter 7, Thomas Alva Edison was a problem-solving leader. However, the company he founded, General Electric, and its major competitor, Westinghouse, became more product than applications driven in their early stages of development because Edison and George Westinghouse wanted to move the country from gas to electrical power. As the two companies evolved, they returned to their applications leadership. Both decided to avoid regulation by divesting themselves of ownership of their electrical utilities in the 1920s and 1930s.

GE leaders in this period, Gerard Swope and Owen B. Young, determined that rather than *control* by ownership, they could *lead* the electric utilities by providing extensive applications engineering and problem-solving capabilities. Thus, the industry was organized so that electric utilities provided electricity but did not develop the products and systems to do the job. In contrast, the arrangement in the telephone and telegraph system was completely different. Theodore Vail's strategy at AT&T was to be owner and operator in major markets and to be creator and developer of all necessary systems and products.

GE executives listened to their customers, identified real and potential problems, and then offered solutions. Among other things, GE:

1. Engaged in the research and development of systems, products, and services to help the electric utilities be efficient and low-cost producers.

2. Innovated and invested in demand forecasting systems and procedures to help the utilities to be prepared for the growth in demand for electricity.

3. Provided manpower development programs, which included extensive customer education, to train utility executives and technical staff. They planned to have a percentage of graduates from GE's own company technical program (called the "Test Program") and the business program (called the "Business Training Course") to work for the utilities.

4. Supported the utilities when they presented their cases to the federal and state regulatory agencies. Most often, the utilities were seeking rate *decreases*. Good management and improved, lower cost equipment allowed the price of electricity to decline over the first seven decades of the century.

5. Stimulated demand for electricity through promotions and the development of attractive consumer products. GE's theme of "living better electrically" was buttressed by the introduction of such appliances as toasters, irons, dishwashers, clothes washers and dryers, refrigerators, ranges, air conditioners, and heat pumps. The utilities were able to increase capacity in advance of demand by purchasing larger and more efficient systems. Everybody benefited (Westinghouse, too).

6. Provided financing to the utilities when they needed it, although the industry was so strong that it was rarely needed.

Throughout this era the American standard of living improved. Appliances freed people from much of the drudgery of domestic chores. Entertainment variety proliferated with radios and televisions. Electric utility companies grew and prospered; their stocks became popular, safe investments. GE and Westinghouse grew and prospered, too. Regulators and local governments benefited because rates declined for citizens and the companies paid handsome taxes. It was win/win for all.

But nothing lasts forever. The producers of electrical equipment and systems lost sight of their mission. Instead of competing, they decided to collude. The "Great Electrical Conspiracy" involved price fixing and market share manipulation. All the major companies (GE, Westinghouse, Allis Chalmers, and others) were found guilty, and many key executives went to jail. This happened for complex reasons, and I am not expert in all the ramifications. It is sufficient to say that the conspiracy altered the relationship between the utility companies and their suppliers, which, in turn, significantly changed the industry. No longer do the utilities rely on GE and Westinghouse to be their problem solvers. Price and product have become the key criteria for getting orders. Former friends are now foes, and the win/win situation is now lose/lose.

The first response of the utilities to the conspiracy was to purchase equipment from foreign manufacturers. By the end of the 1980s, there were no U.S. producers of power transformers and switchgear. Next, because the utilities could not rely on the consultative help of the product providers, many of them were less able to plan and to influence the regulators.

These changes jeopardize the entire electrical industry. New product development has been limited since the late 1970s. Many electric utilities have moved from a growth to a harvest strategy. For many years, no new equipment orders were placed. As a result, many U.S. equipment and systems companies have either gone out of business, dramatically reduced their product offerings, or merged. In addition, most of the major electrical utilities have not been able to fund fossil or nuclear projects. Existing nuclear projects have become so expensive and time consuming that they have been discontinued or sold. Further, they have become so politicized as to affect the utility companies' overall viability. The Shoreham facility is a good example. Long Island Lighting and Gas was forced to sell its newly constructed, Nuclear Regulatory Commission approved, nuclear plant to New York State for $1. New York plans to decommission the unit and convert it to a conventional fossil-fuel plant. That will cost billions of dollars and delay the generation of electrical power—a classic lose/lose situation for the company and the citizens of New York.

NOT EVERY A/C LEADER MUST BE A GIANT

In today's business and industrial world, no single company can provide every product and service needed to solve all their customers' problems (as GE used to do for the utilities companies). As a result, many companies are in the business of offering solutions to customers by integrating the products and services of other vendors. This is not a new phenomenon. Most large applications leaders have used the products of other vendors to fill out their lines and solve problems. The change is one of degree; in the current market, the large firm adds little value and relies more on the contributions of others.

Currently, many younger and smaller companies are the consulting and applications leaders in the information, communications, and other high-technology markets. They help their customers install telephone systems, establish and implement complex transaction and communications networks, and so on. They lead in the design and development of the projects and then subcontract or vend other key components—contracting and installing the hardware, doing the software and protocols, and so on—from others.

Ross Perot is an excellent example of this type of leader. Perot was a successful salesperson for IBM until he became dissatisfied with the company's move from provision of services and applications to product and production emphasis. Perot formed Electronic Data Systems to provide a combination of problem solving, applications software, and facilities management. He created a new market segment dedicated to helping companies solve their data and transaction processing needs by providing both systems and third-party services. EDS became a dominant player in the market, and Perot sold his interests to General Motors and became a billionaire. In 1992, Perot offered his leadership and problem-solving skills to the American public to solve national and global problems as an "independent" presidential candidate.

SERVICE CAN BE THE SOLUTION:
TWO APPROACHES

You can become an applications and consultative leader in two ways:

- Develop a method for solving problems that can be replicated and applied to a number of areas. Here, the focus is on the process.

- Become the expert in a specific industry or business and concentrate on solving a variety of problems in this chosen area. Here, you focus more on the content.

Consider the following three service examples. The first two are process oriented; the last is content directed.

Providing a Solution to Payroll Problems

In 1949, Henry Taub determined that many small- and medium-size companies were having problems managing their payrolls and reporting to the government. Payroll had become more complex with the increasing variety of withholdings for employee benefits and federal, state, and local taxes. Taub established a company, called Automatic Payrolls, to handle those problems for clients. In 1949, Taub had eight accounts; 40 years later, he headed a $1.6 billion multinational corporation. Taub changed the company name in 1961 to Automatic Data Processing (ADP) and expanded to include shareholder services and computer networks. Success can be attributed to Taub's vision and leadership and to the missionary sales ability of his partner, Frank Lautenberg.[2]

Solving Tax Preparation Problems

Henry W. Block developed an entire industry around the need of individual citizens to pay taxes. And H&R Block still remains the leader in tax preparation services. Block also stimulated the use of computerized transaction systems to reduce paperwork and permit individuals and small businesses to file their tax returns, make payments, and get refunds (for a fee) through electronic filing systems. In 1990, almost three million filings were made by computerized systems from Block offices in all 50 states.

Believing his company could help solve legal problems in the same way, Block established a subsidiary, Hyatt Legal Services, to provide low-cost legal services to individuals and small businesses. However, this venture was not successful, and Block spun off the new business and concentrated on his established tax service.

Conquering the Weight Problem

Weight Watchers and Nutri/Systems have learned that a significant number of Americans are interested in looking good and feeling good about themselves. Specifically, they have discovered that 60 percent of the women in the United States believe they are overweight and have difficulty solving the problem on their own. Both companies have established a systems approach. Clients attend meetings at which they support each other and get advice from trained staff. A personal counselor (consultant) is assigned to each participant to help her (or him) reduce in a systematic and health-sustaining manner. Both organizations want their clients to be satisfied and to keep the weight off so that they become living testimonials to the success of the programs.

Long-term success requires a permanent change in eating habits. Clients are advised to buy food branded under the program's name. Heinz, the owner of Weight Watchers, sells Weight Watcher products to clients and the public in supermarkets. Nutri/Systems sells its brands exclusively in its own outlets and only to its members. Both have learned how to value-price. Memberships are relatively expensive, and so is the food. In 1990, Nutri/Systems charged an average of $612 to join and about $50 a week for food. Weight Watchers is somewhat less expensive. Both companies are doing quite well.[3]

THE CARETAKER A/C LEADER'S GAME PLAN

Whether the enterprise is process or content oriented, the leader's game plan is much the same. It consists of 12 elements or plays.

1. Select clients who recognize that they have a problem and are willing and able to pay for its solution.
2. Select clients who want a long-term relationship.
3. Use relationship pricing.
4. Practice the art and science of listening and learning.
5. Offer "one-stop" convenience and economy by adding services.
6. Meet or exceed the customer's expectations.
7. Standardize and formalize the approach without becoming too mechanical.
8. Apply what is known in new and different ways.
9. Avoid the "man who came to dinner" syndrome.
10. Be willing to recommend the best, even if that requires using the services of others.
11. Protect the "know-how."
12. Promote by example and testimonial.

Play 1. Select Clients Who Recognize That They Have a Problem and Are Willing and Able to Pay for Its Solution

This element is similar to one in the risktaker problem solver's game plan. The difference here in the caretaker mode is the focus on the client's ability to pay. The risktaker is on a mission and doesn't usually feel concern about money until the problem has been solved. The caretaker A/C leader is more practical and develops decision-making criteria to identify the potential customers/clients who can actually pay to get their problems solved. The caretaker also avoids costly situations that require first convincing customers they have a problem.

Play 2. Select Clients Who Want a Long-Term Relationship

Customer selection is not critical when selling a commodity product. It is, however, vital for leaders in A/C enterprises because they are pursuing a customer-intensive strategy. The very nature of the problem-solving function indicates that customer relationships are important. These leaders should be looking for customers with whom they can develop a strong and lasting mutual respect. That means avoiding clients who are interested in a quick fix or who believe the problem-solving process can be easily replicated and implemented internally by their own people. The client should be seeking a long-term relationship and help with a number of problems.

Ideally, the client's problems are interrelated and integral to the client's total business. If there is only one specific functional problem, it likely can be solved relatively quickly and any follow-up work will be done internally. Further, the client's problems need to have some relationship to the past successes of the problem solver. If both client and consultant are novices with no past experiences on which to build, they have what I call a "junior achievement project." In this case, it is unlikely that the consultant will be able to generate sufficient confidence to establish a lasting relationship with the client.

Play 3. Use Relationship Pricing

Consultative leaders want to minimize the high costs of selling their solutions. One reason for developing long-term relationships with clients is to not be constantly selling. The key is to convince the clients they are getting value for the price they are paying. It may mean providing low prices for the loyal customer. If clients believe the consultant is taking advantage of them, they will become disenchanted

and begin seeking help elsewhere. I have found that companies succeed when their fees are based on results and customer satisfaction
and not on costs or competition. Prices must be based on the expectation of a lasting relationship and not on a single event. The consultative leader might set different fees for different situations, and even
these may vary from case to case for a particular client. This is relationship pricing.

Sharing the Risk

A variation of relationship pricing is sharing the rewards and risks
with the customer. The management consulting firm of Bain and Company practices this approach. Bill Bain's company has built a reputation for implementing strategically based solutions. Bain has been
willing to link part of its remuneration to the success of its solutions.
Bain can do that because its leadership has sufficient experience to
predict outcomes and estimate how much the solutions will reduce the
client's costs or add to the client's profits.

This form of pricing can be risky. Should the problem solver's advice
not yield the anticipated results, the management company will lose
fees and, worse, damage its reputation. However, achieving the expected results enhances both the consultant's fees and reputation. And
for a consultant, a good reputation means a good business. The key here
is to minimize risk with experience. For instance, a consultant who
links payment to the success of recommendations for improving productivity or losing "weight" probably seems impressively brave to the
client. The consultant, however, is confident because his past experiences indicate the advice should indeed improve productivity for the
client if properly implemented. Thus, the consultant can leverage his
fees and reputation by sharing the risk in relative safety.

On the other hand, if the problem is so great that improvements are
unpredictable, the consultant should not use the risk-sharing method of
pricing. In this case, the more traditional "time and materials" approach
is appropriate. Proper pricing entails setting expectations that are attractive to the client but relatively easy to meet. The consultative leader determines prices and measures of achievement through front-end
evaluations, education, and negotiations with the client. Remember,
long-term relationships are important.

Play 4. Practice the Art and Science
of Listening and Learning

Product-driven and sales-driven leaders begin with the question:
What am I selling? The A/C leader, on the other hand, is truly

interested in determining *what the customer is buying* and what the customer expects from the purchase.

That subtle shift in focus means the A/C leader must know customers well enough to articulate what they want and expect. And that requires the ability to listen attentively and to learn from what the customers say. The customer may not really want what the leader has to sell. That could mean the leader has the wrong product, but it may also mean the customer is confusing the solution and the symptoms of the problem. I have witnessed a number of situations where disturbing numbers led a customer to think that a quality control program was needed, when, in fact, the problem was a poor accounting system. The customer had mistaken the results for the problem. The consulting leader had to listen carefully to the client, separate the cause from the results, and communicate a proper solution.

Play 5. Offer "One-Stop" Convenience and Economy by Adding Services

Over the past few years, many companies have increased their utilization of third-party service organizations to manage and operate their facilities. By doing so, they reduce their labor force and acquire specialized skills not directly related to their own product lines or services. They can then focus on managing their own businesses without having to be expert in unrelated areas. Therefore, they contract with Pinkerton, ADT, or Brinks for security; Marriott, Trusthouse Forte for food service; and a host of other vendors for computer networks, travel arrangements, copier centers, transportation systems, and so.

Recently, some of these service companies have been trying to integrate a wider range of functions in order to offer full management services to businesses that then would not have to deal with multiple vendors. Further, a single company providing multiple, integrated services can likely reduce the cost per service to the client. That would be a good fit for a company with the primary need to control costs rather than obtain expert, specialized service (an integrated service firm may not be as good in every area as a specialized service company). Once again, listening to the needs of the customer is critical.

In the past decade, a number of Big 8 accounting firms have diversified into other application areas in an attempt to become single-source management and financial consulting firms. Several advertising agencies, including Scatchi and Scatchi, have acquired specialized consulting firms for the same reason: to become one-stop providers. Other consulting firms have also expanded to offer both specialized and general services. Some have been successful, while others have failed. The difference has been the ability to meet customer needs rather than to provide just "bundled" services. This requires a continuing search for what the "customer" is buying, what they really need and not a reversion to what I want to sell.

In the consumer finance area, many banks and brokers have increased their offerings in hopes of becoming full-service providers to their clients. Companies such as American Express and even Sears and GE have gotten into the game. Sears began by financing customer purchases at its stores to stimulate sales. It then acquired All State Insurance, picked up Coldwell Banker for real estate service, and later bought Dean Witter Reynolds to provide customers a full range of investment opportunities. Sears also bought savings and loan institutions in California for banking services and began offering the Discover credit card. In short, Sears hopes to provide a complete range of financial services. Unfortunately in late September 1992, Sears' core business—its retail stores—became an endangered species and so its "confused" leader decided to dissolve the union of financial services and refocus on retail.

American Express has employed essentially the same approach. AMEX has leveraged its travel card to provide security brokerage, international financial services, insurance, and private banking services to its customers. GE followed a similar route by leveraging its credit company and acquiring firms such as Kidder Peabody to offer a full array of financial services to companies and consumers.

In the industrial and commercial area, the Bechtel Group has been an applications and consultative leader. Bechtel is one of the world's largest construction and engineering firms. It works on a variety of projects, including electric power generation from different sources (nuclear, fossil, solar, hydro), environmental cleanups, oil and gas pipelines, chemical plants, transportation systems, mining, telecommunications networks, and buildings. Warren Bechtel founded the company when he was 26. He led the construction of the northern California highway system and the Bowman Dam. His son Stephen took over and weathered the Great Depression with massive works projects, including the Hoover Dam. The company is now run by the fourth generation of the family; Riley Bechtel is the current CEO. Bechtel is building the new airport in Hong Kong (among other major projects there), managing the tunnel construction between England and France, and helping to reconstruct Kuwait.[4] Bechtel—a full-service construction and engineering firm—demonstrates that an A/C leader can work both on small jobs and on multi-billion dollar projects.

Play 6. Meet or Exceed the Customer's Expectations

"Promise what you can deliver and deliver more than you promise."[5] This quote from James Robinson, CEO of American Express, highlights a key element of the game plan of a successful A/C leader. I continue to stress how essential it is not to over- or underpromise. (Robinson's advice to "deliver more" simply indicates that if you miss the target, be sure it is in the customer's favor.) By and large, leaders understand the expectations message. It is also vital they appreciate that the expectations must be established early in the relationship with the client; waiting until the problem-solving process is underway is too late because expectations will already be formed by both sides, and disappointments will surely follow.

The skilled generalist consultative leader needs to spend a great deal of time with the CEO and immediate confidants of the client company to make clear what can be achieved and what cannot be. The leader should try to satisfy the one individual in charge, either the CEO or a member of the senior management group.

When a service becomes a business it takes a different type of leader.

Our discussion has focused on how some leaders use "service" as a means to distinguish their product from their competitors. However there are many recent examples where companies have moved "service" from a "means" to an end in itself. For instance GE changed its credit company from a means of selling appliances, to a major multi-billion dollar financial services company. This took an entire different leadership style. The caretaking leaders of GE CREDIT were not suited to lead GE CAPITAL.

I have been involved in several such transformations. Under the leadership of Carole St. Mark, Pitney Bowes created Pitney Bowes Management Services. This new unit provides mailing, copying and fax services to customers as an alternative to selling the equipment. It was highly successful and made a major acquisition to enhance its growth in this new business.

Play 7. Standardize and Formalize the Approach without Becoming Too Mechanical

After selecting the firm's area of expertise and focus, the A/C leader must develop a package that can be *replicated with ease and effectiveness by trained professionals and support personnel*. Completing this vital task may be as simple as getting answers to the right questions, or it might involve using more complex, computerized "artificial intelligence approaches." These computer programs allow users to build on the experience and success of others by comparing data from their problem to similar situations that have been resolved effectively. In this manner, A/C leaders can improve the quality of their recommendations and accelerate the problem-solving process.

Play 8. Apply What Is Known in New and Different Ways

At times, customers may not be able to explain their problem precisely, and the leader and his team may be required to experiment with new applications of existing products or technologies. For instance, when the oil crisis drove the airline industry to seek ways to reduce fuel consumption, the two jet engine producers, GE and Pratt and Whitney, were able to apply the technological know-how they had acquired from their military contracts to this commercial situation. Today, the process is in reverse. The military is receiving the benefits of the experience and know-how gained by these firms in the commercial market. Application know-how may not be customized, but it can be modularized; that is, the leader can create new uses by combining or modifying what is already known.

GE Plastics performs a similar applications function for clients by finding ways to replace metals with plastics. GE labs determine the customer's unique needs and problems and then work in partnership to find solutions. For instance, GE was one firm that helped the auto industry meet EPA gas mileage requirements by substituting lightweight, durable, and attractive plastics for heavy and corrosive-prone metals. GM's 1991 model Saturn even uses synthetic materials in the side panels. GE Plastics has built applications labs in Europe, Detroit, and Tokyo to be close to the major auto companies and thus be ready to keep the problem-solving partnerships working.

Task 9. Avoid the "Man Who Came to Dinner" Syndrome (Know When It Is Time to Leave)

The consultative leader must avoid losing objectivity as a result of becoming too entangled with the customer's problems. Even worse, the leader may become "part of the problem" and not be able to separate personal feelings from the solution. That is, the leader feels like part of the client's team and is unable to point out the client's faults and poor procedures. (The lead character in the play *The Man Who Came to Dinner* stayed well past his welcome but had no trouble pointing out his host's shortcomings.)

The essential question for the consultant then is: When do I leave? The first sign is the loss of objectivity I just described. The second indicator is an inability to come up with creative new solutions. Beware of forcing your preferred process on inappropriate situations. Third, changes in key personnel may mean it's time to go. A new CEO should have the opportunity to hire a new consultant with fresh insights into problems.

Obviously, long-term, continuing relationships with clients are important, but the A/C leader needs to step back periodically and assess the progress that has been made. Consultants are guests and not permanent members of the household. In a large consulting company, the team can be rejuvenated by seeking ideas internally from others in the organization. The leader's decision to leave or continue must be based, however, on what provides the best service for the customer.

A relevant story concerns a highly reputed consultant and his relationship with General Electric in the 1950s. This consultant was one of the major contributors to GE's decentralization strategy (today, the expression would be "empowerment at the lowest possible level of the organization"). He became a frequent speaker at GE's annual management meetings, where he was introduced as "one of the GE family." Once reality caught up with the trite phrase and he recognized that he truly had become part of the family, the quality of his consulting help declined. He had lost the objectivity and detachment necessary to give hard, honest advice. Belonging had become too important to him.

I have personally faced this dilemma of either changing my relationship with the client or moving on, and so have most consultants. The problem has cropped up for many accounting firms that have moved into general management consulting while remaining the primary accountant for the client. Conflict of interest can become an issue. What if the accounting unit discovers that the consulting arm was responsible for a major loss of funds or market position? The answer from a professional and ethical perspective is clear, but the political and practical aspects of losing a major revenue source introduce some uncertainties. What to do? The A/C leader who loses the ability to offer a client honest and objective service needs to "leave the table."

Play 10. Be Willing to Recommend the Best, Even if That Requires Using the Services of Others

A companion to knowing when to leave is knowing your own strengths and weaknesses. No one can do everything and solve all the problems. The A/C leader must put aside the temptation to attempt things beyond her capabilities or she may endanger the client relationship. A failure with part of the problem for which the leader has inadequate expertise can undermine the client's faith in the consultant's ability to succeed with what she does so well.

I have always like the assertion of the hired maid that "I don't do windows." I have told a number of clients what I can't do, and they have respected my honesty. After declaring these limitations, however, the consultant should recommend vendors or problem solvers who can help in the weak areas. Doctors and lawyers learned this technique long ago. They always refer patients or clients to specialists who have the specific expertise they lack. They know the dangers of giving advice beyond the range of their knowledge.

The A/C leader must overcome the fear that not doing the entire job may mean losing the account or not receiving all the necessary funding. The fear has a basis. Clients have limited resources; spending in one area takes away spending in another. However, the caretaker leader must take this risk. The core mission is to help clients solve their problems. Besides being the right thing to do, it is good business. I have found that clients appreciate that the leader is taking a chance. They will likely either fund the projects or let the A/C leader be the integrator and monitor of the other problem solvers. That is a real win.

Play 11. Protect the "Know-How"

Problem solvers are usually not able to protect their creative applications with patents or copyrights. True, their materials—manuals, case studies, and other teaching aids—can be packaged and copyrighted. However, success resides in the people who apply those materials and ideas. Thus, the only protection for the A/C leader is good faith.

Unfortunately, many of the leader's trained consultants may move on to their own businesses, taking the leader's approach with them. In the consulting business, we create our own competition. The major competitors for the Boston Consulting Group have been their own alumni. Strategic Planning Associates, Bain and Company, and other firms are owned and operated by people who started at BCG. Consultants often leave for positions with their company's clients, who now get the job done internally. Other service professions, such as law, advertising, and public relations, also operate this way.

Although it may be impossible to keep people from striking out on their own, the A/C leader can protect the integrity of the firm's problem-solving process through strict training and auditing procedures. Early in my career, I was trained in the problem-solving and decision-making approach developed by Chuck Kepner and Ben Tregoe. This excellent approach was successful only when instructors and consultants knew the material well and did not deviate during applications. Kepner/Tregoe selected their trainees carefully and put them through an intensive two-week program. When they finished training, the instructors and consultants were not only skilled in teaching the process but expert in applying it. Quality control was maintained by on-site audits. Chuck Kepner, Ben Tregoe, or a top staff member would attend the sessions to make sure the instructors were following the process, using the cases properly, and providing quality sessions.

This sort of systematic discipline is critical for internal protection. The A/C leader can also choose from several other strategic options to protect proprietary practices:

1. *Packaging.* Materials can be modularized and controlled by the leader so that it is difficult for others to replicate them. Special manuals, application cases, instructor notes, or computer software packages can be protected by copyright.

2. *Updating Materials.* The methodology can remain the same, but the techniques used to apply or teach the concepts should be modified periodically as the experience of the experts dictates. This step is analogous to the product innovator having the next generation ready to counter the moves of the copycat competition.

3. *Legal Protection.* The leader can use contracts that contain noncompete clauses to make clients and consultants aware of their moral and legal responsibility to protect the integrity of the approaches. However, the leader should go to court to fight a violation of contract only when it threatens the survival of the problem-solving process. Often, negative publicity can have more clout than the courts. Large companies in particular do not want to appear unethical. So, shine a light on the thief of your "intellectual property" and make a loud yell of protest.

4. *Limitation of Personnel.* Carefully limit the number of instructors or consultants authorized to apply or teach the concepts. Kepner/Tregoe's approach improves the chances of maintaining control, although it does limit growth. Obviously, the more people using the process, the greater the potential revenues and profits. The trade-off between profits and security must be considered carefully.

5. *Limitation of Provider.* Remain the sole provider of the service; do not license it to others. Here, the firm is both owner and operator. This method is especially appropriate when customers want the results but not the product or equipment. This approach also limits growth, of course, because it restricts use even more than option 4. Still, circumstances may make that the best path to follow.

Play 12. Promote by Example and Testimonial

A beautiful aspect of this game plan is that the satisfied client often becomes the most productive part of the sales effort. Clients are grateful when their problems are solved. They may "testify" for you by:

1. Giving speeches, writing articles, or even appearing in advertisements. They may do all or any of this on their own time for no, or a minimal, fee.

2. Allowing you to use their offices or facilities as demonstration centers. They may let you bring in prospective clients to see how your process works and hear the endorsement of the satisfied client.

3. Becoming a partner and sharing information and results.

Tom Peters is one of the most successful consultant leaders in the 1980s. He has articulated a set of common sense rules in his presentations and books (*In Search of Excellence* was the first) and has gained quite a healthy following of CEOs who are willing to share the podium, coauthor articles, and appear on audio- and videotapes. These clients are now his best salespeople.

The Dale Carnegie program has been able to achieve the same results. Participants go forth as a missionary sales force. Their efforts allow the consultants to concentrate on their offerings and not be too concerned with direct sales and promotions.

Testimonials are not only effective and time liberating, they enhance the consultant with a noncommercial image.

THE RIGHT TEAM FOR THE CARETAKER APPLICATIONS AND CONSULTATIVE LEADER

The A/C leader needs a team that will stick to the proven and recommended approach and not deviate or improvise. The game plan must be carefully designed and implemented to assure a high degree of success. In this regard, the caretaker's team resembles a highly structured football team, following elaborate plays drawn out in detail, with each individual player adhering to an assigned role. The team can not afford prima donnas or uncontrolled creative forces. However, individuals must also be sufficiently flexible and innovative so as not to appear mechanical.

Because the team must have continuity, rewards should be structured so that consultants feel they have a share of the firm's success. As I discussed earlier, the leader does not want trained people to leave and become competitors. For this reason, many consultant firms have a large number of "partners," who are required to make a personal and financial commitment and so have a stake in the success of the company.

Team members must know their limitations, that is, understand what the problem-solving process can and cannot do. Therefore, they will be selective and not try to move into unchartered waters that might prove to be treacherous and unnavigable. If they can't do a job, they must have the humility and good judgment to call in the required outside expertise. Most likely, the client will appreciate their honesty. To establish and enforce this discipline, the leader must select team members carefully and weed out those who are not doing the job or failing to conform. The leader also needs to keep tight control over pricing and contract negotiations. Even after their problems have been solved, clients might still not believe they are getting value for their money if the fees are set too high.

The sales force should be small because only the leader, senior management, and (as described earlier) satisfied clients will do the "selling." Team members must protect the reputation of clients that endorse the firm. Clients should never be placed in a situation where they appear to be hyping the service and making unrealistic promises.

A/C caretaker leaders need team players who are constantly looking to help each other. The firm may have several projects in process at the same time in the client's organization, which means consultants will be competing against each other for the client's time, attention, and funds. Nonetheless, they must all be willing to share resources and work for an integrated solution. But they must always tell the client what they know, regardless of how that information might reflect on a team member (remember the accounting conflict of interest example I described earlier). Team work is critical, but it is always in service to the client.

Team members should be sensitive to how people in the client's organization think and feel. Understanding the politics and culture of the client's business can be particularly important when solving problems that have been caused by or exacerbated by the client. To avoid putting the client in a poor position, consultants must frame the solution carefully within the reality of the situation. However, they cannot sacrifice their integrity to avoid hurt feelings.

Team members must be able to communicate in the client's language and present their advice in clear, simple terms. They may have to communicate differently to senior management than they will to those responsible for implementing the solution. One of the variables is depth of input. If the material is too detailed for senior management, they may not really understand the recommendations and discount the findings as tactical. On the other hand, if the implementors consider the consultant's communications too shallow, they might disregard the recommendations and be lost for what to do next.

The consultative team must present a solution that can actually be implemented. I have seen a large number of consultants' studies and evaluations that were not. Many consultants seem to feel they are not responsible for the practicality of their advice. That attitude will not build a long-term relationship with the client. The consultant team should work with the client, which does not necessarily mean they have to do everything. In some cases, they may have to take action themselves, in others, they merely lead and guide.

What could be termed "selling the solution" is often a complex, time consuming, and continuous process. It is complex because the consultant must solve a problem and not just attack the symptoms. It is time consuming because the consultant must listen to the client and specify the problem. It is continuous because one step in the problem-solving process will affect the next, and so on. The team needs to understand the techniques of "consultative selling" because, in most cases, it will be a team effort. Advertising is one industry that understand this truth. It is impossible to have a meeting with only one member of an advertising firm. The leader always comes with a team. Each team member focuses on a specific part of the presentation, while the leader (a partner in the firm) monitors and integrates. They practice the "team sell" deliberately to get more than one perspective on the client's needs and on the potential solution.

TWO ESSENTIAL SKILLS FOR THE PROBLEM-SOLVING COMPANY

An applications and consulting firm must have a variety of capabilities to be successful, as I have delineated throughout the chapter. Regardless of whether it specializes in one problem area or helps clients with a wide range of problems, however, the company must possess two pervasive skills.

1. *The company should be there when needed.* Consultants must be available when the clients need them and not just when it is convenient for the consultants. This obvious business truth is not recognized by many problem solvers. Imagine going to the dentist with a painful toothache and being told the next available appointment is in several days, or visiting a bank for a loan to close a major deal and being informed funds will not be forthcoming for weeks. Impossible. But consultants put off clients who need immediate help solving business, advertising, productivity, or personnel problems.

   The client wants help when it is needed, not later; problem-solving leaders must have the skills and infrastructure to respond. If necessary, they should have emergency personnel on call and an answering service to relay messages to someone who can respond: 24 hours a day, 7 days a week, 52 weeks a year, and on major holidays. Their situation is analogous to the product innovator who cannot afford stockouts that give the competition an opportunity to enter the market. For problem solvers, responsiveness is more critical, since they may not get a second chance to keep the client happy.

2. *The company must always keep current.* Keeping current has two dimensions. The first entails being abreast of, and being skilled in, what is happening in the profession. The problem solver must know the "best practices." For instance, if the tax laws have changed or are in the process of changing, clients should reasonably expect their tax accountant to be up on the changes and be ready to provide advice based on the new rules. The second dimension involves keeping current with the client's business and its needs. Has the client moved into new markets? The consultant must determine how this development affects their relationship and the client's needs.

The real winners are those who are up to speed in both dimensions. Keeping current with the client's business may take some extra effort. The consultant may have to hire people who have worked in that field. For instance, an on-the-ball problem solver might be able to alert a client to one of the many opportunities provided by specific market segments. Consider the case, described by the *Economist*, of serving Japanese tourists in Britain. The magazine points out that 1 in 30 tourists visiting Britain in 1988 were Japanese. That represented a problem for both British merchants and the tourists because most of the Japanese visitors did not speak English and also expected a different kind of service. Unfortunately, the entrenched British merchants regarded the Japanese as an annoyance rather than an opportunity (the visitors were highly affluent and willing to pay "top pound" for the goods they wanted). Instead of catering to the tourists' special needs, the merchants put them off. As a result, several Japanese-owned stores opened up in London to serve Japanese customers. Japanese saleswomen sold Burberry coats, Wedgewood china, and other highly marked up, traditional English items. The shops made an astonishing profit, which might have gone to the established stores had they or their consultants been current with the latest possibilities.[6]

TIMING

When is the most appropriate time for the caretaker consultative leader? There are five special situations.

Situation 1. When the Customer Has a Critical Problem and Is Willing to Pay for a Solution

The A/C caretaker strategy is more viable when the customer has a problem, or several interrelated problems, whose immediate solution is vital to the business. In this case, the leader must move with alacrity to do the job. Obviously, the fit between the customer's needs and the consultant's expertise must be considered, but that should be secondary if the leader's team has the potential ability to complete the task to the client's satisfaction.

As I have mentioned, GE Plastics was willing and able to jump into the auto industry's problem of meeting EPA fuel efficiency standards, even though GE had no direct experience in the car business, because leadership had faith in their people, because the client's need was immediate and extreme, and because the client was willing and able to pay for a solution. Electronics companies also helped by designing fuel injection systems and computers that could control acceleration and thus improve fuel efficiency.

Situation 2. When Regulatory and Other External Changes Create Opportunities

Just as the auto industry must contend with tightened fuel efficiency requirements, so must other industries cope with new legislated or regulated conditions. For instance, most heavy industries must reduce smokestack emissions, electrical utilities must conform to tougher pollution and safety regulations, and nuclear reactor operators must develop community evacuation plans in case a unit malfunctions. All these developments present opportunities for companies to help solve problems of compliance. Compliance is a term that refers to the ability to capitalize on a customers need to meet specific regulations, laws, or standards. Some of these are a result of federal, state or local governments, such as the need for electric utilities to meet smoke emission standards or the requirements of food processing companies to meet specific packaging or information requirements. Many companies have been able to develop solutions for companies to meet these standards. Perkin Elmer, under the leadership of Gaynor Kelley, has provided instruments and systems which enable their customers to identify and verify increasingly stringent air, water and soil environmental regulations. In addition, through a combination of his and the leadership of Riccardo Pigliucci, P.E. has developed a highly innovative instrument which facilitates PCR (Polymerase Chain Reaction) and has had a profound impact on genetic research and molecular biology. This has given them a major lead in the emerging DNA bioscience market. It is an excellent illustration of the willingness of these leaders to take risks and move the company from a purely analytical instrument business to an applications and problem-solving company. Instruments have become their means of helping to solve major societal and environmental problems.

Broader social and political upheavals also provide unique opportunities for the problem solver. In Eastern Europe and what was the Soviet Union, such changes are proceeding at an amazing rate, offering unprecedented possibilities for application/consultative caretaker leaders and for risktaker problem solvers to adapt structures and improve quality and productivity. They will also have major opportunities to train personnel to operate in a freer economy.

Situation 3. When Old Solutions No Longer Work

Sometimes incumbent leaders are reluctant to abandon ways of doing business that have gone from being tried and true to tired and toothless. Because they don't want to discredit the traditional, they open opportunities for the problem solver. A new solution that is unique and protectable is a vehicle for market leadership.

Consider an ongoing problem for retailers: How do I price-mark my goods for sales and inventory purposes? The traditional solution was to mark everything by hand. The next solution was the price marking gun, which did the job more efficiently but still was a mechanical process. Lately, many stores have converted to the barcode printing and labeling system—those postage-stamp-size, white patches with black lines that are printed right on the package and are meaningless to the consumer but can be read and recorded by special scanners. Merchandise is usually barcoded at the factory or wholesaler's warehouse. Items are scanned at the store, which records them into the inventory system and loads the prices into the store's computer. When an item is purchased, the retailer scans the barcode, and the computerized cash register rings up the current price and prints out an itemized sales slip for the customer. The retailer also has a record for inventory.

Symbol Technologies has been a leader in developing the barcode system. The problem-solving company took away a significant share of business from the traditional price-marking companies (the "gun" makers), while actually creating a new market segment. New solutions can create new markets for equipment and total systems when the old equipment and systems no longer meet the customer's needs.

Situation 4. When the Customer's Business and Strategy Are Changing

Change of any kind creates opportunities for leaders who can adapt or know how to help others adapt. Today, major companies in all industries must adapt to the requirements of the international marketplace. What does that mean?

1. Many companies will have to obtain products and components from offshore. Consequently, firms that know how and where to purchase goods offshore will have excellent opportunities as sourcers or importers.

2. Companies will seek partners and allies in different parts of the world to deal with local laws and regulations. Thus, those who can help form those local partnerships will have significant growth potential, especially if they have contacts in Eastern Europe.

3. Companies must be able to attract and retain local management and motivate the local work force. Some Japanese operating plants in America are demonstrating less than optimum skill in this area; as with Americans and Europeans abroad, they reserve the best jobs for themselves and alienate the locals (in this case, ironically, Americans). Perhaps local consultants could help, here and everywhere.

4. Companies will also have to deal with local governments, which is even more complicated than described in situation 2, because politics and the special character of bureaucrats enter the equation. Again, leaders with expertise can help these firms—and themselves.

Major changes are also emerging in the American marketplace that reflect changes in society. For instance, the aging population creates both marketing and staffing problems for companies who suddenly have older customers (or would like to) and older employees, both with different needs. You may have noticed senior citizens behind the counter at McDonald's (fewer teenagers available in the work force) as well as the hamburger giant's appeals to an older clientele (not only the menu, but bingo during the slack periods between breakfast and lunch).

Marriott Corporation is attempting to address the needs of older people with Retirement Inns, which provide nice accommodations and extra services. Bill Marriott's company is also looking after the special needs of executives who are away from home working on major projects. His Residence Inns offer more living space and amenities for longer stays; they are, in effect, efficiency apartments with hotel services. Marriott illustrates how a customer-driven company solves problems generated by changing market conditions.

Situation 5. When Problem-Solving Skills or Applications Can Be Used in Other Ways

In the previous chapter, I mentioned how the Institute for Infantile Paralysis and NASA were able to apply the talents and skills originally dedicated to solving one major problem to other important concerns. On a more everyday level, consultative leaders can do the same thing. For instance, I have been able to adapt and use the process of strategic thinking to help others set priorities and develop effective strategies. At the company level, I have advised staff organizations how to move from a subservient reactive mode to a more anticipatory and proactive stance. I have also applied the process to teach individuals productive ways to think about their own personal and career development.

This concludes my discussion of problem-solving leaders—risk-takers and caretakers. In Part Four, I will describe creative leadership styles in selling and marketing.

FOUR

THE MARKETING LEADERS

Chapter 9 discusses risktaker sellers. These leaders focus on innovating how they sell, where they sell, and when they sell. *How* deals with the way the customer is addressed, *where* deals with the location, and *when* deals with timing. Rapid expansion and growth as well as a continuing attention to the customers' needs and desires are necessary to protect selling creativity. Selling leaders have a short window of opportunity and must capitalize on it.

The caretaker marketer builds and institutionalizes the selling innovation of the risktaker seller. Chapter 10 focuses on these leaders, who establish long-term relationships with vendors while developing systems that meet customer expectations. They have the team and abilities to "put and keep it all together."

9

Risktaker Sellers

Leaders must be unique. They gain competitive advantages for their firms by creating innovative products, solving complex problems, or applying existing concepts and approaches to new situations. I have described these types of leaders over the past five chapters. Here, I want to examine another variation: the risktaker leader whose unique talent is selling.

Some gifted people appear to be able to sell anything—a product, a service, a way of life, or even a means of protesting. These individuals focus on the *means and not just the ends*. They love the process, the thrill of selling, and are less concerned with *what* they are selling.

Of course, selling is a means of implementing any strategy. Unless the customer buys the product innovator's new invention, it will fail. To stay in business, problem solvers must sell their ability to solve the customer's problems or apply their techniques to the customer's situation. Selling leaders, however, are in the business of selling. They take products and services, often made or developed by others, and sell them to the public, to businesses, to government, and so on. Some call these leaders, merchants.

Leaders in this category exhibit their talents by creating new ways of selling or by enhancing existing methods. Not all of them are in business. Politicians, educators, religious leaders, scientists, and others in every conceivable field have distinguished themselves by the way they have sold ideas, policies, programs, and themselves. Ronald Reagan, the "Great Communicator," was a master at selling his point of view to the American public. Franklin D. Roosevelt's famous "fireside chats" over the radio reduced fear and built confidence that America could solve its economic problems. John F. Kennedy was perhaps the first to mold the power of television to his political purposes. These are just a few examples; we all could think of many recent sellers of distinction in such disparate fields as religion and commerce.

This chapter will be dedicated to the risktaker leaders who create new and different ways of selling. In the next chapter, I will distinguish between these leaders and caretaker marketing leaders who often follow them and who are motivated to enhance their achievements and make them more profitable.

CREATIVE SELLING

Since the late 1890s (and probably since the beginning of humankind), risktaker merchant leaders have been convinced the key to success is in "how and where you sell and not just what you sell." Often, they have taken the same products available in other outlets and sold them in ways the customer found more interesting and convenient. Many of these creative selling channels were for consumer goods, but others have opened for customers in business, industry, and government.

Selling approaches are differentiated by these major factors: (1) how, (2) where, and (3) when the goods or services are sold. (Other variations include customer service, price, and image.) The "how" is the process used to sell, as in directly to the customer or through third parties or via such technologies as the telephone. The "where" is location of focus—city, suburban, rural, or regional. The "when" is time of day, week, or year. The key for all three elements is finding the method, place, and/or time that is best for the customer. That or some other special feature (service, price, or image) provides the leader a competitive advantage.

Developing a creative selling approach is similar to developing an innovative product. Leaders start with an idea that they believe is consistent with the needs and wants of the potential customer. This belief often comes from insights or intuition rather than comprehensive market research. To succeed, they must not only be right, they must plan well, have good timing, and be lucky. Just like the product innovator.

Many people think that great sales geniuses are more in tune with their customers than other business leaders. In fact, seller leaders are as much product driven as customer driven, as internalized as those whose focus is developing the product innovation. However, once they succeed in implementing their concepts, they must keep in close touch with the customer to make sure their merchandising approach continues to satisfy.

THE DIFFERENCE IS "HOW"

For certain types of risktaker sales leader, the very pro
supreme. There are many ways to reach a customer, but these ...
are committed to their way.

Selling Directly in the Home

Most consumer products have been sold directly in the home. Brushes,
soaps, cosmetics, books, vacuum cleaners, insurance, milk, Bibles, magazines, and many more items have been peddled at people's places of
residence. Sellers capitalized on the customer's desire for ease and
convenience in purchasing certain products. The glory days of home
selling occurred before World War II, when most women were house-
keepers with limited means of transportation and communications. In
addition to helping women who couldn't get to the store or phone in
an order, innovative sellers offered products not found in traditional
retail outlets. Customers were willing to pay premium prices for the
convenience and for the company. Some sales approaches were quite
innovative; let's look at a few.

Using Housewives to Sell to Housewives.   Once upon a time, a book
salesman named David McConnell began giving away small bottles of
perfume to housewives who listened to his sales pitch. When he discovered that the perfume was more popular than the books, he founded the
California Perfume Company and marketed beauty products under the
Avon brand.[1] McConnell's simple strategy was to recruit housewives to
do the selling. Commissions were small, but women who used the products were happy for the chance to earn discounts on Avon items and to
get out and socialize at other people's homes. The strategy worked because of this motivated sales force and because they were selling high-
quality products at a reasonable price. Low costs and high margins
made Avon very profitable for many decades. Later, it fell on hard times,
but current CEO Jim Preston is successfully turning the company
around.

Starting in 1974, Avon undertook a number of unsuccessful diver-
sion moves to compensate for its anticipated decline in its traditional
home direct-selling business. Among these diversification moves was
the acquisition of Tiffany (prestige jewelry store), Mallinckrodt (hospital supply and chemical company), Foster Medical and 60 other
medical and health care providers. Each of these acquisitions proved
to be unattractive and not compatible with Avon and were sold. Jim

Preston, a long-term veteran of Avon took over the company and returned it to its core focus and direction. He has given new life to the company by a series of aggressive and focused moves in global markets. Avon has prospered in the developing nations, such as Mexico, Brazil, Eastern Europe and recently in mainland China. These countries lend themselves to the expertise of Avon in selling direct to consumers in their home, using part-time workers. In addition, Jim has expanded the selling approach of Avon in the United States. Avon is now more aggressive in selling via catalog, telemarketing and in non-home environments, such as offices and other workplaces.

Jim clearly demonstrates the ability to evolve change after major surgery has been performed. Simultaneously with this strong return to the core business, he has successfully fought off the attempts of Irwin Jacobs, Amway, and members of the Mary Kay management team to take over Avon.

What lessons can we learn from the Avon story? First, make sure you are selling the right product. McConnell recognized that perfume should be the end product and not the means to sell books. Second, be aware of how economic and social changes are affecting your strategy. Avon has discovered that it can no longer attract and motivate sales representatives in the same way in contemporary America. The company has had to offer rewards similar to those of the competition in domestic markets; it has gone across the border to apply the old techniques. Third, understand that all innovations have a limited life cycle. Leaders must adapt or die.

Making It More Fun to Buy.   Mary Kay Ashe thought the best way to sell beauty care products was to have a party. Essentially, she expanded the one-on-one home selling approach to a group experience. Customers found this a more attractive way of socializing; salespeople liked it because they could reach more people more efficiently. Mary Kay's "beauty consultants" were also motivated by greater monetary and prestige awards. They could make big money and even win the use of a pink Cadillac for two years if they really excelled. The car has become a trophy as coveted by beauty saleswomen as Oscars are by movie actors. Mary Kay's sales approach continues to work; her company felt prosperous enough to consider participating in the acquisition of Avon.

The home sales party method has been appropriated by other merchants, the most famous being Tupperware, which was very successful in selling high-quality plastic cookware and housewares products in the 1960s and 1970s. Parties have also been held to sell clothing, gifts, toys, and financial planning services. It is a powerful sales tool that has not yet reached the end of its possibilities.

Demonstrating Products Door to Door.   The vacuum cleaner salesman at the doorstep has become a cliché of American life. The tradition began in 1910 with Electrolux, a company founded by Swedish
salesman Alex Wenner-Gren. Electrolux men knocked on doors unan-
nounced and offered to demonstrate the effectiveness of their machines. The homemakers were impressed with the vacuum's superior
performance. A little moderate-to-hard closing sell and the demon-
strator had another order.

Two elements seem to be critical to successful door-to-door sales:
The product has to be unique or of superior quality; the product
should be available only from the sales rep and not through regular
outlets. Electrolux scored on both counts. I should point out, however,
that some firms have sold well door-to-door without meeting those
conditions when the customers only *believed* the products were unique
and not available anywhere else.

Bringing Cars to the Door in Japan.   Property is so expensive in
Japan that automobile showrooms are too costly to operate. Therefore,
Japanese have had to develop other ways to sell autos. Toyota sells its
Corolla to people in their homes. And so do the other car makers. Ac-
cording to the *New York Times Business Magazine*, 50 percent of auto sales
in Japan are made in the home.[2]

As you would expect, the Japanese approach this sales effort systematically and scientifically. The sales team draws a profile of every
household in its geographic area and periodically calls for appoint-
ments to talk with potential customers in their homes. During these
visits, sales reps update the household profile: How many cars of what
age does the family own? What makes with what features? How many
children are in the household? What use does the family make of the
car(s)? When does the family think the car(s) will need replacement?
(Can you imagine an American auto dealer having this information or
even wanting it?) The Corolla rep will match the family's needs with a
car in the brand's line. If the family is interested, the rep can handle
all aspects of the sale, including financing, trade-in, and insurance.
It's one-stop service, and the company comes to the buyer's house.

The Japanese are motivated to sell this way by considerations other
than expensive real estate. They know that customer research and personal service builds long-term relationships. This focus differentiates
the service-driven leader from the product-driven leader. *The service
leader is interested in repeat business and not just a single sale.* Japanese auto
companies make it clear that the dealer will fix any problem the owner
encounters with the car, at no cost to the owner. Sometimes this guar-
anty includes insurance problems. Agents continue to update customer

files after the sale. They send congratulation cards when someone in the family gets married or graduates; they send condolence cards when a family member dies.

Why don't the Japanese employ this powerful strategy in the United States? One reason may be that Japanese cars are built to order in Japan but in advance of the order for the United States. However, once they build more cars in U.S.-based factories, Japanese companies may have short enough supply lines and sufficient control to provide the extra service of personal, at-home sales.

Selling to Your "Friends and Neighbors."   Led by John Fairfield Dryden, the Prudential Insurance Company pioneered the selling of small, straight-life insurance policies to urban, low-income consumers. The company recruited agents to sell in their own neighborhoods to capitalize on the inherent familiarity and trust. Years later, in the 1980s and 1990s, a number of innovative insurance companies have been attempting to apply this strategy to medium and higher income segments. Agents are now self-styled "pension consultants" whose focus is on helping clients prepare for life after retirement. They may sell at the country club or church rather than in the home. The sales entry is still the same, however: Buy from a friend and neighbor who understands your needs.

"Neighbors" are also selling "health" products door to door, perhaps because trust from familiarity is critical to sales for such items. For example, Nature's Sunshine Products sends its reps out to their friends and neighbors to sell herbs, vitamins, cosmetics, coffee substitutes, and water purifiers. Interestingly, the company has had compensation problems similar to Avon's. Sunshine has been forced to establish a bonus program and offer greater medical benefits to its friendly and neighborly employees. The concept of neighborhood sales is still valid, but sales reps must now be treated as professionals and not as casual workers.[3]

Giving the Distributor the Responsibility.   Amway is another innovative, direct-selling company. Founded in 1959 by Richard De Vos and Jan Van Andel, Amway sells its products to regional distributors. The distributors select their local salespeople and are responsible for their training and performance. Amway sells liquid organic cleaner, nutritional supplements, personal care products, cookware, educational books for children, and legal and travel services. The company took its successful approach to Japan in 1979 and is reported to be the seventh fastest growing company in that country.

Making Home Deliveries. Before World War II, milk, groceries, and other food products were commonly delivered to the home on a regular basis. Economic and social changes, which I have already mentioned, forced the end to that sales approach. However, the old technique has been revitalized for other products. The most notable risktaker seller in home delivery is Domino's Pizza. Tom Monaghan and his brother borrowed $500 and opened their first store in Ypsilanti, Michigan in 1960. At the time, pizza was a mom-and-pop business, challenged only by the emerging franchise giant, Pizza Hut. Monaghan decided his competitive edge would be guaranteed delivery within 30 minutes of ordering. By 1988, his company has grown to over 5,100 stores with over $2.3 billion in sales and $6.1 million in profits.[4]

Pizza Hut has reluctantly paid the ultimate compliment to its competitor by copying Domino's delivery service and even mentioning Domino's by name in its advertising. In addition, Pepsico, which owns Pizza Hut, is experimenting with the same home delivery sales concept for Chinese and other ethnic foods.

Selling Directly in the Office

The Avon and Tupperware methods can be used in the workplace to sell (for example) office equipment, supplies, and products to businesspeople. Sales reps schedule convenient times or make "cold calls" (they just show up) to demonstrate their products. Almost all office equipment has been sold this way, most often by equipment manufacturers. For instance, Pitney Bowes has been highly successful in selling postage meters, small copiers, and dictation equipment to small and medium-size businesses via a strong, direct sales force.

John Patterson, founder of National Cash Register, was one of the early risktaking pioneers of business direct selling. He established an aggressive, highly motivated, well trained, missionary-style sales force to sell cash registers to retailers. The distinctive sales approach made NCR a leader with the dominant share of the market. However, Patterson fell victim to the over zealousness that characterizes many risktakers. He was sentenced to jail (though he didn't serve) for tampering with products and spying on, and even bribing, competitors.[5, 6] Risktakers become so intent on controlling that they may violate laws, albeit often unintentionally.

In the preceding chapter, I described IBM as a strong, applications-driven company under the leadership of Thomas Watson, Jr., and John Akers. However, from its inception, IBM has also been a strong, sales-driven company in the NCR image. Indeed, Thomas Watson, Sr., learned the selling art from Patterson at NCR. When the two men had a falling out, Watson left NCR to run the struggling Computer-Tabulating-Recording Company, which was to become IBM. One of his first moves was to establish an aggressive, professional, direct sales organization.[7]

What did that mean? Both NCR and IBM stressed that sales- and servicepeople should look and act like professionals. Men had to wear dark suits, white shirts, and conservative ties. (Watson didn't want servicepeople looking like handyworkers or sales personnel reminding customers of the loudly dressed, phony salespeople of legend.) In addition, IBM people would act like professionals because they were so well trained in proven sales techniques and skills and so well versed in the features and capabilities of their own and the competition's products. Dedication to IBM was inculcated through the singing of company songs and pledging allegiance to the company and to maintaining the quality of its service. Strange how this sounds so Japanese today. But these approaches were quite common in the United States before World War II. Likely, the Japanese learned their loyalty-building tactics from the best companies in the world at the time: IBM, NCR, and, even my old alma mater, GE. General Electric had rigorous dress codes and company songs, and it demanded complete, lifetime loyalty from its people as late as the 1950s.

Another company with a long history of success in direct sales to the work-place is Snap-On Tools. The business was established in 1920 as the Snap-On Wrench Company by Stanton Palmer and Newton Tarble, both salespeople. Snap-On was a distribution business whose sales reps demonstrated tool sets at customer's work sites. By 1940, the company had more than 500 salespeople and was making hard tools for the military. Tool shortages for civilian use during the war forced sales reps to begin carrying excess stock with them on the road. In time, these reps selling retail to mechanics became independent dealers with their own regional territories. Snap-On retains the strong market position won through its direct sales network by investing in the development of unique tools.[8] Once again, sales may be the driving force, but the product must also have a distinctive quality.

Restocking the Shelves, Automatically

Some innovators have been able to build ongoing relationships with customers from direct sales and so create a continuing revenue stream. Zee Medical is an excellent example. The company helps businesses comply with health and hygiene regulations by providing bandages, ointments, and emergency equipment. Rather than periodically selling these products, Zee Medical offers a contract that allows it to restock customers on a continuing basis. This arrangement offers convenience and security for both parties.

Different vendors provide similar services in other office areas. Some, for instance, guarantee customers will always have a supply of paper and other consumables; some provide maintenance services. All such vendors free the customer from having to continually make decisions about routine matters that have nothing to do with their core business activities. For the company providing the product and/or service, the sale is converted into an annuity, that is, guaranteed income. The supplier also does not need to compete continually on price. Major competition comes annually, which can be more effectively managed. Normally, the margins are much higher in these types of arrangements.

Direct selling to the business market is similar to direct selling to the home. Both require trained, loyal, enthusiastic salespeople who are willing to meet the needs of the customer by making sales calls that suit the *customer's* convenience. (Successful door-to-door salespeople always come back if they knock at the wrong time.) Risktaker seller leaders reward their people generously with high commissions, entertainment, and ego gratification. They cement loyalty with good treatment and no-layoff policies. In some firms, salespeople are literally treated like royalty. Even when business is down, top performers receive extravagant trips, dinners, and awards; poor performers are sacrificed.

Selling by Mail

Direct sales does not necessarily require person-to-person contact. In the United States, where we are fortunate to have universal, reliable mail service, selling by mail has become a viable option for an increasing number of products. (It is less popular in other countries where mail service is not universal and much less reliable.)

Of course, the most famous catalog sellers in history are now much better known as storefront retailers. Giant merchants Sears and Montgomery Ward were initially catalog risktakers in the early 1900s. In fact, Aaron Montgomery Ward became the first general merchandise mail order company in 1872. In 1885, Ward pioneered the policy of "satisfaction guaranteed, or your money back," which differentiated the company from the hucksters and con artists in the business.[9] Richard Sears, who started as a mail-order merchandiser of watches, distributed a general catalog of merchandise, in partnership with Alvah C. Roebuck, the very next year. They offered money-back guarantees to their principal customers, farm families. In those days, rural customers looked on the catalog as more than a means of purchasing the goods they needed; it was a way to dream. In fact, the Sears catalog was called the "Dream Book" by those who read it for pleasure.

Neither Sears nor Montgomery Ward is considered to be a catalog innovator today. That title belongs to specialty and upscale marketers such as Land's End and L.L. Bean. Their merchandise has some prestige appeal and they offer some unique items not readily available in traditional stores, but the critical selling point is still the convenience of home shopping, especially for those too busy, or disinclined, to handle the hassle of the malls. However, catalog sales may have become too popular for their own good; overexposure may be reducing their appeal in some cases.

Using Technology Creatively

The telephone, television, personal computer, and facsimile machine have been and will continue to be used to create new and innovative ways of selling.

The telephone in particular is a major force in direct selling. The telemarketer calls prospective customers, makes a pitch, and tries either to get orders on the spot or schedule a sales call. Selling over the phone requires special skills and resources and must fit the product offering. Usually, the technique works best when the customer is familiar with the product and knows how to use it. In that case, both the seller and the user save time and money. Since the product is often a commodity, pricing makes the difference. If the product is new or complex, however, telemarketing is best employed to set up a sales appointment.

Phone sales can also be combined effectively with a catalog. Here, the telephone is more of an ordering than a selling device. A number of specialty catalog companies permit ordering merchandise over the phone when the customer gives a credit card number. Again, the process works best when the merchandise does not need personal demonstrations or complicated explanations. However, some selling does go on while the order is being placed. A few innovative companies have trained employees to entice customers to increase their orders by asking questions and making suggestions, much as high-service retailers have always done. In catalog phone sales, the leaders have been consumer electronics and camera stores, especially a company called 47th Street Photo.

The Home Shopping Network is an innovative risktaker in another technology-based, direct-selling approach. HSN sells specially purchased merchandise over cable television. The format combines entertainment with sales presentations. Viewers shop in the comfort of their own homes and place orders by mail, phone, or facsimile machine. HSN now provides catalog service so customers can purchase items at any time over the phone or through third parties. For instance, the Network has an arrangement with doctors. Doctors become agents of the Network and can sell prescription medicines or over-the-counter drugs listed in the company's catalog and split the profits.[10]

Some innovative firms have taken advantage of the explosion in personal computers to sell stocks, bonds, and other financial instruments via the computer. Subscribers are linked to a computer network through their own computer and a phone hookup. They can then access information and make purchase decisions while logged in.

Sears and IBM are also exploring the concept of computer sales through a joint venture called Prodigy. As of 1989, the partners had invested over $600 million, and that figure is expected to eclipse $1 billion before the network is completed. In 1990, Sears and IBM announced that Prodigy had over 1 million subscribers. Prodigy will give subscribers access to 500 products and services, ranging from airplane reservations to grocery shopping. Users of the system can bank at home and purchase, sell, and place options on stocks and bonds. But Prodigy offers more than home shopping by computer; it is also a combination of magazine, electronic mail, and interactive advertising system.[11]

Both Sears and IBM claim they are looking to the long term and not for a quick financial payoff with Prodigy. They believe a technologically sophisticated, easy-to-use system will grow into a major merchandising force. They view Prodigy as a transactional advertising business and expect to make their money by selling ads to and receiving transaction payments from businesses wishing to be part of the network, and possibly by filling purchase orders from subscribers. While skeptics point out that this type of service has failed in the past, IBM and Sears have had the financial resources to invest for the long haul and the abilities to systematically work out the bugs as the system grows. Further, improvements in the technology and increases in the number of personal computer owners bodes well for future success. However, both partners must be willing to stay the course despite short-term profit pressures. In 1992 both were restructuring and under considerable revenues and earnings pressures that may cause one or both to disengage.

Should Prodigy succeed, it will make a major contribution to the long-awaited home transaction business. As with most merchandising systems, success will require quality products and services as well as rapid and predictable response and delivery. Both the system and the offerings must meet customer expectations. The novelty appeal of the technology will wear off if the product is not good. Early satisfaction is vital. If the initial users are pleased, they will spread the word and encourage others to experiment. Subscribers will become "missionary" salespeople, and growth is likely to be dramatic. The pioneers with the vision and commitment will gain an early dominant share and reap their deserved rewards.

Facsimile is another technology apparently destined to be applied as a selling device. Already, a number of companies permit both consumers and businesses to place orders and to purchase goods via the fax. Some firms are beginning to experiment with using the fax to sell, as one would with the mail. Fax is, in fact, electronic mail, hard copy over the phone lines. The problem: many customers view fax selling as intrusive as telemarketing. The seller leaders in this technology must make offers that recipients will view as truly valuable.

THE DIFFERENCE IS "WHERE"

Sometimes it is not only how you sell but where that creates a competitive advantage. Certain risktaker leaders who have focused on location have been extremely successful. In some cases, they were the only ones who knew, "You *can* get there from here."

Moving from the Country to the City, Gradually

Many well-known merchandisers have had humble beginnings in rural America. Sears, Montgomery Ward, JC Penney, State Farm Insurance, Wal-Mart, and others have profited from starting small in rural areas and then selectively and gradually migrating to the major urban markets.

As I related earlier, Richard Sears created a great catalog sales business by catering to the wants and dreams of the rural population of the United States. General Robert Wood took over in the 1920s and built the company into a retail giant before his leadership tenure expired in the mid-1950s. The growth of Sears was founded on the General's anticipating and adroitly exploiting two major trends. First, he understood the changes the automobile would have on rural life during the 1920s and 1930s. He established a chain of retail stores throughout the countryside so that farmers could drive to purchase many of the same items they had been buying from the catalog. He also began adding Sears's brands of products. (Interestingly, Sears tires were sold under the name All State in 1925; the insurance company didn't exist until 1931.)[12]

General Wood also foresaw the tremendous changes coming in the United States after World War II, particularly the growth of the suburbs, which was made possible, in part, by increased auto use. Wood built Sears stores all over suburbia and gradually made the company the nation's largest retailer. In contrast, Montgomery Ward, which had migrated from the country to the cities with Sears, missed the boat—or rather, the commute. Sewell Avery, CEO at Ward, was convinced that the United States would suffer a recession after the war. Avery canceled expansion plans to the outer city areas and instead bet on the vitality of the city centers. Thus, Montgomery Ward failed to prosper from the postwar boom, lost major share, and almost went under. (Ironically, General Wood was an executive at Ward before he took over at Sears. He quit because, at the time, Avery was unwilling to open retail stores to complement Ward's catalog business.)

State Farm Insurance also began in rural areas and grew into other parts of the United States. State Farm was founded in 1922 by a retired farmer, George Mecherle. (You're never too old to be a risktaker; many leaders start new ventures after retirement.) Mecherle's company started selling policies to members of farm bureaus, even training bureau secretaries to sell to the membership. During the 1940s, the bureaus decided to share some of State Farm's success by beginning their own lines of insurance. State Farm was forced to relocate its business to metropolitan areas and by the early 1950s had a full-time agent system in place. The move suited the company. In 1991, State Farm had 17,500 agents, serving 25 million households and carried 57 million policies. Policyholders rated satisfaction with the handling of claims very high. State Farm was #1 in both auto insurance with 21% share and homeowners insurance with 18%. They recognized that success depended on sharing the profits. Their agents, in 1990, had a median income of $148,000 per year, with 172 agents earning more than $500,000.[13]

Finally, Sam Walton is the latest risktaking merchandiser to understand the value of the rural United States. Walton recognized the opportunity created when Sears and the big discount chains focused exclusively on the major suburban and urban markets. As a result, America's small towns often became the domain of mom-and-pop stores. In 1962, Walton was positioned to take advantage of the situation. He had begun his career as a JC Penney management trainee and later leased a Ben Franklin franchised dime store in Newport, Arkansas. By 1962, he owned 15 Ben Franklin stores under the Walton Five and Ten name. After Ben Franklin management rejected his suggestion to set up discount stores in small towns, he and his brother James (Bud) opened the first Wal-Mart Discount City in Rogers, Arkansas.[14]

Walton opened a number of small- and medium-size variety stores in towns like Rogers. As his volume grew, so did his purchasing clout. Thus, he was able to offer national brands to Wal-Mart customers at discount prices. This approach allowed him to knock out the local competition and become a near monopoly in his markets. Wal-Mart's success often resulted in the decline of the downtown in rural America. Wal-Mart continued to expand geographically and grow rich. In 1990, Wal-Mart had revenues of over $32 billion, an ROS (Return on Sales) of 4 percent, and an ROTC (Return on Total Capital) of 18.8 percent. With 1,725 stores, it was the largest retail chain in America.

However, Sam Walton did not become complacent. He started a new chain of Sam's Wholesale Club, which are giant bargain stores open to the public on a membership basis. Before his death in April 1992, he also began experimenting with giant supermarket/discount stores called Hypermarkets. In addition, the present leadership is testing a new concept, vendor stores, which grant extra space to preferred vendors who make special commitments to the store. In 1988, Mr. Walton was succeeded by David D. Glass who appears to be the classic caretaker leader.[15] The original Wal-Mart concept exemplifies how small companies can grow by focusing on market segments that are ignored or undervalued by the large-volume, financially driven players. Successful risktakers seem to have a unique view of the market that gives them a competitive advantage.

Consider the case of Carl and Dorothy Bennett. They also found a market that was being ignored by the big chains. The Bennetts built a chain of discount stores, called Caldors (*Cal* for Carl; *dor* for Dorothy), in the affluent suburbs of Fairfield County in Connecticut and Westchester County in New York. Discounting had been invented in New York but not aggressively rolled out of the metropolitan area. Caldors prospered under the leadership of the Bennetts but floundered after they sold the chain to Allied Stores. Recently, the chain was sold to its own management and is now embarking on another high-risk play.

Tightening the Geographical Focus

Long ago, the Atlantic and Pacific Tea Company (A&P) was led by George Hartford and his two sons. In 1912, son John opened a new store employing a low price, "cash and carry" format that did not allow credit or premiums. Four years later, the company adopted a strategy of putting a "store on every corner" and thus blanketing American cities with A&Ps. They became a very early version of the convenience store.

John Hartford's format was a departure from the traditional mom and pop grocery in which clerks filled the customer's order from a very limited stock. He recognized that the spread of refrigerators and ice boxes to many urban homes would allow customers to buy food in larger quantities once a week instead of purchasing whatever was needed on a daily basis. He reasoned that customers would be willing to serve themselves given the possibility of a greater variety of products. The self-service approach and the no-credit policy reduced labor and finance costs; the multiple locations greatly increased A&P's buying power. The combination permitted the company to lower prices. Customers were attracted to the bargains, the better selections, and the convenient locations. Also, the store's "Anne Page" brand became very popular, contending with national brands in many parts of the country.

Over the decades, A&P grew with the size and vitality of the American cities it served. By the 1950s, it was one of the largest and most profitable chains in the world (a $5-billion business). At that time, the locational strategy that had worked so well for A&P became a trap. The buying population moved, but A&P did not. The problem was ineffective leadership. When John Hartford died, the Hartford Trust took over. Management decided that paying dividends was more important than reinvesting and innovating. Besides missing the shift to the suburbs, A&P declined to expand the supermarket format to include nonfood items, as the competition was doing. An antitrust suit in 1949 also contributed to management's timid leadership. The great company nearly went under. It was saved by a surgeon leader, James Wood, by a combination of massive store closings, strategic acquisitions and strict cost controls.[16]

THE DIFFERENCE IS WHEN

It has always amazed me how many retailers and businesses keep "banker's hours." They seem to think that their convenience should be more important than the customer's needs. Automobile dealers are a grand example of this concept. They might pay attention to the innovative scheduling of Southland's 7-Eleven stores. The name itself was conceived to demonstrate their difference from other stores; 7-Elevens were open from 7 o'clock in the morning until 11 o'clock at night, 7 days a week. (Now many are open around the clock.)

Essentially, Southland expanded A&P's location strategy to include time. The company correctly decided that customers would find it useful to have access to strategically located, small stores where they could select from a limited number of food items, beverages, and household goods. In the process, 7-Eleven assumed convenience store leadership.

Other companies are trying to replicate Southland's success through the use of new technologies. Electronic kiosks are now emerging as a means of selling 24 hours a day with a minimum of human intervention. Machines allow customers to select what they want from electronic and visual displays, place an order, and pay for it with cash or credit card. Depending on the item, the customer either gets immediate delivery from the machine or gets it very soon by special delivery from a centralized warehouse. These kiosks are more sophisticated versions of vending machines that have been popular sellers of gift items in high traffic, public locations. They are especially useful for renting videos, in effect expanding store hours without the need for personnel.

For businesses that must have people on duty to do the selling, the liberalization of "blue laws" or "Sabbath laws" has been a boon. Just a decade ago, it was difficult to find stores open on Sundays or late at night because of restrictions of local ordinances. Risktaker sellers challenged the laws, and now many stores are open 24 hours a day, seven days a week. People can buy at their convenience.

THE DIFFERENCE IS SERVICE

Remember Stew Leonard's two rules of business: *Rule 1: The customer is always right. Rule 2: If the customer is ever wrong, refer to rule 1.* Selling leaders who distinguish themselves by the quality of their customer service embody those rules. Stew Leonard is a wonderful example.

Stew Leonard began as a milkman. He inherited the Clover Farms home milk delivery business from his father. The Clover Farms truck and distribution center was located in my hometown of Norwalk, Connecticut, near Route 7. When the state condemned the property by eminent domain 25 years ago to build the Super 7 Highway, Stew built a small milk store on the Westport side of town.

It was a pleasant little store that sold quality dairy products at a reasonable price; it even had a small animal farm for the kids. Over the years, Stew kept expanding both his floor space and the variety of his product offerings. Today, Stew's place has been declared by Ripley's to be "the largest dairy store in the world." It is recorded in the "Guiness Book of World Records" as having the fastest moving stock of any food store in the world. It is, however, much more than a dairy store. It is a complete "farm stand" where you can find fresh fish, meat, vegetables, baked goods, and so on. The store is always crowded and generates over $100 million annually in revenues from over 100,000 shoppers each week.

At Christmas, you can purchase your tree and decorations at Stew's. In 1989, his one outlet sold 25,000 trees, the largest number in the area. In the spring, Stew's store sells garden supplies, flowers, bushes, and fertilizers. Both seasonal specials maintain the establishment's standard of high-quality merchandise at reasonable prices.

What is Stew Leonard's secret? I'll discuss his approach in more detail in the next chapter, but for now the short answer will suffice: Customer service. Stew really knows his customers. He continually seeks their advice on what to do next. He tries to be highly visible in the store, walking about and talking to customers. From the beginning, a suggestion box has been prominent at the exit, and Stew actively encourages customers to participate. A sign in the store proclaims that over 100 suggestions are received per day. These informal measures are augmented by in-depth focus group studies conducted by professional researchers.

Stew found that his customers were interested in being entertained; they wanted to enjoy the experience of shopping for food. As a result, the store features mechanical animal characters that act, sing, and talk. Staff members costumed as animals wander about the store relating to the customers. And, of course, the original real animal farm is still there.

Stew's caters to the upscale consumer with first-class products. Staff are trained to be pleasant and customer oriented. He highlights his best employees by displaying pictures of the "employees of the month" for current and past years. At the checkout counters, displays feature the career growth of employees.

The store has the latest in automated checkout systems that allow the rapid movement of large numbers of customers and purchases, at the same time providing detailed records for customers and management. This automated accounting is an integral part of the stocking plan. The store features sales from truckload purchases. Stew has in place a system that allows him to buy direct from local farmers and also to get volume discounts from suppliers; he advertises these relationships in the store and on his packages. Frank Perdue, the chicken king, is proudly depicted recognizing Stew's as his largest "single store" customer. Westport neighbor Paul Newman's salad dressings were introduced at Stew Leonard's and are displayed under a picture of Stew with the actor. Newman uses the store to market-test his products.

Stew advertises locally, but his reputation is global. He has been highlighted in Tom Peter's *Passion for Excellence* and other national bestsellers. A favorite speaker at conventions and a guest on talk shows, Stew can command $15,000 an appearance, which is close to top dollar. He is a disciple of Dale Carnegie and promoted by that organization. Japanese visitors come by the busload because the store has become a tourist attraction.

Although Stew Leonard is very active in promoting his establishment, he is in the process of turning over the business to his children.

They have opened an even bigger store in Danbury, Connecticut. Incidentally, that Super 7 Highway has still not been built.[17]

For all Stew Leonard's success as a risktaker leader, driven by sales and service, his operation still faces problems. One is parking. His location has forced him to add parking lots on the other side of a busy highway, which customers find difficult to cross with shopping carts. Success has also bred another problem. The store is always crowded and so is not as pleasant a shopping experience as it once was. The new store in Danbury, fortunately, has wide aisles, plenty of floor space, and ample parking. The original facility is trying to address the overcrowding issues (cars and people) but still has a way to go. The difficulties represent a classic case of a risktaker not being prepared for success—at least not in the amount that Stew Leonard has enjoyed. It will be interesting to see how his operation copes in the caretaker phase.

THE DIFFERENCE IS SELLING VOLUME: DISCOUNTING LEADERS

The original innovative, lower priced, volume merchandisers were five-and-ten cent stores. The first risktaker leader in this area was Frank W. Woolworth in the late 1890s; others, including Kresge and McCrory, soon followed. Modern discounting can be traced to Korvettes in New York, a regional chain of stores that later moved national. As I related in Chapter 4, the success of the discounters in the 1950s meant the end of "fair trade pricing" in consumer hard goods and electronics. No longer could manufacturers determine who could sell their products and control retail price.

Before the discount chains, consumers could only get "almost whole-sale" bargains if they "knew somebody" or had literally "joined the club." Master's stores in New York were "club" stores catering to the civil servants of New York City. That is, they sold goods to the police, firefighters, sanitation workers, and other city employees at below retail price. Because the stores were a huge success, Master's expanded its customer base, eventually to the general public. Manufacturers sued both Master's and Korvette's and lost. The Age of Discounting had begun.

Today, there are discounters in all retail and wholesale markets. KMart, Wal-Mart, Target, and hundreds of regional chains can be classified as general merchandisers. Volume discounters in specialty areas include Toys-"R"-Us, Rickel's, Grossman's and Home Depot (the last three are fighting for leadership in the home improvement segment). Many of these companies are expanding into Europe and, more slowly, into Japan.

The club membership approach to volume selling is also doing very well. Perhaps the most successful retailer is a not-for-profit organization: the American Association of Retired Persons (AARP). Led by Ethel Andrus, a retired school principal (again, age is not a barrier to risk-taking), AARP has grown to 32 million members worldwide. Members are able to purchase lower cost health and accident insurance as well as get discounts on prescriptions, travel services, hotel reservations, and car rentals.[18] Of the "clubs" normally categorized as retail organizations, with no age or other significant membership restrictions, Sam's Wholesale Club is number one, and Costco is number two. Both of these offer a limited variety of low-priced, brand name merchandise.

THE DIFFERENCE IS PRESTIGE

The flip side of price consciousness is concern for image. Discounters differentiate themselves with low costs; other sales leaders offer something extra for those customers for whom price is no object. They offer prestige, elegance, a special shopping experience that can't be had by everyone and certainly not at KMart. Bloomingdales, Lord and Taylor (in New York), Dayton Hudson, and Saks are a few of the traditional retailers who cater to the upscale customers in the clothing and housewares areas. In jewelry, Tiffany's, Gucci, and Cartier are internationally known for providing the best quality and at the highest prices. Chanel has been able to move from a fragrance house to a boutique with prestige accessories and products. And because these stores have status, they attract customers who are not rich and famous but who want to acquire that association along with their purchases.

The need to be entertained appears to be increasingly important in the high end of the market. Customers want shopping to be a pleasant and diverting experience. They are willing to pay more to get more than the merchandise and to enjoy what they are doing. Many stores provide comfortable surroundings for shoppers and televisions and magazines for those who are waiting. They also sponsor shows in the store for their customers. The upscale shopping malls can provide those services and atmospherics on a shared basis and thus reduce the overall costs to individual stores.

THE INTUITIVE GAME PLAN
OF THE RISKTAKER SELLER LEADER

Risktaker leaders whose unique talent is selling must devise a game plan that consists of five critical plays:

1. Identify a new (real or perceived) way to sell.
2. Protect the selling innovation by rolling it out rapidly.
3. Select the location that fits your product or service and sales approach.
4. Focus on a specific type of consumer or business and know how to target.
5. Match the approach to the product or service life cycle.

Play 1. Identify a New (Real or Perceived) Way to Sell

Frequently, innovative selling ideas are creative applications of old approaches to new situations. For instance, the high-volume, low-margin discounting, full-offering approach used by Toys-"R"-Us to market toys is really not very different from the method used to sell consumer electronics or clothing. When Charles Lazarus decided to shift from children's furniture to toys in 1958, he opened a 25,000-square-foot store and offered a 20 to 50 percent discount. In 1983, he extended the concept to children's clothing: Kids-"R"-Us. As of 1989, the chains had grown to $4.7 billion in revenues with a consistent ROS of 6.5 to 6.7 percent.[19]

A second means to innovation is to examine how technology might be used to gain a competitive advantage. The experimental partnership between Sears and IBM in Prodigy is one example. Video-based shopping is another. Here the customer examines the product or service on television and places the order electronically or via the mail. The more successful participants combine shopping and entertainment. The Home Shopping Network integrates game and variety shows into the shopping programs. I've already mentioned telemarketing, facsimile machine selling, and electronic kiosks that are open 24 hours a day. Picture phones that combine voice, data, and video will become popular. The phone companies plan to supply these services, but they have been fought by the cable companies, newspapers, and other media concerns who fear competition in the emerging transaction and advertising businesses. The new phone technology would require regulatory change and the conversion from analog lines to fiber optics and digital systems.

Electronic signage and transaction systems are transforming the selling process. Electronic signage utilizes technology that enables store managers to change the shelf price or promotional message electronically using a communications network. It is similar to the highway signs that use RF (radio frequency) to transmit information to motorists by communications and video displays. This allows firms to change prices rapidly and frequently. Thus, they can adjust immediately to competition and even offer specials during a selected period of the day and not have to physically change signs or price markings. Turner Broadcasting is moving to gain a dominant position in the in-store checkout business, which will enable Turner to broadcast into stores and advertise products to the customer waiting in the checkout line. CNBC/FNN, the NBC cable affiliate, is planning to offer television in airports for the traveling public.

Play 2. Protect the Selling Innovation by Rolling It Out Rapidly

Innovative sellers are plagued by their inability to patent or copyright their concept or presentation format. Charles Lazarus at Toys-"R"-Us established a competitive difference not only by his application of an established selling approach but by his willingness to bet on the concept by rolling it out selectively and rapidly. He was supported and financed by Interstate, which he later took over.

The process has worked for hundreds of seller innovators because speed and presence preempts the competition. This part of the game is absolutely vital, since most selling modes are easily replicated and cannot be protected. Thus, leaders must determine where their company needs to go and how it can get there rapidly. Obviously, financial support is critical to the successful completion of this step.

One way to roll out rapidly with other people's money—and still maintain control of the new selling approach—is franchising. All the major auto and consumer goods manufacturers have used franchising to roll out their *products*. Today, retailers are franchising to protect and roll out their *merchandising formats (that is, selling techniques)*. In fact, franchising became a national obsession in the 1980s.

The Howard Johnson restaurant and motel chain was one of the early successful franchise operations, but the undisputed champion for the past decade has been McDonald's. In general, McDonald's has adhered to the principle of seeking franchisees who would be working partners—people who are willing to provide "sweat equity" as well as financial capital—and limiting them to one franchise. Carvel, a northeastern ice cream franchiser, focused on individuals lower on the economic ladder who might be willing to make the franchise a family business. Lately, however, McDonald's and other franchisers have increased the number of company owned and operated stores. Not only are these stores more profitable, they make it easier for the parent company to experiment and to maintain control of quality and delivery of the merchandise.

Another franchising approach is for the risktaker to offer complete regions or geographic areas to franchisees and permit them to manage the area and operate as many outlets as they can staff and afford. This approach accelerates growth but possibly at the expense of control over the franchisees. Burger King and Gino's have been advocates of the regional method. GM's Saturn has employed it as an incentive for dealers to take the risk with a new automobile.

Training is absolutely vital to successful franchising. Those who represent the company must be well schooled in the qualities of the product or service; the accepted ways of selling; and, most critically, how to run a business and make money. Sound training helps keep franchises stable and reduces turnover in ownership. McDonald's indoctrinates its franchisees at the company's famous "McDonald's University" (called "Hamburger University" by some) in Oak Brook, Illinois. Other companies are comfortable that their selling and servicing systems can be taught sufficiently "on the job."

Play 3. Select the Location That Fits Your Product or Service and Sales Approach

The old saying in real estate that the three most important elements of a property are "location, location, and location" applies just as well to retail businesses. I described how Sam Walton and the Bennetts selected geographical locations that would permit their companies to grow without having to take on the giant merchandisers. Walton opened Wal-Marts in small, rural communities; the Bennetts placed Caldors in affluent suburban counties. Leaders must also think about specific sites within the target areas. The sites must fit the product being sold. For instance, fast food outlets must be easy to find and convenient to get to when people are hungry. Office supply stores should be convenient to businesses or be willing to make free deliveries. Discount stores can be more remote because customers will seek them out to get lower prices.

Howard Johnson restaurants were always located at exits on all the major interstate highways where they were convenient to the traveler and did not usually face direct competition. (HoJos had the exclusive food service franchise at the rest stops on the Pennsylvania Turnpike, a limited access highway that was extremely inconvenient to exit.) McDonald's also selects locations with great care; the company was also very fortunate to take over highway locations when Howard Johnson began to fail. Burger King appears willing to follow McDonald's from spot to spot, picking up the overflow after McDonald's has built the traffic. Prestige stores such as Chanel, Sharper Image, Laura Ashley, and Brooks Brothers select spaces in prestige shopping malls specifically targeted at upscale consumers.

Location is also important for technology-based selling. Telemarketers must operate where the local phone companies have installed modern, responsive networks and distribution systems capable of providing uninterrupted, reliable service. For instance, Prodigy has been rolled out very selectively. The first offering was in the affluent, high-tech community of Atlanta, Georgia, which also has a telephone system with over a 100-square-mile area for "local calls." Catalog selling is localized as well. Postal zip codes are used to determine appropriate places to send particular catalogs, whose merchandise fits the demographic profile of the area.

Play 4. Focus on a Specific Type of Consumer or Business and Know How to Target

Risktaker seller leaders cannot be confused about their customers. They must recognize that certain types of outlets and sales techniques will appeal to certain types of buyers. Obviously, you wouldn't expect to find an exclusive mall in a destitute neighborhood or strong telemarketing sales where there is poor phone service. Matching customer and sales approach is a validity test for the game plan.

Leaders must determine who is most likely to be attracted to their best selling mode. They cannot, for instance, use computers to sell products or services to people who hate computers. Women who are not social by nature might resent the Avon lady approach or not attend Tupperware type parties. If the business customer doesn't want her fax machine used to solicit orders or doesn't like cold call selling, then those techniques will fail to sell her anything.

Often, the means of selling will be self-selecting, and it may not have universal appeal. This truth eludes many companies. They become so locked into one selling approach that they cannot even consider an alternative. I know one company that is convinced that its products can only be sold by its own direct sales force. Another firm is equally fixated on using only distributors. Both will have problems as their markets change. Once again, leaders must adapt, or their companies will suffer.

Changing demographics should inspire leaders to change sales techniques. Consider the Hispanics in the United States; they represent the country's fastest growing minority population. Hispanics are projected to number over 40 million in the United States by the year 2015, which will surpass the number of African Americans at that time. In fact, the Hispanic population is already the largest segment of the New York City market. Many firms are paying attention. Metropolitan Life increased sales to Hispanics by over 150 percent in 1988 by advertising nationwide in Spanish. Coors has built Hispanic market share for its beers by sponsoring festivals celebrating Columbus Day in Miami and Cinco de Mayo in Los Angeles.

Many marketers have discovered that the Hispanic segment must be broken down further. The Puerto Rican, Mexican, and Cuban populations have a common language but entirely different cultures. They therefore respond to different selling approaches, advertising, and products. These differences can be understood only by people who share the culture. Consequently, many companies have found it preferable to hire and train the right Hispanics than have an already skilled Anglo try to learn the subtleties of the various cultures.[20]

The approach is similar to hiring locals in foreign countries to do selling, or at least to participate in the essential decision making. The same principles apply when selling to Asian populations in the United States, another rapidly growing market segment, or segments. Leaders must recognize there are vast cultural and linguistic differences among those who have come from Japan, Korea, China, Taiwan, and so on, and they must find and train people who understand those cultures to make selling decisions.

In fact, accepted folklore to the contrary, the United States is not a single homogenized market, or even a grouping of regional markets. Of course, I see McDonald's, Kentucky Fried Chicken, Marriott, and Holiday Inn outlets everywhere I travel around the country, but I continue to be amazed at how different people are. And their different values and lifestyles may provide new marketing opportunities. For instance, the Midwest lags the East Coast and West Coast in adopting new styles and fashions. Thus, different types of products and services will appeal to different regions. These variations have not received enough attention.

Targeting is becoming increasingly popular, however. R.J. Tobacco, a database pioneer with over 40 million names in its mainframe computers, is now able to mail out premiums that are tailored to individual life styles. This trend in direct marketing and advertising will flourish.

Play 5. Match the Approach to the Product or Service Life Cycle

Obviously, the product line must fit the distribution and selling approach. In addition, leaders must recognize when the product has moved along the life cycle curve and so needs to be refitted with a new selling method. When personal computers were introduced, the manufacturers understood that they would need a retail structure that could provide direct selling both in stores and on business sites. Salespeople would have to demonstrate the machines and guide customers to the particular models they needed. Thus, sales staff would have to interview customers concerning how the computers would be used as well as how often; they could not simply be order takers. However, as the products became better known and as customers became better able to determine their own computer requirements, such well-informed, direct sales help became less necessary. Smart sales leaders then abandoned most of their direct sales efforts and adopted approaches better suited to mature offerings. In general, as products become more like commodities, self-service selling through catalogs or electronic technologies becomes appropriate.

While some selling approaches are appropriate for certain products and services, that does not mean that others can't be adapted or modified to do the job. One would suppose, for instance, that auctioning artwork would require direct selling techniques. But Anderson Auction of Troy, Ohio, has been able to sell high-value art of all types by phone and mail. Anderson sends a catalog to prospective buyers that provides a picture, description, estimated value, and minimum price for each item. After reviewing the collection, customers mail in or, in some cases, phone in their bids. When all the bids are in place, bidders can change their bids by phone. The process continues until a sale is made.[21]

THE RISKTAKER SELLER'S
TEAM AND TALENTS

The leader must be enthusiastic, a real cheerleader. She must believe in her selling approach—the how, where, when, or whatever that makes her unique—and be able to get others to believe as well. She should be highly verbal and visual. Frequently, that means attaching her name to her enterprise. Most of the major consumer retail stores or organizations were named after founders: Sears, Kresge, JC Penney, Bloomingdales, Macy's, Gimbels, Nordstrom, Lord and Taylor, Mary Kay, Lauders, and so on. That is not just ego, it is personal commitment. When the leaders who take over have the same personal drive, the company continues to thrive. When the institution adopts an esoteric corporate name, like International Dry Goods, it signals a move from being sales to production driven or, even worse, cost driven.

The best leaders are always personally selling themselves and their services. Mary Kay Ashe was always a great personal motivator; she was very visible and made her top people very visible, too. Ross Perot is another top salesperson. It is said he left IBM to start his own business because he could not give the personal service to his customers that he thought was necessary. Ironically, IBM flourished originally because of the sales personality and leadership of Thomas Watson, Sr., and he learned his techniques from the master salesperson, John Patterson of NCR.

The late Sam Walton was known for his ability to motivate Wal-Mart management and the entire work force. He adopted the concept of "associate" from JC Penney. Wal-Mart people are "associates," not employees. Associates are given information about the total operation (costs, freight charges, profit margins, etc.) that most companies hide from their managers. Wal-Mart sets profit goals for each store, and if the store exceeds those goals, associates share in the additional profit. The company also pays bonuses when the store achieves lower-than-expected shrinkage, that is, losses from theft. Associates also know they can talk openly with management if they have problems.[22]

It is also important that sales personnel look and act as though they have pride in their organization. As I noted earlier, Thomas Watson, Sr., learned from Patterson at NCR the value of a sales force that dressed and behaved in a professional manner. This lesson does not apply only to the corporate elite of years gone by. Dominic Longo's Toyota dealership is the largest auto dealership in America. For years he has had a strict code for sales staff: no smoking, gum chewing, loud shirts, wild ties, or bad language. Longo never advertises on price; instead, he touts the location, the inventory, and his ranking for service. As a result, his operation is very profitable, and over 60 percent of his sales are from repeat business or referrals. Further, his good service and high tone, honest approach has been very effective in selling cars to women.[23]

While enthusiasm and professionalism are keys to success, the risktaker leader should recognize that sales-driven people are highly motivated by money. As much as they love the art of selling, they are energized by financial rewards. Many retailers have discovered that if they increase incentives, they will be able to get more revenues per salesperson. This has always been true in direct sales. Companies that rewarded the sales force by commission had higher revenues than those that paid a straight salary. Nordstrom, an upscale retailer with an excellent reputation for customer service and quality products, owes its success, in part, to its sales incentive program that promotes loyalty and effectiveness. Nordstrom salespeople know that if they make the sale, they will benefit.

Finally, the sales force should know more about the product than the customers do, especially when the company's offerings are very technical. An extremely knowledgeable staff that can share its expertise with the customer is one of the advantages stores such as the Home Depot have over their competition. Further, training must keep up with changes in the product, which is a real challenge in fields defined by rapid technological development or where products are moving upscale.

Toyota recognizes this truth and put over 500 salespeople through an intensive training program when it introduced its luxury Lexus brand.

TIMING

When will the risktaker sales leader be most successful? When any one of these five situations arises.

Situation 1. When the Customer Wants a Different Way to Buy

Everything is cyclical. What appealed to the preceding generation will often not appeal to the current one. That is as true for sales approaches as it is for clothing styles, entertainment, food, music, and so on. Few seem to want to be "old fashioned" (like their parents). You can bet that if the current generation likes to shop in malls, the next generation will like stand-alone stores or home shopping. If the current generation is interested in bargains, the next will likely brag about "paying retail" (or, for the snobbish, "above retail"). However, since there are only a limited number of variations on the sales theme, trends will eventually repeat.

Where is the opportunity for the risktaker seller? Look for the industry where selling has been done the same way forever, where sales are sluggish. For instance, the auto industry today is crying for a change. Americans love cars but find going to the dealer's show room an unpleasant experience. Salespeople are often defensive and sometimes adversarial. Some ignore the customers, while others swarm all over them. Few seem oriented toward service. Frequently, customers cannot figure out the difference between one model and the next and between one model year and the next. "Improvements" consist of more gimmicks and higher prices. Price stickers are hard to understand and some may well have been doctored by the dealer. Great service after the sale is promised but often not delivered. "Service" (and I use the term very loosely) departments are interested only in making money, which they do. Prices for parts and labor are higher at the dealer than at other outlets, with no break for customers who bought their cars from the dealer. Often, the car isn't fixed; in fact, it seems to come out with more problems than when it went in. In sum, people are unhappy.

Yet, no one in the auto industry (except Honda) appears to be interested in long-term customer relationships and future sales. Worse, auto manufacturers are not getting along with their dealers. Dealers are taken for granted and forced to increase inventory, especially in poor selling periods. The dealer's profit margins have eroded, and many of them have gone into receivership. Although American carmakers have improved the quality of their products and have tried to respond to the complaints of their customers, they have not looked for new, creative ways to sell cars. They should learn from the leaders in other fields. For instance, they could:

1. Move closer to the customer by owning and operating their own dealerships, especially in areas where they lack a strong and consistent dealer network. By establishing closer ties with the customers, they could build better, lasting relationships.

2. Increase the use of technology-based selling. They could combine television and computers in an interactive system that would allow customers to describe their needs. The auto companies, or perhaps some third-party agency, could then help car buyers select the best fit.

3. Model an approach after Toyota's home selling methods in Japan, which would improve customer relationships for the long term.

I don't claim to have all the answers for the auto industry. I do believe, however, that there is always a need to challenge the current selling approach with innovative thinking. This requires a risktaker selling leader.

Situation 2. When the Current Leader Becomes Arrogant

One of my favorite sayings is: "When you start to believe your own press releases, you are in trouble." I have always found that companies start to falter when they begin to get extensive press coverage or are featured on the covers of major business magazines. I often observed while at General Electric that after a feature article appeared about one of the units or its leader, the business began to decline, and in come cases, it disappeared. Consequently, the best time to innovate and possibly leapfrog the incumbent is when he is collecting his awards ("retailer of the year," "entrepreneur of the decade"), being lauded for record revenues or earnings growth, and constructing his trophy headquarters building.

A number of sales-driven leaders have, over the years, succumbed to the idea that their approach would succeed forever and always keep them on top. But arrogance is the downfall of all leaders who believe in their own immortality—Hitler, Napoleon, and other giants of history and business. In 1979, Sears announced in its annual report and in major publications that it was going to be the "store of the future." The future came and went quickly. In fact, in consumer products (and national politics) the life cycle of success is getting shorter and shorter. Once customers sense a leader is "getting too big for its britches," they start to look for someone else. In America, we always root for the underdog to knock off the leader.

Situation 3. When You Have the "Right" Approach at the "Right" Time

Intuition and luck are a potent combination. Consider that home shopping with the Avon lady and at the Tupperware party fit perfectly in needs of the female consumer during the 1950s and early 1960s. In the 1970s and 1980s, however, when women entered the outside work force in record numbers, these two selling approaches were no longer "right." Similarly, shopping centers and shopping malls were/are "right" for the growing suburbs because they create a sort of "town center" that has been lost with urban flight. They also fit because they were/are convenient, efficient, and accessible by car. Perhaps in the near future, time constraints will make shopping at home, in the office, or while in transit the perfect fit for the buying public. Selling through the electronic media will then become an important mode for innovation. And down the road, aging yuppies and senior citizens may desire an approach that is more communal but still private. A combination of catalogs and the party plan could be "right" for that time.

Situation 4. When There Is a Perfect Fit with the Product or Service

Obviously, there is no one right sales approach for all products and services. In general, complex offerings require direct communication with expert salespeople, and commodities must be easy to purchase, perhaps taking advantage of self-service mechanisms. Successful sales leaders understand what their product or service requires in terms of explanation, sales style, purchase frequency, and convenience and will construct an approach to fit. That is all part of being sensitive to the needs and wants of the customer.

The 24-hour convenience food store is a good fit between product and delivery system in urban areas because many people work during traditional grocery shopping hours. Domino's rapid delivery service can quickly satisfy the pizza cravings that college students and partygoers develop at odd hours. The Home Depot's massive warehouse stores, which contain over 40,000 home improvement items, fit the needs of the typical do-it-yourselfer—because they are staffed by pleasant, knowledgeable craftspeople who are willing and able to answer questions (and even offer seminars). Home Depot also provides special services for the professional contractor and so is responsive to both sets of customers.

Situation 5. When New Products Require New Ways of Selling

Consumer products that exploit new technologies often require new specialty outlets that can explain how the things work and service them when they don't. For instance, when television was introduced to the public, many television stores (or dedicated departments within big stores) were opened to sell and service the sets because no other retail mechanism was totally equipped to handle those tasks. The same was true with the introduction of personal computers, video and audio electronics, cellular phones, and other consumer electronic products. Early in the life cycle of technology-based products, salespeople are the key to building customer confidence. As the product matures, skilled salespeople and on-site servicing become less critical.

Over and over again, the cycle is repeated. And with change, comes opportunity for innovation for insightful, intuitive, seller leaders who are willing to take the risks.

10

Caretaker Marketers

Because product innovator and problem solver risktakers are mainly concerned with growth, they have difficulty making immediate profits. However, it is not unusual for the seller innovator risktaker to be highly profitable during the early and rapid growth stages of the venture. The primary reason is that expenses often lag revenues, and even though there may be inefficiency in the system, the returns on sales and investments are quite often high at this stage. This unexpected profitability can be both a problem and a blessing. Making money is a blessing because it builds confidence with the investors, the employees, and even the customers. It can become a problem when the risktaker's ego is so inflated with praise that he relaxes and refuses to adapt when the market and the competitive situation change.

Normally, the growth of outlets or orders begins to slow and the inefficiencies and excess costs begin to show. Then the profits drop dramatically or even disappear. At that point, the risktaker seller leader should step aside and appoint a caretaker leader to succeed him. Thus, we see the leadership cycle follow the business/product life cycle, as it does for product-innovating and problem-solving enterprises. Caretakers usually follow risktakers. The caretaker's mission is to build on the creativity and innovation of the risktaker while implementing systems and practices that will promote the orderly growth of both revenues and profits.

First of all, caretakers cannot be complacent about maintaining the competitive advantage gained through the selling innovation. Because the leader's approach can be easily copied, caretakers must continue to innovate. Consider that Korvettes and Masters were the early leaders in discounting; A&P, the leader in food stores; and Gimbels, the trendsetter in mass market department stores. All failed to continue to innovate and stay ahead of the competition. All have been merged into other chains or disappeared. In contrast, Wal-Mart continues to experiment with new ways of selling and meeting a broader group of customers.

Second, caretakers must be more selective than risktakers in how the business is to grow and be financed. Caretakers need to target the most appropriate customers and expand in markets that will optimize the company's way of selling. Thus, leaders will have to increase investment in sophisticated consumer and market research, rather than relying on their own intuition. Keeping in touch with the customer as Stew Leonard does (see Chapter 9) through suggestion boxes, focus groups, and just wandering around is vital.

In addition, the caretaker-led business should grow with its own funds and reduce its reliance on franchises. Franchises become less useful as a business matures because they are difficult to control and manage. They may not be committed to maintaining the overall image and reputation of the seller, and they may take short cuts in implementing the game plan that will sacrifice quality. As I mentioned in the previous chapter, McDonald's and other fast food chains have increased the number of company owned and operated outlets and even defranchised those that were not meeting company standards.

Location management is even more critical to the growth plans of caretaker leaders. Not only must they put into place highly sophisticated procedures for site selection and management, they must anticipate changes in the environment that could impact the quality of sites far in the future. Recall that the genius of General Wood at Sears was his ability to foresee the growth of the suburbs and the impact of the automobile on American society. Today, the leader must be sensitive to global as well as domestic changes. For instance, Avon has been able to replicate its past U.S. success in the developing nations, and Toys-"R"-Us has targeted Japan for much of its future growth.

In summary, caretakers cannot focus too much on the bottom line. They must leverage past successes by making the company more organized and systematic about its markets, customers, competitors, and technologies.

THE CARETAKER MARKETER'S GAME PLAN

Specifically, caretakers need to emphasize the following plays:

1. Maintain efficient systems that optimize the inventory and the response to customer demands.

2. Recognize that customers have short memories.

3. Practice innovative and flexible pricing.

4. Create and meet customer expectations.

5. Develop a partnership with key vendors.

6. Put it all together and keep it all together.

7. Experiment with other approaches.

Play 1. Maintain Efficient Systems That Optimize the Inventory and the Response to Customer Demands

Regardless of the company's sales approach, the caretaker leader must develop logistical and support systems that can deliver products and services efficiently and reliably. As the original innovative sales approach matures and is replicated by others, customers will be more demanding about getting what they want when they want it, because they will be able to shift to competitive vendors.

Consider what happened to the innovative catalog showroom stores that opened in the 1970s. These chains tried to combine the advantages of catalog orders and discount stores to provide instant delivery. That was great in concept but, as it turned out, poor in execution. These were the steps in the plan:

1. The seller determines the most popular seasonal merchandise.

2. The seller purchases the goods in volume and establishes local outlets with large warehouses in the rear.

3. The seller develops an attractive, price-competitive catalog and mails it locally.

4. The consumers read the catalog, select what they want, go to the local store, purchase the products, and take them home.

The process was clean and simple. However, it did not solve three major logistical problems. First, the customer often had to fill out forms at the store that could have been filled out at home, and still had to wait in line. Second, the store quite often did not have the products, and store personnel appeared reluctant to order out-of-stock items. Third, stores had problems in those inflationary times maintaining the prices listed in the catalog, which had to be printed six months before mailing. As a result, customers were hassled and frustrated.

Stockouts, especially of popular or sale items, plague traditional retail stores as well. I have witnessed this problem personally in the Norwalk, Connecticut, Caldors store. This successful discount chain has (as described in Chapter 9) failed to maintain standards since Carl and

Dorothy Bennett sold their interest in the stores. Commonly, local stores do not have the items advertised in the chain's weekly promotional flier. The "excuse" of store management is that the ads are developed at headquarters by people with little knowledge about, or concern for, the local availability of the products. To appease the disappointed customers, stores provide rain checks so that items can be purchased at the sale price when they finally become available. This arrangement is not satisfactory for the store or the customer. The sale items are often "loss leaders" designed to pull customers into the store in the hope that they will purchase other, more profitable, products. When the sales item is not available, not only is that sale lost, but so is the good will of the customer, who may not purchase anything from the store, then or in the future. This system failure is all too common—I do not want to single out Caldors—and cannot be tolerated by caretaker leaders. Reliable and consistent service is essential for repeat business.

Wal-Mart is dedicated to maintaining its competitive position. The company has invested heavily in a strong, technologically based, logistical support and response stem. For instance, Wal-Mart maintains a sophisticated "six channel satellite" system that gathers store data for the master computer, transmits credit card approval in five seconds, and tracks the company's complex distribution network. The satellite also allows headquarters to talk to every store simultaneously as often as desired, sharing merchandising information and reducing telephone costs. Wal-Mart's system includes the ability to order directly from manufacturers and to deliver with its own fleet of trucks. Inventory is managed efficiently and cost effectively through a series of mechanized conveyors and computer bar codes. Interestingly, Sam Walton was able to overcome his dislike of computers and listen to his experts in this area.[1] Leaders not only have to hire smart people, they have to let them work.

Play 2. Recognize That Customers Have Short Memories

Because customers have short memories, a company's advertising and promotional campaigns must be consistent with, and thus reinforce, the sales approach. If the sales edge is low price, for instance, the advertising must remind the customers that they are getting the best value for their money. If the differentiation is prestige, the advertising should stress image and special services associated with the purchase.

For promotions, the media must also fit the targeted customer. For instance, airlines and other travel-related companies have used frequent traveler or guest clubs to build loyalty and awareness. Many merchants have introduced preferred membership clubs to retain customers and encourage loyalty. Credit card purchases allow sellers to track and analyze how much of what type of merchandise the consumer buys. They then can target sales and special events at those who will be the most interested.

Play 3. Practice Innovative and Flexible Pricing

As with advertising, pricing strategies and policies must fit the business's product line and image. Discount stores must maintain low prices. But prestige stores such as Tiffany, Chanel, and Gucci also use price to reinforce their exclusivity by concentrating on items that appeal to the very rich or those who desire to appear rich.

In the past decade, pricing strategy has been expanded to include the terms and conditions of purchase, and many sellers have used creative approaches to distinguish themselves from competitors. For instance, some companies offer their customers very high trade-in value on their used merchandise. This technique has been popular in the "exclusive" clothing and furs markets as well as in the boating and automotive fields. It has been adopted when sellers want to stimulate demand and encourage "planned and accelerated obsolescence." A few enterprising firms have created new businesses to sell the used merchandise at reduced prices down market, while preserving their exclusivity and maintaining prices in the original business. Renting and leasing have also become popular for automobiles and other high-ticket items, but the seller must have a strong balance sheet and cash flow position.

The history of Pitney Bowes is illustrative. Although Pitney Bowes is a manufacturer and product-driven company, it has also been sales driven since its founding. Walter Bowes and Arthur Pitney formed the Pitney Bowes Postage Meter Company in 1921. Not only did Pitney obtain a strong patent on his postage meter, he had congressional authorization of its use. These strengths coupled with the decision to rent rather than sell equipment contributed to a positive cash flow and earnings and a near monopoly in the business for over 50 years. Dealing from an established position, management has diversified product line and sales terms. Customers can now lease, rent, or purchase—and they can use the Pitney Bowes Credit Corporation to finance. The latter is a nice innovation for the company. It assures professional management, supports sales, and contributes to earnings.[2]

The clubs that develop customer loyalty and repeat business can also employ innovative pricing arrangements. Club members can earn points with each purchase, which they might apply to other items. The points system is analogous to the trading stamps system, most popular in the 1950s and 1960s, in which stamps are redeemed for merchandise at the stamp company's stores. The club approach is more powerful, however, because customers use credits (points) in the sales outlet, which builds trade and loyalty.

Play 4. Create and Meet Customer Expectations

Often, great salespeople are so talented that they oversell or sell at the wrong time. Products have been sold at the wrong time if they are not available when the customer *expects* them. The seller must set realistic expectations that the customers can accept, even if they need or want the merchandise earlier. For example, it appears that many custom furniture companies have convinced their customers that it is unreasonable to expect delivery in less than several months. Further, they have successfully associated the waiting for delivery with exclusivity and personal service. Of course, the real danger to the caretaker leader is that customers will expect service *sooner* than it can be given. The leader's task is to set expectations that can be met consistently so as to build lasting customer relationships.

Even with the sophisticated logistical systems in place, stockouts can occur when companies surprise themselves with their success. Perhaps leaders have been burned by overly optimistic forecasts from the sales force. Nonetheless, they must take the risk and invest in sufficient inventory to meet possible demand. In a sales-driven strategy, the leader must capitalize on the demand that has been created. Caretakers may be less likely to bet on intuition than risktaker leaders, but they should be more willing to invest in sophisticated forecasting and projection techniques. Today's computerized "point of sale" information retrieval and analysis systems are capable of recording the sale, describing the type of user, tracking the level of inventory, projecting the optimum level of inventory, and placing orders with vendors automatically. More than record-keeping devices, they are an integral part of the caretaker leaders' total information and planning process.

Play 5. Develop a Partnership with Key Vendors

In the past, sellers and vendors have often had adversarial relationships, in which each attempted to achieve a win/lose position and fought for a few cents of margin. Neither was willing to accept the risk or cost of carrying too much inventory. As a result, neither possessed optimum ability to respond to customer expectations.

Fortunately, many U.S. companies have learned a better way from the Japanese. The Japanese have always had a tightly integrated supply system. It was a key element of the pre-World War II "zaibatsu." It is now known as the "just in time" or "quick response" alliance between sellers and suppliers. In the United States, companies are now allying themselves with suppliers in a totally integrated, information and transaction network in which both parties assume the risks. The plan works on mutual trust and shared information. They tell each other what they need to know, they make commitments, and they establish a win/win situation.

For example, Wal-Mart has invested over $600 million in five years to install a system which permits its over 2000 vendors to see immediately how well their merchandise is selling. This enables the vendor to become a partner and assume the responsibility of tracking and shipping to assure that there are no "stockouts." This reduces the traditional adversarial relationship between retailers and their vendors.[3, 4]

Play 6. Put It All Together and Keep It All Together

I called my first book, *Putting It All Together*, because that is the essence of any strategy. However, the caretaker leader must take one more step and *keep it all together*. Many sellers have had the right game plan in place but were unable to keep it from falling apart. But one who appears to have kept it all together is Nordstrom, the upscale retailer.

Nordstrom is a $2.3 billion, family-operated business, based in Seattle, that has an almost obsessive commitment to treating its customers well. It has attracted legions of loyal shoppers and generated high profits. Nordstrom opened its first East Coast store in McLean, Virginia, and reached a sales level of over $100 million in the first year. In addition to its prestige department stores, the company operates a youth chain called Place Two and a discount chain called Nordstrom Rack. The department stores are elegant and feature classic rather than trendy merchandise. They focus on apparel, shoes, and accessories and have enormous selection and inventory. Dressing rooms are larger than usual.

But Nordstrom's real competitive advantage is its employees (who call themselves "Nordies"). Nordstrom's buyers are given a great deal of latitude in what they select for the store. Sales staff are hired because they are nice and like people. They go beyond normal customer service by helping to solve problems, offering suggestions on merchandise, and delivering items themselves. Customers do not have to search out staff for assistance. Employees are young, often college educated, and interested in careers in retailing. Nordstrom pays them well, and with commissions they can earn $30,000 annually, with opportunities for promotions. Employees are given practical training and constantly urged to meet sales and service standards. Those who do well are given special awards and recognized publicly. The pictures of "Customer Service All-Stars" are displayed prominently in the store.[5]

Play 7. Experiment with Other Approaches

Leaders are understandably reluctant to change or even modify their chosen selling approach. They make take refuge behind the sometimes harmful adage, "If it ain't broke, don't fix it." Unfortunately, our favorite things are sometimes "broke" before we like to admit it. Leaders must avoid this "wishful thinking" trap.

As usual for caretaker leaders, the answer is a system, in this case, an ongoing surveillance system of current and potential customers. Employees or consultants can gather data and make suggestions, but the leaders themselves must recognize long-range implications and take action. Avon was aware of the socioeconomic trends that would hamper its way of selling; the company had hired a large consulting firm to do a study. But management could not make the changes indicated. Like many other companies, they were afraid to move away from the tried and true.

Leadership is about honest analysis and bold action. That means noting the competition's methods and examining alternative ways of doing business. Maybe the company can try a pilot project to see what the pluses and minuses are for different selling approaches. Customer needs change. And so does the technology. Caretaker leaders must be aware of how these developments impact their current practices and whether they offer opportunities for fresh approaches.

THE CARETAKER MARKETER'S TEAM

Throughout the book, I have stressed that leaders are not leaders unless they can command the efforts of a talented team that fits their leadership style. The caretaker marketer needs several sets of players with specific skills.

Competitive Salespeople and Competition Watchers

Good salespeople enjoy the challenge of competition. Many can clearly and effectively communicate competitor's sales and product strategies and tactics. Leaders need to tap into this analytical source when formulating strategic plans and actions. They should establish an organized and systematic process for including the *objective* (salespeople tend to rationalize and exaggerate) assessment of the competition by the sales staff.

Further, the leader needs people to examine all sellers, regardless of whether they are current competitors. They should track how customers' discretionary income and expenditures are being allocated and not just focus on companies that sell the same way they do. For instance, many sellers ignore video selling because they believe, perhaps mistakenly, that it does not compete for the same sales dollar. In fact, many of their current customers may decide to switch to what could be for them a more convenient and interesting way of purchasing. The caretaker leader cannot omit this consideration.

Customer Research Professionals

You can't meet customer expectations if you don't know who the customers are and what they want. The risktaker depends on intuition; the caretaker hires experts to do demographic and psychographic profiles. Market researchers can also spot changes early enough for leaders to frame a strategic response. Research must be focused and segmented; it cannot deal in generalities. Further, staff must be sufficiently pragmatic to convert data and trends into actions.

Good research saves good sales approaches from failure by notifying leaders when the sales technique is not appropriate for the customer base. Warehouse selling provides a good example. A decade ago, several companies, including Levitt's Furniture, began warehouse type operations. Their outlets were plain and located in areas that were difficult to access. Customers had to haul their own merchandise, which usually meant they needed a truck. The sales force was not service oriented and not even very knowledgeable. Early predictions said customers would accept these conditions to get lower prices. The predictions were wrong. The sales approach did not fit the customer's needs and expectations and failed.

Advertising and Promotion Talents

Advertising and promotion are important to assure that the customer does not forget the unique value the company offers. Because advertising must be consistent with the sales approach, indeed, with the total business strategy, advertising and promotion people should be included in strategy development so that they may think and behave strategically and not like technocrats. Leaders must also approach advertising and promotion consistently and competitively, as an investment and not an expense.

I have witnessed a number of situations where the advertising was not supportive and actually decreased the effectiveness of the business strategy. In one instance, a company's attempt to upgrade a product line and focus on the upscale consumer was defeated by advertising and promotional programs that stressed price and implied a lower level of quality. While the sales force was telling retailers the company was increasing the upper end of the line, the customers were being pulled into the stores to purchase the lower priced merchandise.

Location Finders

Selecting the proper locations takes highly specialized and analytical talents. The process pertains to all modes of selling. Deciding where to locate the catalog response center, the telemarketing center, or the direct mail operation is as important as determining where to put the store. If leaders do not have these skills, they must hire people who do.

Even if leaders can specify the location for a store, they may need someone with real estate negotiation skills to make the deal. Prime property is always in demand; everyone wants their shop in the highest traffic area in the mall, on Main Street, or off the highway exit ramp. Getting there early helps. If the property has not yet been developed, then talented people are needed to make the purchases without prematurely accelerating the value of the land. For example, Walt Disney spent years unobtrusively collecting the rights to the land around Orlando, Florida, that was to become Disney World.

Those who reach their customers indirectly through the mail or by phone will need expertise to properly site their response and communication centers. They must have—or hire experts who have—knowledge of the technological sophistication and available capacity of the local telephone carrier and interstate or global carrier. They should also know the character of the local work force. Ideally, they want a place where both the communications network and the labor force are highly sophisticated and underutilized. Citicorp selected the Far West for its credit card operation; some firms are locating in Puerto Rico and other Caribbean Islands. Many parts of the country have a talent pool of women who want to work part time and who have the personality and intelligence to do the job well. Some of them can work in their homes, thus taking advantage of the emerging "electronic cottage."

People doing the siting must also understand the business implications of local labor, zoning, and environmental regulations and the opportunities afforded by local tax incentives. Many states and developing nations are willing to finance any business that will provide jobs and increase economic growth.

In sum, the company must be able to hire or buy the services of people who can identify the location, do the value assessments, establish a purchasing strategy, negotiate the deal, and put the whole package together.

Acquiring real estate involves dealing with zoning, taxes, and environmental concerns and with local, state, and even federal agencies.

Purchasing Planners

As I described in Chapter 9, Sam Walton made a success of Wal-Mart by employing a rural location strategy. While Walton was certainly a risk-taker seller, he and his successor, David Glass, also made the transition to caretaker marketer through a well-researched purchasing plan. They studied his customers and determined they were primarily interested in national brands and in relatively standard, not very exotic, products. Further, they found their customers were very nationalistic and would prefer to buy American made products. Obviously, discount store customers were attracted to low prices, but they were also concerned about quality and reliable performance. After collecting data about customer purchasing habits and desires, Wal-Mart purchasing professionals were able to develop a consistent and effective strategy. They sought companies that made products in the United States, and "buying American" became a cornerstone of the store policy and advertising. They arranged to deal directly with manufacturers, bypassing representatives and agents, to get better prices and have access in event of a quality problem. This arrangement also fit Wal-Mart's logistical and transactions system.

Logistical Experts

These skills have often been underestimated by selling organizations. In recent years, however, logistics has become the cornerstone of retail and sales-driven companies. A variety of skills and talents are involved.

First, someone on the team must be able to automate the order processing, shipping, and invoicing. Over 20 years ago, a leader of a discount hardware chain proudly told me that "My MIS [management information system] manager is my highest paid employee." The leader clearly understood the power of information technology in business operations. It is even more true today. If you don't know which and how many of your products are selling, where they are stored, and how sales respond to advertising and price promotions, you can't be a marketing leader. Information management and data processing will become more critical in the future as companies try to balance meeting customer needs with keeping a minimum inventory on their shelves and in their warehouses.

Warehousing must be well planned. Merchandise should be properly stored and easy to find and move. Many companies are using computerized bar code systems (like those in retail stores) to monitor the flow of items in storage. When warehouse personnel scan the items, the data is automatically stored in the master computer. Scanning allows the computer to keep track of what is on the shelf, what has been shipped (and when), and when it has arrived at its destination.

Information flow and goods flow management are important, but cash flow management is the heart of the company. Bills should be paid at the optimum time, not too early and not too late. Cash flow experts know when to collect the company's money and how to keep it earning, even for the short term.

Cash management is enhanced by good communications and training. In the past, store managers would have to travel to headquarters or another central location to hold meetings. In businesses selling trendy merchandise, such as clothing, managers would meet with buyers to provide insight into what was needed and to learn about changes in the line. These meetings were expensive and time consuming. Today, many companies have installed their own television networks for two-way communications between the stores and headquarters. Thus, meetings can be held more cheaply and more frequently, allowing everyone to be informed and remain current.

Technology can also accelerate the transfer of other types of information and transactions. Electronic data information systems (EDIs) permit companies to order goods by computer and monitor their location and the amount in inventory. Electronic funds transfer devices can be used to move money around more quickly and reduce the float of checks and even credit transactions. Voice mail and voice response systems are used by trendsetting companies and will become as common as the telephone in selling. Salespeople are coming to love how cellular telephones keep them in touch with the office and with customers. Portable facsimile machines now permit the customer and salesperson to send in orders and get written confirmation.

The lesson here is that successful marketing-driven leaders will need to have access to creative and innovative applications people who are skilled in all forms of communications and information and transactions processing. These people need not necessarily be on the payroll, but they need to be available on demand. The real competitive advantage in marketing may come from creative applications of technology. Support and logistical services that back up the traditional sales force may become the essential element of success.

Innovative Pricing Experts

Finally, the caretaker marketer's team needs professionals who can guide pricing practices and policies. One skill is determining where pricing decisions should be made. Some markets are national, some regional, some local; and the competition may well be different from one to the other. The leader has to decide how much authority the local management should have to respond to competition. Too much centralized control could cost market position against an aggressive discounter; too much local discretion could result in abuses by local managers.

Another pricing skill involves the creative use of terms and conditions, such as the trends in renting, leasing, trade-ins, and clubs. The team should study these approaches and implement them (if at all) in harmony with the total selling strategy.

In general, the caretaker must be more of a marketing leader than a selling leader with the attributes of a professional manager, who can change approaches when conditions indicate.

Unfortunately, in recent years too many sales-driven companies have needed the services of surgeon or undertaker leaders. Sometimes, the companies have failed because the leadership change came too late. Famous retailers (e.g., B. Altman's and Gimbels) as well as innovative chains (e.g., Crazy Eddie) have died because management did not see it was time to stop growing and regroup. Debts mounted and the stores' relationships with customers deteriorated until nothing could be done to save the establishments. Timing is vital. Leadership style must reflect the particular needs of the company in its current life cycle phase.

PART
FIVE

SYSTEM
AND PRODUCTION
LEADERS

Chapter 11 describes system network risktakers. These leaders have the same long-term commitment and dedication as problem solver risktakers. They are truly visionaries. Their systems and networks often take decades to design, develop, and build and then require long-term investments and expense for maintenance and upgrading. These leaders need the sensitivity and skill to deal with many stakeholder groups, since their systems are often monopolistic and have a major impact on society.

Chapter 12 deals with leaders who are focused on "how" the product or service is produced. Production leaders have the ability to know how and where to produce the product and assure that it meets the changing needs of the customer. They are students of and are willing to adopt, adapt, and improve on the "best practices," regardless of who has developed them. These leaders take the "slogans" (Quality, Productivity, Empowerment) and integrate them into the total business strategy and implementation plans. Though they are flexible and adaptive, production leaders avoid faddism.

11

System/Network
Risktakers

We hit the light switch, and there is light. We pick up the phone and talk to people in all parts of the country and around the world. We turn on the television and see events live from Kuwait. We relax in public parks and recreation areas. All these things we take for granted, never thinking about the people who designed, developed, and implemented the giant, complex, and capital-intensive systems and networks that are part of our daily lives. But they all started with individuals who had the vision and the willingness to bet their careers and even their personal fortunes on making them a reality.

These system and network builders are risktaker leaders. They are comparable to the problem solvers I discussed in Chapter 7. They make lifelong investments in projects with the realization that they may never be recognized in full for their achievements. They see the big picture, the total system, not its components. They strive to build the best first and then think about how to get people to use what they have made. In some sense, they are idealists, although they never question in their own minds the value of what they are creating nor doubt that it will eventually become popular.

EARLY SYSTEM/NETWORK BUILDERS

Theodore Vail—Communications Risktaker

Theodore Vail had a vision. He saw the potential of creating a pervasive communications system that would be available to all people. He saw a system that would allow an individual to talk with someone in the same town or at some distant location in the country. Indeed, he recognized that the telephone network would only work if there were connectable phones in every home, office, and public institution. "Universal service" became the strategic driver. Vail took the risk of investing in the "long lines" that connected local systems (which he also acquired) with each other in one giant network. The complete system was integrated under the company he led & developed: American Telephone and Telegraph, AT&T. (AT&T was officially formed in 1899, but it wasn't until Vail took command in 1925 that it grew aggressively.)

Vail also established Bell Laboratories to (eventually) provide AT&T with new products and new materials (and later new software packages) that would improve and evolve the system. He staffed it with world class scientists and engineers and permitted them to do basic scientific research in hopes that their experiments would some day yield practical applications (long and short term) for the system. Bell Labs invented the semiconductor and integrated circuits. In 1956, it won a Nobel Prize for the transistor, which has made the entire information age possible. In 1961, it developed the first communications satellite. Over the years, Bell Labs has been awarded more than 25,000 patents.

The second part of Vail's system strategy was Western Electric, the manufacturing company responsible for converting laboratory research findings into high-quality products for the system. By controlling the manufacturing, AT&T assured itself of reliable components and the best network in the world.

The business units—the third element in the integrated system— were created to sell, install, and maintain equipment and service. The Long Lines Division developed a national and global network that enabled customers to call any part of the world at a reasonable rate. AT&T also owned and operated local telephone companies in all the major markets and linked them and the independent companies to the network. These companies distributed local service and installed, maintained, and upgraded equipment used by business and residential customers.

Thus, AT&T was in control from the invention in the lab to the connection to the customer. It made all the products and sold them to other telephone companies to ensure compatibility with the system. AT&T demanded and received national and local monopoly status, and it had a highly skilled staff of experts to deal with government regulators at all levels. AT&T negotiated favorable terms with the regulators that permitted it to guarantee reliable service and reasonable prices. The Bell System was considered a "natural monopoly," but it still constructed effective barriers to entry that prevented other companies from using the network or connecting non-Bell equipment.

Vail and his successors had created the largest total integrated system and network company in the world. It offered one of the most widely held stocks that paid large and predictable dividends. It was called the "widows and orphans" stock because it was safe as an annuity but could also grow. AT&T continued to lead and prosper because it balanced the interests of all its stakeholders—customers, regulators, stockholders, employees, and technology experts.

As I have pointed out before, however, no strategy succeeds forever. As AT&T grew, it became more complacent and increasingly slow to change. Its reluctance to offer the most innovative systems and equipment encouraged smaller companies to challenge its monopoly status. The first losing confrontation occurred when the courts, in the Carterphone decision, allowed vendors to sell equipment that could be hooked up to the AT&T network. Next, MCI (founded by John Goeken and led by Bill McGowen) won the right to operate a competing long distance service. Ultimately, AT&T's caretaker management realized that it would lose the war in the courts, if not in the marketplace, if it didn't reach a negotiated settlement. Thus came the famous breakup of a few years ago.

After all the trauma, AT&T and the regional Bell companies are still driven to have the best and most effective networks in the world. Each continues to invest in system improvements, and each seeks to control as much of the system as possible. AT&T appears to be looking for direct access to customers, bypassing the local operating companies. The regional Bells are trying to overturn the original consent decree, which will enable them to establish their own national and global long distance services as well as produce their own equipment. Under the leadership of Robert Allen, AT&T has continued to perform selective surgery to enhance its competitive position, while targeting specific markets and applications.[1]

AT&T still has one of the best R&D labs, the manufacturing company, and long lines capability. It is moving aggressively into information and transactions networks and systems. However, AT&T is no longer in complete and dominant control. Other major companies, in the United States and elsewhere, can do the research, make the products, and provide long distance service. Extensive competition exists in all areas of the industry, and profitability is no longer attainable at the traditional levels and certainly no longer assured. Vail's vision came true, but it could not last forever.

Robert Moses—Risktaking Civil Servant

Throughout the book, I have emphasized business and industrial leaders and have not spent a great deal of time describing leaders in the nonprofit sector. In many cases, I could have illustrated key points with people from the public sector. In systems and networks, one such individual so personifies the qualities of the risktaker leader it would be unforgivable to leave him out.

Robert Moses was defined by his grand vision. During his long reign (1934 to 1968) as chairman of the Triborough Bridge Commission, he led efforts that produced all the major highways, parks, and recreational facilities in New York City, lower Westchester County, and Long Island. If you were to ride into New York on the west side, you would be traveling on the Henry Hudson parkway, a product of Moses's leadership. You would pass a marina and parks that were his creations. As you progressed southward down Manhattan, you could go through the Battery Tunnel or turn up the east side on the FDR Highway. These, too, are the result of the genius and leadership force of Robert Moses. If you journeyed out to Long Island, you would see parks, including Jones Beach and its huge outdoor theater, that are part of his legacy.

As a lifelong public official, Robert Moses never accumulated much personal wealth. He was, however, one of the most powerful and influential men in the history of New York City. He served under a number of mayors and governors, and in most cases had the clout to do what he wanted without interference from them or any of the unelected "bosses." The Triborough Commission was completely independent, did its own financing and planning, and was controlled by Robert Moses for decades.[2]

Unfortunately, Moses was unable or unwilling to groom a strong and innovative successor. After he retired, the power and influence of his job, which he had created, disappeared, and no one emerged who could restore it or take his place. As a consequence, the highway systems, parks, and bridges that he developed, financed, and operated have not been improved or, in many cases, even well maintained. No leader since Moses has put together a master plan for the next generation of infrastructure for the area. A sad example is the New York City West Way, which was supposed to replace the West Side Highway (which has literally fallen down). It was conceived in the Moses style over 25 years ago to include underground roads, new parks, new apartments, and office buildings. Unfortunately, the project required that land be reclaimed from the Hudson River. Environmentalists and other political interest groups have stopped construction. Today, there is no highway and no clear planning direction. Traffic is a mess, pollution is increasing, and everyone (and the environment) is suffering. Had Moses established a successor, the story might have been different and the infrastructure of the New York City area might be in much better shape.

Risktaker innovators often neglect to prepare the systems they build for success after they are gone. There are several reasons: (1) Many leaders seem to believe they will go on forever, (2) they believe only they can do the job and so fail to delegate responsibility, which would help underlings develop, (3) they are afraid that a designated successor will become a competitor and try to assume power before they are ready to relinquish it. Leaders in several instances have fired successors just before they were scheduled to take over or made life so unbearable that they left. Large firms in private industry have a better record of implementing systems for leader succession because they have strong boards that can enforce discipline and assure continuity. (No political leader in New York really wanted a new figure like Robert Moses whom they could not control.)

CONTEMPORARY SYSTEMS RISKTAKERS

There are still leaders today who have been able to create a competitive advantage by establishing unique systems. The following five examples are all involved in some fashion with communications.

Frederick Smith and Next-Day Delivery

Consider what Frederick Smith has accomplished in just over two decades. You can now take a letter or small package to a Federal Express outlet, a third-party store, or a drop box—or have it picked up at your home or office—pay a premium, and be confident that the letter or package will arrive at its destination on time and in one piece. You also know that if the letter or package does not arrive on time, it can be traced. You don't have to worry about insurance because you have faith that your letter or package will get where it's going.

Contrast this experience with taking the same package or special letter to the U.S. Post Office. You will wait in a long line and then have to deal with personnel not exactly oriented toward service. You will pay less than at FedEx, but you will worry that your letter or package may not arrive on schedule, or if it does, that it may be damaged. So, you will probably pay extra for insurance, to recoup your losses when the package disappears into the "deep hole of undelivered mail." To be fair, the Post Office has improved, and the Express

Mail service is better. However, like many people, I still don't have the same degree of confidence in the USPS that I do in Federal Express.

Frederick Smith is one of my favorite examples of a system risktaker. At age 28, he gambled his $4 million inheritance, plus $80 million borrowed from venture capital, to launch Federal Express. He envisioned a national service that could deliver packages and special letters within 24 hours. His innovative system consisted of a centralized hub and a fleet of his own planes. He selected Memphis for the hub because it was his home and because it was centrally located. Customer's packages would be picked up by FedEx trucks by evening, driven to the airport, flown to Memphis on FedEx planes, sorted, placed on other FedEx planes, flown overnight to the destination cities, and delivered the next morning by local FedEx trucks.

At the time, no other vendor guaranteed next-day delivery, used a hub system, or had its own planes. Smith had to construct a major infrastructure before he could deliver a letter. It was an incredibly risky and ambitious undertaking. Now, however, all the major competitors, including the Post Office, have followed his lead. Even the commercial airlines have exploited the hub concept for efficiently moving things, in this case, passengers.

Smith did not rest with his success. He worried that facsimile would become a threat to his express mail business, and rather than wait to be displaced, on July 2, 1984, he started his own fax and distribution network, called "Zap Mail." He created a dedicated system similar to the old Western Union telegraph system, only Smith's depended on high-speed satellite transmissions. But the launch was destroyed with the ill-fated Discoverer manned spacecraft. Smith's Zap Mail never achieved the quality required. Smith also underestimated the penetration and growth of personal fax machines in homes and offices. Zap Mail could not compete, lost hundreds of millions of dollars, and so was abandoned.

In 1989, Smith took another gamble in hopes of protecting his business. He became a truly global small package and letter delivery service by acquiring Flying Tiger International, the world's biggest heavy cargo airline, for $880 million. The Flying Tiger had many problems to overcome such as integrating Tiger's unionized workforce with FedEx's nonunion crew and more-costly-than-anticipated maintenance on Tiger's aircraft. From 1989 to 1992 FedEx's overseas operations losses totaled $629 million. However, the acquisition included landing rights in the Pacific Rim countries such as Australia, Malaysia, and the Philippines, providing a competitive advantage over rival United Parcel Service. Another growth opportunity Smith has created has been his inventory management and response system.

Smith is utilizing his 432 planes and his trucks as a worldwide network of mobile warehouses, allowing customers to use just-in-time inventory systems for parts and goods sourced globally and delivered overnight or second day. The game is still not over, but Smith continues to demonstrate his willingness to take risks and make long-term commitments.

Smith describes the operation as "converting aircraft into 500 miles per hour warehouses." FedEx contracts with companies to supply parts and supplies overnight to their customers on request. That means the suppliers must allow FedEx to store a small emergency inventory in its warehouses and distribution centers. The system provides rapid, reliable service for customers and allows FedEx to optimize its systems and warehousing.[3, 4] Smith is demonstrating that not only is he a risktaker who builds systems, but he has the vision and the daring to take risks to protect what he has created.

Craig McCaw and the Wireless Telephone System

Risktaker Craig McCaw might be the Theodore Vail of the 1990s. At the age of 40, he has taken a number of strategic actions to build a national network of wireless communications. Vail did much the same thing with the wireline telephone business in the 1920s and 1930s. McCaw's mission is to consolidate the independent cellular operators in America's 733 individual cellular markets into a single, integrated national network to be known as Cellular One. The network's elements will be owned by McCaw's partners and allies, but McCaw would control the interconnections. According to *Forbes*, McCaw predicts that "in the future, telephone numbers will be associated with people and not places. You won't have to be bound by a plug on the wall and a six-foot cord. People who call your number will be connected to you wherever you happen to be."[5] (Interestingly, AT&T offered a 700 service in 1992 that enabled individuals who continued to be AT&T customers to have a lifetime telephone number.)

To achieve this dream, McCaw beat out BellSouth in a battle to acquire Lin Broadcasting. Lin had 25 million pops (interconnection centers) and held controlling interest in cellular systems in Philadelphia, Houston, Dallas, New York, and Los Angeles. McCaw calculated that by combining Lin's assets with his 45 million pops he would be much closer to his envisioned total system. He has bet his company to make the bid, assuming a significant amount of debt and risk. He paid $3.4 billion for the property, equal to $350 for each potential cellular customer. To service the debt and make the other investments pay off, he must penetrate at least 8 percent of the national market. In 1991,

2 percent was signed up. In addition, McCaw will have to invest in new equipment to standardize the systems and to add such customer enticements as information services to enhance the revenue stream. McCaw has already allied his company with AT&T to rebuild the federal government's telecommunications network.

McCaw and his three brothers own 32 percent of the company and have 88 percent of the voting stock. (British Telecom owned 22 percent of the company.) In November 1992, AT&T announced it was negotiating to buy a third of McCaw for $3.8 billion and it might eventually buy control. McCaw stated that AT&T and McCaw are natural allies.[6] McCaw is in the tradition of the great system builders of the past. He is committed to his vision and will take both personal and business risks to be successful. He is competitive and doesn't hesitate to challenge anyone in his way. It is too early to tell whether he will be recorded in history as a leader of Vail's stature, but win or lose, he has been a true systems builder and risktaker.

Modern Day Sarnoffs

General Robert Sarnoff was one of two visionary leaders who created the broadcasting industry as we know it today. (The other was William Paley of CBS.) Sarnoff was working in the telegraph business with Marconi when Marconi ventured with General Electric and Westinghouse to form the Radio Corporation of America. Sarnoff became vice president of marketing and sales. He recognized the potential of radio to become a national news and entertainment powerhouse. In contrast, the management of GE and Westinghouse viewed RCA as a provider of telecommunications for business, industry, and government and not a significant consumer opportunity. Sarnoff led a successful coup, which culminated in GE and Westinghouse being forced by the Franklin D. Roosevelt Administration to divest themselves of ownership of RCA. Sarnoff became CEO of the now independent company, serving as president from 1930 to 1948 and chairman from 1947 to 1970.

Sarnoff began to build his business much as Theodore Vail had with the telephone system. He created a network to connect the smaller independent stations and provided entertainment shows and news coverage to provide national and international programming. He also built his own research laboratory and manufacturing company to develop, make, and sell broadcasting equipment and to stimulate the growth of consumer radios and, later, televisions. Sarnoff recognized the potential of color television and developed the system that became the industry standard. Under his leadership, RCA and its broadcasting arm, NBC, became the leaders in radio and television.

Sarnoff had built a magnificent integrated system, as Vail had done. But like AT&T, the system would not survive long after the creator's passing. RCA strayed into other businesses and neglected the core. The company deteriorated and was acquired by GE, in 1986 one of the original founders. The consumer electronics business was sold to Thompson Electronics of France, and GE is still evaluating whether to divest NBC.

Ted Turner

I would grant Ted Turner equal status with Sarnoff as a risktaker network leader. And I am not alone in that assessment. *Time* selected him "1991 Man of the Year" because of his visionary network building. In 1970, Turner acquired a small Atlanta UHF television station (WTBS) and developed it into one of the major stations in the region. WTBS became a "superstation" when Turner began selling its programs by satellite to cable systems around the country. He bought the Atlanta baseball and basketball teams (Braves and Hawks) in 1976–1977 and broadcast their games along with a collection of old TV shows and movies. By 1979, his station reached 5.8 million homes.

A year later, Turner launched the Cable News Network (CNN), which broadcasted news, mostly live, 24 hours a day. CNN reached 1.7 million homes its first year and gradually spread to more and more cable systems and around the world. CNN now provides 24-hour news service in countries that have censored news in the past. Its coverage of the war in Kuwait in 1991 earned the network worldwide prestige on par with the major U.S. networks.

In 1986, Turner tried and failed to take over CBS. Instead, he bought a film library of 3,700 movies from MGM/UA for $1.4 million, a risky venture that caused Turner Broadcasting to struggle with heavy debt. Turner was bailed out, however, by 31 cable operators around the country who recognized his importance to their business and the industry. Turner used the vast resource of films he acquired to start Turner Network Television (TNT). He outraged many critics by colorizing several of the black and white classic films. But the new network grew as the other Turner offerings did with the appeal of the old movies and extensive sports programming, including the NBA and the Olympics.[7]

Turner has built an impressive series of television, radio and cable networks (and more are planned) against all predictions by the experts. He has demonstrated that imagination, commitment, and long-term perspective can wound or even topple the entrenched giants. As with McCaw, it is too early to know if Turner will endure personally or be pushed aside by his investors and partners. But there is no question that he has exhibited the type of risktaking leadership I have been describing.

John Malone

Although he was not the founder of Tele-Communications, Inc., John Malone has been the innovative leader who has made TCI the largest cable system in the United States. Malone was one of the operators who provided Ted Turner with the capital to stay afloat in 1986 and (with the 21 percent of stock he received for his financial support) spearheaded the creation of TNT. Malone's company has also helped launch three other cable networks—Black Entertainment Television, the Discovery Channel, and American Movie Classics—and owns half of the Showtime network.[8]

Malone's vision extends beyond the traditional view of cable. He has a game plan to make TCI a leader in communications, video on demand, and advertising on the local level. He is experimenting with a local telephone company service bypass system and a personal communications network, called PCN, which would be a lower cost substitute for cellular radio. Malone's partner in PCN is McCaw; his partners in the video-on-demand venture are AT&T and U.S. West (the regional teleco in the far west). Video on demand would permit cable subscribers to use their remote control to select from a listing of 1,000 movies and special events and schedule the showing at their convenience for a fee. It is a natural extension of currently limited offerings of "pay per view." Not content to build on others' know-how and technologies, Malone has led the development of the cable industry's own R&D lab. This laboratory is concentrating on compression technology and digital systems that will permit cable systems to carry up to five channels on frequencies that now can carry only one. Like McCaw, Malone is moving to create a system that will encompass both entertainment and communications.

Stuart Z. Levin

Although not as well known as Turner, Malone, or McCaw, Stuart Levin is a true systems risktaker leader. With the backing of MCA, Inc., and Paramount Pictures, Levin has formed the TVN Entertainment Corporation, which hopes to provide television programming via satellite for subscribers living in rural areas who cannot get, or may not want, cable. TVN's expectation is that people with backyard satellite dishes will pay premium prices for movies and special programs because they will find it more convenient to phone in orders than rent from video stores or hook up to cable (if either are available with acceptable quality and in quantity). Technology developed by General Instrument Corporation of San Diego has cut down on piracy and is now standard for satellite dishes. Technology developed by AT&T electronically identifies the name and address of the caller ordering the programming. The Videocypher, developed by Levin, provides decoding capabilities. With that protection built into the system, movie studios such as Paramount and MCA Universal are considering satellite transmission more fondly as an outlet for their films and are willing to provide financial backing.[9]

Levin believes that satellite programming's prime has arrived, and he is trying to get a system in place to take advantage of the opportunity. (Operations were scheduled to commence as this book was being written.) Levin plans to start selectively in only 3.4 percent of American households that have satellite dishes, most of these concentrated in Nebraska, Idaho, Wyoming, Montana, and Vermont. It is not certain this venture will succeed, but it is worth tracking to see if entrepreneurial system risktakers can still make it in the United States.

THE SYSTEM/NETWORK RISKTAKER'S GAME PLAN

These leaders need to complete five critical plays to implement their game plan successfully:

1. Build the best system possible well in advance of demand.
2. Maintain control of long-term financial resources.
3. Be prepared for success and the reaction of pressure groups.
4. Invest in system maintenance and improvements to sustain position.
5. Groom a caretaker successor.

Play 1. Build the Best System Possible Well in Advance of Demand

Building the best and most efficient system possible involves using the most advanced technologies in the hope that they will yield superior results. It is an expensive gamble. Fred Smith bet his inheritance on a risky express mail system. More than that, he bet his pride and reputation that his idea was right and could be made to work. Craig McCaw did that when he scared off BellSouth with his self-described "maniac" intensity and drive. Smith was just enough ahead of his time to be first with a system that was needed. Time will tell if McCaw can put together a system that will eventually satisfy market demand.

Play 2. Maintain Control of Long-Term Financial Resources

Risktaker system leaders are engaged in projects that are usually highly capital intensive and have long-term paybacks. Thus, leaders not only need long-range financial support but arrangements for maintaining personal control if they are to reap the rewards of their efforts. As I pointed out in an earlier chapter, many product innovators never gained personally from their innovations. It was the Morgans, Rockefellers, and Mellons who profited from the inventions of Edison, Westinghouse, and Durant.

The same fate looms for the systems builder. Despite unloading cable systems, taking on British Telecom as an equity partner, and selling southeastern cellular systems to Contel, McCaw still has an enormous debt ($3.6 billion in 1990). If he can't afford to finance and if his stockholders become too uneasy, McCaw will join the long list of innovators who had the idea and took the risk but were not rewarded financially. Ted Turner's acquisitions have also placed him in financial jeopardy, and he may not be around to see the final triumph of his networks. Stuart Levin, on the other hand, seems well buttressed by strong financial partners who also have a ready stock of programming. These resources may be sufficient to sustain him during the long lead time required to get the system operating in the black. However, only time will tell.

Play 3. Be Prepared for Success and the Reaction of Pressure Groups

As risktakers begin to succeed, they must be prepared for the inevitable targeting by competitors and/or government regulators. If a system or network dominates a market, others will attempt to gain a foothold. For instance, two decades after Fred Smith demonstrated that the hub concept was viable and efficient, major competitors have copied his approach.

Some things are too expensive to replicate. Certainly, more than one electric, telephone, gas, or water company in a geographic area is redundant and unnecessary. However, in the early development of these industries, competing companies serviced the same market. The ensuing problems caused the formation of "natural regulated monopolies." As we saw in the history of the telephone system, natural monopolies were only regulated when the owners got greedy. Had they simply provided cheap universal service, they would have been left alone. Instead, they came under the scrutiny of the government and citizens' interest groups.

More recently, cable systems have traveled down this path. Originally, cable companies were awarded monopoly franchises and were tightly regulated by local or regional governments. The reasoning held that it would be too expensive to install extensive underground and above-ground wiring without assurances of a captive market. Major cable companies, spearheaded by John Malone, have been able to deregulate the industry, allowing local cable companies to raise fees and still maintain geographical exclusivity.

However, there are already signs of change. Some cable companies have elected to "harvest their systems" by raising prices without investing in new equipment or programming, by changing "basic" services to "premium," and by eliminating certain channels. Cablevision of Long Island and Connecticut has, for instance, removed the Madison Square Garden Network from its system because the network wanted to shift from being a premium to a basic offering. Customers became upset over losing their favorite sports programming and complained to the government. At the time, all the government could do was threaten re-regulation. But that threat could become a reality if enough citizens remain riled. A Federal law was overwhelmingly passed in September 1992, aimed at regulating cable and encouraging more competition and price reductions.

Play 4. Invest in System Maintenance and Improvements to Sustain Position

Major systems need a lot of care to remain viable. The American infrastructure—bridges, roads, public transportation, water and sewage treatment, and so on—has in general been poorly maintained, and too little has been invested in improvements. State and local governments faced with difficult financial choices have deferred maintenance and transferred capital funds to other programs that have vocal constituents. Since it normally takes many years of neglect to generate a crisis, those elected officials responsible are often out of office when the deterioration reaches critical mass. At that point, repair and rebuilding becomes extremely expensive.

All successful system operators continually invest in maintenance and improvements. This often requires having extensive research and development facilities like the Bell and RCA Labs. AT&T and the regional Bell companies have, among other more mundane matters, invested heavily in digital systems in anticipation of their future use in voice, data, and video transmission. They have added fiber-optic cables to provide more services to customers in large metropolitan areas and even across the Atlantic. Cable companies such as Time Warner, Cox, and Tele-Communications are investing in systems that will enable them to increase interactive communications and transactions. FedEx continues to lay out hundreds of millions of dollars to improve its systems and increase its ability to offer rapid and reliable services.

A risktaker leader can't become complacent. However, if and when a leader decides to stop innovating or invest at a slower rate, he can truly "cash out" on the investments over a period of time. Systems and networks are very attractive to the "harvest and divest" undertaker leader.

Play 5. Groom a Caretaker Successor

Even if risktakers do everything I have prescribed, they will still have trouble building a business and keeping it viable for the long haul. That job usually falls to the caretakers, who are better fitted psychologically for that sort of planning and management. Leadership style corresponds to system life cycle just as it does to product and business life cycles. Thus, even though we associate the great systems with their risktaker founders, the caretaker leaders who followed made them what they are today. The final task of the risktaker leader, therefore, is to groom a caretaker successor and, when the time is right, get out of the way. It is interesting to note that McCaw, Malone, Turner, and Smith all continue to lead their companies, when it may be time to transfer leadership to a caretaker.

WARNING: AVOID GREED

Leaders must learn to accept the rights of the system's various stakeholders and balance their diverse needs. This truth is particularly compelling when the risktaker has been given an unfair competitive advantage, even if they do not enjoy a complete monopoly. For instance, the government has established duopolies, mandated two competitors, in each cellular radio market. Originally, one of the competitors was to be the indigenous teleco and the other was a nonwireline company. At the time I am writing, this ruling is still in effect. However, in almost all major markets, the nonwireline competitor has been acquired by either another teleco or a company, like McCaw's, that wants to develop a larger, more integrated system. If the two competitors respect their positions and do not become greedy, they will prosper and their status will not be challenged. However, if they begin to collude or change the rules to suit their own interests, they will surely face tougher regulation.

The situation is similar to that of the cable companies described earlier and not unlike the "Great Electrical Conspiracy," which I lived through personally and detailed in Chapter 8. GE and Westinghouse decided to sell off their equity in the regulated parts of the electrical industry to investors or the public. However, GE and Westinghouse understood that in order to keep the systems and equipment modern and efficient, they had to control their customers, the electric utilities. They maintained this control by remaining the strategic planners and market forecasters and researchers for the industry. They also provided training and management development at all levels. GE and Westinghouse performed their tasks well, the system worked, and everyone prospered—until greed and selfishness prevailed. The manufacturing companies colluded on prices and divided market share. They were caught, trust evaporated, and the industry has never been the same. Everyone suffered. In fact, by the next decade, the United States could be electrically deficient.

Greed is a potential danger for all major infrastructure monopolies and cartels. It appears that too much success can make people very myopic and internalized. They forget that the public and the government are watching. Abuse can cost them their power far faster than it took to acquire. System risktakers and the caretakers that follow should actively watch for the signs of corrupting self-absorbtion, the temptations of greed. Perhaps they can avoid that path to destruction.

THE SYSTEM/NETWORK
RISKTAKER LEADER'S TEAM

Systems and network teams must possess a significant level of sophistication. All of the systems/networks I have been describing have four things in common:

1. They are all high technology intensive and complex.
2. They provide services to the user.
3. They are capital intensive and require long-term financial support.
4. They are, or could be, regulated.

The skills required by the team respond directly to those four characteristics.

First, leaders need technologically skilled people who can put together and operate complex systems. They should be up on the state of the art in their technological field but still focus on what is doable, on what can operate in a reliable manner. Team members must anticipate changes in technology that will have a long-term impact on their system. I mentioned how John Malone initiated an industry-wide lab to investigate compression and digital technologies. Malone is well educated. He holds two Master's degrees and a PhD in operations research and worked at Bell Labs.[10] Malone knew they would change the way cable systems operate, both in terms of quality and cost. All the giant system players—AT&T, GE, RCA, and so on—have had strong R&D laboratories and staff organizations.

Since all systems are service businesses, team members should possess a service orientation; that is, they should be responsive to customer needs. Customers don't care about the technological beauty of the system; they care only that it works, that it delivers the service. If the system is down, it must be repaired and service returned rapidly. Electrical utilities, telephone companies, and cable companies should have—and many do have—rapid response systems to address major outages. Team members will also need good communications skills to let the people know what is happening and to listen to their concerns.

The system/network leader needs people with strong financial skills. Some members must have the cost accounting and forecasting abilities required to cost out the system and services for the short and long haul. Others should be able to negotiate for long-term financing. Further, they must be able to keep the investors happy by demonstrating that their investment is well managed and therefore secure. Team members must meet financial expectations and keep surprises to a minimum.

Finally, since many systems qualify for monopoly status and/or involve the public domain and trust, the team must have people who can deal with regulators, or potential regulators, and interest groups. That involves negotiating good regulations. "Good" regulations protect the public interest and permit the risktaking organization to make a reasonable profit and defend its market position. That is no simple task, and those talents are often difficult to find. Negotiators cannot be just lobbyists and bureaucrats; they must be able to communicate to the government and the public what it takes to be a successful systems player.

TIMING

When is a new system needed? Here are three general situations that offer an attractive opportunity.

Situation 1. When the Current Leaders Are Complacent

Ted Turner brought CNN to maturity in the mid-1980s when the three major networks were changing leadership and concentrating on short-term financials. Strange as it may seem, all three of the new leaders focused on improving the profitability of the news segments of their networks. NBC was (and is) led by Robert Wright, a senior executive with GE, which had acquired RCA, and a close associate of CEO Jack Welch. ABC was taken over by Tom Murphy (and now led by Dan Burke) of Capital Broadcasting, and CBS had been acquired by financier Larry Tisch.

Wright, Murphy, and Tisch believed that news should be profitable. Instead of investing in the people and equipment to maintain and improve worldwide coverage, they began cutting costs. This strategy might have been acceptable had they been competing against themselves, as they had been for decades.[11] However, there was a new player in the game. While the networks were cutting back, CNN was increasing its global coverage and adding staff. However, the cable network was not encumbered by high-salaried news anchors and so could expand service at significantly lower costs. And because the news was on 24 hours, CNN could get maximum programming use out of its people and their coverage. While network news operated as unprofitable loss leaders for the majors, CNN made money. Turner took advantage of the vulnerability of the current share leaders and won.

Situation 2. When the Market Is Ready for Your Unique Idea

Frederick Smith created his own timing. He recognized that the publicly owned and highly politicized U.S. Post Office could not provide the service he was proposing. In fact, the Post Office seemed unable even to conceive a need for a high value, premium delivery service. The launch of Federal Express coincided with the growth of high value, financial, accounting, and legal services. The firms that provided those services needed quick, reliable deliveries and could pass the costs along to their clients. Even had the Post Office been able to compete (as it is trying to do now), the FedEx concept and execution would have prevailed. Smith had the right idea at the right time.

Situation 3. Technology Leapfrog

Often the technology is available and not being utilized by the caretaker incumbent. Cable, cellular, fiber optics, and compression techniques are not new. They have been available for more than a decade and ready to be applied. However, the telephone and broadcasting companies were not excited about investing millions, if not billions, of dollars, to substitute for their existing and highly profitable systems. This is the type of situation that is highly attractive to the risktakers who are outsiders and have nothing to lose, and everything to gain by using a new technology and leapfroging the incumbents.

12

Production Leaders: The Difference Is How It Is Made

System/network builders are distinguished by their willingness to gamble on major projects before there is any proven demand. Production-focused people have a similar personality, although their ambitions run to a smaller scale. These leaders (and they come in all styles) are convinced they have found a competitive advantage in how their company's offerings are produced.

Perhaps the most famous production leader in American business history was Henry Ford. His great genius resided in *how* he produced cars more so than in the cars themselves. In fact, Ford's autos were physically unappealing and relentlessly functional to the point of dullness. Competitors developed more sophisticated cars with more "sex appeal," but Ford was able to make his cheaper and quicker. His special contribution to manufacturing was the assembly line. Ford reasoned that production would be more efficient if the car came to the worker, and each worker specialized in one aspect of building the car. He put his concept into practice on a scale that started a revolution.

During the past 50 years, many leaders have distinguished themselves by their creativity and dedication to making high-quality products at the lowest possible costs. Their efforts have taken the form of new production methods, new equipment or tools, or new relationships with vendors that have made assembly easier, faster, and/or more efficient. For the most part, these talented individuals have labored in obscurity except within their own plants or industries. But they are as much leaders as any I have depicted in this book.

THE PRODUCTION LEADER'S INTUITIVE GAME PLAN

This leader has to complete 10 plays in order to implement a total production game plan.

1. Focus on *how* the product is produced.
2. Seek the "better way."
3. Determine *where* to produce.
4. Understand total business costs, not just labor costs.
5. Remember that everything is relative to the competition.
6. Know what is proprietary.
7. Avoid ego trips and complacency.
8. Keep current and reinvest.
9. Make vendors partners.
10. Keep the game plan simple so everyone can understand it.

Play 1. Focus on *How* the Product Is Produced

Production-driven leaders are willing to learn from others in order to do a better job. They are dedicated to putting together the best factory, the best logistical system, the best integrated company in the industry. They study the way the product is currently being made to determine where the system is inefficient or overloaded and where it can be improved.

Production leaders in the United States have prospered during three periods of industrial history. The first was from the early teens of the twentieth century to the Great Depression when new ways of producing autos, electrical and telephone equipment, and iron and steel were implemented. New plants were built. Employees were trained to improve productivity while maintaining consistently high levels of quality.

World War II saw the second great production era. America had not prepared for war, although Franklin Roosevelt had tried to get the country to invest in the requisites for what he saw as an inevitable conflict. Business and workers were preoccupied with surviving the Depression and not interested in gearing up for hostilities in Europe. Therefore, when the United States entered the war, it had to develop many skills and resources from scratch. Roosevelt enlisted some of the best manufacturing and production people in the world. They formed teams of engineers and technologists (War Production Boards) to work with production leaders to build the plants that turned out the military hardware. The United States was able to meet not only its own needs but those of its allies around the world. Historically, Americans have responded well to a crisis but often not to its warning signals.

The production boom transferred nicely into the civilian economy from the mid-1940s into the late 1950s when U.S. firms were the dominant figures in all major industries. They built large, new, efficient, state-of-the-art facilities throughout the country that could make high-quality goods at reasonable costs. But improvements failed to continue apace in the 1960s, as other countries began to invest more in top facilities. While the United States became complacent, first the Japanese and then the Germans gained production leadership. Developing nations, especially in the Far East, have also made impressive advances. They show the strength that the United States has displayed in the past: success in highly competitive, commodity industries where efficiency and quality production can separate winners from losers.

Play 2. Seek the "Better Way"

Nearly a century ago, the "better way" was Henry Ford's assembly line. Today, production breakthroughs often involve applying computer technology to how people work. The goal is to improve the efficiency of workers and the quality and amount of their output. That may mean using technologies in new areas. For instance, information and communications systems and software have improved production methods and standards, although they were not originally designed for those applications. Factory methods and know-how have also been applied to service businesses, particularly in the fast-food establishments. McDonald's invested in equipment, training, standards, and procedures to automate food production and delivery. McDonald's complements its sales and marketing strengths with production leadership.

Of course, the Japanese are the world champions at finding the better way. After the war, the Japanese took advantage of the insights and strategic leadership of General Douglas MacArthur, who was military governor of the country, and the considerable help and guidance of American industrial giants when rebuilding their devastated infrastructure and production capability. Of course, America business leaders might not have been so generous with their assistance had they imagined either the power of a rebuilt Japan or the extent to which they would be competing in a global marketplace by the 1970s. However, the Japanese ability to learn really made the difference; they are truly a learning society. They studied the best manufacturers they could find, copied what they could, and improved as they went along. Today, the Japanese are the undisputed production leaders of the world.

Ironically, now American companies are learning from the Japanese, and some are regaining leadership positions in certain industries. To their credit, however, many Japanese firms are not becoming complacent; they continue to invest in new production approaches and facilities. Japanese manufacturers will tear down factories and production lines that still have economic value and utility when they can put something better in their place. They don't wait until everything is completely depreciated before making the changes needed to maintain cost and quality positions.

Automation has always been resisted by unions in the United States out of fear of loss of jobs for the membership. In contrast, because worker–management relations in Japan have been more cooperative and less adversarial, labor is more receptive to change. As a consequence, Japan leads in robot applications and in information and communications systems that control production by evaluating quality and that determine the optimum size and location of facilities. Again, the Japanese demonstrate their ability to learn and adapt.

But all production innovations are not in Japan, and not all are in manufacturing.

U.S. Agriculture: In the Tall Cotton.   Having grown up in Brooklyn, New York, and worked all my life in an industrial environment, I might easily have overlooked one of the best examples of a production innovation strategy: American agriculture. And one of the best case histories in agriculture is J.G. Boswell, described by *Forbes* as the "largest, most profitable and most technically advanced cotton farmer in the world." His company uses "laser guided scrapers to level the soil. Its land is scientifically irrigated by special high volume pumps invented by J.G. Boswell engineers and soaked by water that has flowed through more than 1,000 miles of private canals from the Sierra Nevada mountains."[1]

Boswell's strategy is simple but highly effective. (Most effective strategies are simple and obvious. It is the implementation and commitment that really matters, not the idea or concept.) The company applies the "components of large scale manufacturing automation where ever possible," makes sure raw materials are in supply, and does extensive research in crop production. Its cost is 40 cents per pound of cotton, compared with the industry average of 63 cents. The farm yields 1,250 pounds per acre, 150 greater than average.[2]

Boswell has no doubt profited from his long-term membership on the board of directors of General Electric. His game plan is the same as the great company's was in the 1950s and 1960s. He also supports his cost and quality leadership position with innovative marketing, brand development, and packaging. The Boswell "Diamond B" is the premium cotton brand and is distinctively packaged in protective, heavy, clear plastic instead of the traditional jute. Boswell has invested in the systems and innovations to make his "simple" production-driven strategy work.

Housing: Standardization, Modularization, and Efficiency. After World War II, one production genius was able to apply the principles of mass manufacturing to housing construction. William Levitt created a mass-produced, standard-design home for the hoards of returning GIs desperate for affordable housing. He built 17,447 nearly identical homes on Long Island. This is the largest residential subdivision built by a single developer. He originally called it Island Trees but later changed its name to Levittown.[3] But Levittown was not the answer for everyone or for very long. By the next decade, people wanted more customized, differentiated housing. And just as other carmakers improved on Henry Ford's simple concept ("any color as long as it is black"), other home builders improved on Levitt's basic designs. These modularized, factory-built houses can have all the amenities, including fireplaces, built-in bookshelves, and specialized heating and cooling systems. Unfortunately, their use has been thwarted by resistance from local construction unions, as I discussed in an earlier chapter. Nonetheless, Levitt and his followers have demonstrated that the production-innovation strategy can have many applications. Levitt's strategy was timely but it was not lasting. Modular housing may become popular in the future, when another leader can work with the local officials and craft unions to make it a "win" for everyone.

Play 3: Determine *Where* to Produce

Location is as an important an element in the game plan of the production leader as it is for the seller leader. Deciding where to place the production facility is becoming increasing complex. The leader has to determine the best locations for the manufacturing plant, the centralized processor, the hub, the key warehouses, and so on. Three decades ago, limited transportation and communications linkages restricted options. Plants had to be built in proximity to the markets they were to serve or near major rivers or railroad lines. The development of the interstate highway system, the opening of new ports, and the creation of a large airline network, with bigger planes, has provided a great many more options for leaders today.

This infrastructural growth has allowed many companies to build their facilities in the booming Sunbelt. They were motivated by, among other things, the desire to flee the inflexible and militant unions that had grown strong in the traditional industrial areas of the Northeast and northern Midwest. For instance, in the 1950s, GE moved its Major Appliance Division from Bridgeport, Connecticut, to Louisville, Kentucky, to escape the unions and implement more flexible methods and approaches. GE moved to other locations in the South as well in search of low wage scales. Unfortunately, the unions anticipated the company's moves, and they were entrenched by the time the plants were opened. The Louisville unions proved the most militant, even worse than in the Northeast.

The next attraction was the extremely low wages paid in the Far East. So, in the 1970s, GE led the migration offshore to Korea, Taiwan, Singapore, and later Malaysia and China. The appeal was also the chance to start over by building modern and efficient plants. Some areas, such as Puerto Rico, also offered attractive tax incentives.

However, all things are cyclical, and many companies are returning to the United States. The Japanese are coming, too. Japanese auto and consumer electronics firms are building state-of-the-art plants here because they fear the United States will restrict imports and they will not be able to supply their markets from offshore. The Japanese firms also have been given tax breaks and other financial incentives to locate in America by states or cities hungry for the jobs and economic stimulation that new industry would bring. Ironically, Japanese and other foreign manufacturers are gaining a competitive advantage over existing American companies through these incentives.

Technological advances have made electric power companies more mobile as well. In the past, nuclear and fossil fuel electricity generation centers had to be built near users because power could not be transported long distances economically. Now, huge plants can be constructed in remote areas and power transmitted via extra-high-voltage equipment, thus opening up many location alternatives.

Similarly, improvements in communications technologies have made it possible for Citicorp to locate its credit card operations where it can take advantage of inexpensive labor and facilities. The company has built three large processing "factories" in South Dakota, Nevada, and Maryland. Communications networks are now able to provide reliable transportation of information and data. Today, a company can locate its processing and billing centers any place in the world and be confident of providing reliable service. Some companies have even located their reservations centers in the Virgin Islands.

In Chapter 11, I related how the commercial airlines have copied FedEx's hub system for package delivery to move their passengers.

Today, it is not uncommon to fly to Atlanta (or Pittsburgh, or Denver, depending on the airline) to be rerouted to another part of the world, even to Japan. The hub system is very efficient and increases productivity. However, most passengers really hate the idea because it makes travel slower and more unpleasant. That the airlines use hubs anyway illustrates the difference between being production driven and being customer or market driven. Airlines are network and production-driven organizations. They appear to be more interested in efficiency than customer service or convenience, though their ads and speeches try and create the image of service driven leadership. This is an excellent example of the gap between "saying" and "doing."

The Make versus Buy Decision. A number of companies have opted not to produce at all. Instead, they "outsource" the product from someone else and become a distributor or systems integrator. Almost all U.S. consumer electronics firms and an increasing number of U.S. auto companies are following this path. The game plan is to have another company make the product or component to unique specifications and just sell it or integrate it into the offering that the original firm does make. At this point, the company is no longer production driven, and it must learn to lead in other ways.

Centralized versus Decentralized Production. Deluxe Checking is one of the leaders in the production of personal and business checks. Since it was founded in 1915, by William R. Hotchkiss, the company has focused on providing a "quick, quality response" to customer needs. From the beginning, DeLuxe has striven to give 48-hour service to its banking and consumer clients. Today, over 95 percent of all the company's traditional checks can be printed and shipped in two days.[4]

DeLuxe sustains its competitive advantage by going against conventional wisdom. Most printing companies believe large, centralized facilities are more efficient and economical. They reason that centralization allows them to invest in large presses, buy materials in large volumes, and offer multiple color processing. However, DeLuxe has had success locating smaller plants near the customers. The company has built over 60 regional facilities in the United States and, as I mentioned, has no trouble providing excellent service.

The lesson is not that decentralization is better than centralization; that decision must be made on a case-by-case basis. DeLuxe's case illustrates that production leaders should not be tied to the conventional wisdom or a preconceived approach. Their production strategy, including location decisions, must be consistent with market and competitive conditions.

Going Global.   Globalization can be a powerful force in gaining access to new process expertise and technology, and not just a way to achieve lower labor and production costs. Consider the case of the Stanley Works (a tool company), headquartered in New Britain, Connecticut, which has opened production plants offshore. In fact, Stanley invested 25 percent of its capital budget in 1988 for offshore production. This move represented a shift in the company's traditional "Made Only in the United States" strategy. It was instituted by CEO Richard Ayers, a graduate of the Massachusetts Institute of Technology (MIT) and then but 46 years old, who felt that Stanley had to experiment with new production technologies and locations to preserve its position in the tool market.

For instance, Ayers acquired National Hand Tool/Chiro of Taiwan because that company had developed a cold-forming process that speeded up the production of forged metal products and reduced waste. This technology was used in other Stanley plants, affecting 30 percent of its production processes. Ayers also opened a plant in Bescancon, France, a community known for its skilled watchmakers. Because the watchmaking industry was struggling, the town had already shifted to producing electronic devices used for factory automation. Stanley has been able to apply Bescancon's expertise in flexible automation to the manufacture of small tools and has reciprocated by providing internships to local university students.

Another aspect of Stanley's successful globalization involved learning how to market and brand effectively. When Stanley closed its German plant, sales declined there because German craftpeople are loyal to their national brand. Unlike Americans, Europeans are highly nationalistic and support their country's brands over imports. To avoid this problem elsewhere in Europe, Stanley came up with a sound branding and shipping strategy to support its production-driven strategy. From its distribution center in Rotterdam, The Netherlands, the company ships to other countries in small quantities, bills in local currency, provides instructions in the language of the target market, and has a post office address in each country. Stanley is thus able to cloud the issue of where its tools are made.

Stanley has demonstrated that globabization can be accomplished with finesse to maximize gains in expertise/technology and market penetration. Its approach to local markets may be an excellent model for other firms to adopt and could be critical in the emerging European Common Market.[5]

Of course, European and Japanese companies realize the need for globalization and are taking advantage of their strong currencies to move aggressively. According to *Fortune,* Toyota is planning to "build factories around the world" and to diversify into "electronics, telecommunications, factory automation, and possibly aerospace." In addition, the magazine reports, Toyota will create joint ventures with automakers in Europe as they did with GM in California. Matsushita, Hitachi, and Toshiba are planning a similar strategy. Matsushita will target software companies, Hitachi will look for telecommunications and computer firms, and Toshiba will try to acquire foreign companies in computers, integrated circuits, medical equipment, telecommunications, ceramics, and superconductivity.[6]

Globalization is an important strategic consideration but not an easy move to make. Companies venturing into other nations cannot act like conquerors or empire builders. Workers in any land will resent subordination by outsiders. Nationalistic feelings once aroused can easily lead to trade barriers that will hurt everyone.

Play 4. Understand Total Business Costs, Not Just Labor Costs

Often, managers look at only one part of the production and logistical system and don't see the total cost picture. When companies moved their plants to Singapore and Taiwan, for instance, they expected to operate at a fraction of their previous costs because workers there earned a tenth or even a twentieth of U.S. wages. However, there were other costs to consider—the costs of shipping, managing remotely, and acclimating to new workers, cultures, and languages. It turns out, the total cost of doing business was much more than they envisioned when focusing on that cheap labor. These sorts of costs also play a role in totally domestic production.

The supply chain is the first consideration of the total cost strategy. The leader must factor in where the materials and components come from and how they will be transported to the production facility. Costs include potential transportation delays and damages in transit.

Management distance is the second element. If headquarters is in another locale, or even another country, management is complicated by questions of who has authority, how decisions will be made, and when senior executives will visit local installations (and when local managers will visit headquarters). In foreign operations, this travel and meeting time can be quite expensive.

Obviously, the foreign factor has the greatest impact on the third element of total cost: that is, adjusting to different styles, languages, and cultures (although northeastern companies setting up production in the Sunbelt have had some acclimation costs as well). The local work force must be made to feel they are a part of the company and not just serfs or hired hands. When the Japanese firms built production plants in the United States, they invested a considerable amount of money and time in selecting and training personnel. Workers were taught the Japanese approach to production and made to feel part of the team. Japanese management attempted to establish personal relationships with the work force.

The Japanese efforts appear to be successful now; that is, production appears to be worth the investment. The question is how long the good times will last. New situations normally have a positive effect in the short run. The famous experiments at Western Electric's Hawthorne plant in the 1920s demonstrated that when workers felt they were being treated differently, their productivity increased. I believe the Japanese plants in the United States are benefiting from the Hawthorne effect, as well as the gratitude of people in depressed areas for having steady paychecks. What will happen when the newness wears off, when workers see their upward mobility blocked because the best positions are reserved for Japanese nationals, when the Japanese attitudes toward minorities and women appear? Will the same degree of cooperation and loyalty continue? Remember, familiarity often breeds discontent.

These issues aside, the major point here is that leaders must factor in the total costs entailed in production, not just the obvious one of pay scales. They must do the analysis to assess the related costs and locate the hidden costs.

Play 5. Remember That Everything Is Relative to the Competition

I have seen a number of companies invest heavily in new equipment, new systems, and new plants and feel good about the improvements because they decreased production costs. However, these firms failed to determine how their costs compared with those of the competition. In the 1960s, for instance, most U.S. companies declined to evaluate costs of their foreign competitors; they refused to believe that the Japanese and other Far Eastern manufacturers were much more efficient and had a lower cost per unit.

Many U.S. firms used "value analysis techniques" in which a competitor's product was purchased, dissected, and analyzed as to how much it would cost the *American* firm to make. Unfortunately, they were asking the wrong question. The right question is: How much does it cost *my competitor's plant* to make the product using *its* systems and methods. Answering that question means knowing the competitor's factory layout, production methods, quality of work force, source of materials, and so on. This is a difficult task. Nonetheless, the leader must perform the ongoing, in-depth evaluation of the competition to maintain any hope of achieving a production advantage. The Japanese, Koreans, and Taiwanese all manage to do the job. They visit, listen, and select the practices that will work best for them. Recognizing manufacturer "know-how" can provide the real advantage.

Play 6: Know What Is Proprietary

When I was with GE, I was always amazed at how freely the company shared confidential information with outsiders. There appeared to be little concern for security or for using production expertise as a competitive weapon. GE invited large numbers of people into its plants and offices; company professionals and managers wrote papers, gave out supporting documentation, and offered training and educational courses. The Japanese would annually come to learn firsthand what GE did and determine the strengths and shortcomings of its methods. Their teams represented all aspects of the business, and members listened intently, took pictures and made notes. This openness seems still to be part of the GE culture. Jack Welch and his senior executives continue to share their knowledge of management techniques. Many case studies, videos, and articles are published on GE's approach to management and production.

The IBM and the Japanese Approaches. On the other hand, IBM has followed a radically different approach throughout its history. The computer giant was so secretive that it would often constrain its suppliers and vendors from informing anyone that they were even working with IBM. This extreme may not have been without harm either, for it so insulated IBM that the company became too sure that anything it did was unique and unsurpassed.

The Japanese appear to have staked out a middle ground between GE's openness and IBM's secrecy. It has been my personal experience that the Japanese are willing to share their expertise, but you must work for their cooperation. That is, when I visited Japanese facilities, I could observe and ask questions, and they would answer the questions that I asked but would not volunteer information. The key to a successful visit was preparation and a desire to learn. Learning from others requires humility and a determination to listen and evaluate without prejudging. The problem for many Americans is that we tend to be more interested in talking than listening to and learning from others' experiences.

Production leaders must recognize that *how* the company makes its products is a key asset that deserves proprietary protection. It may be necessary at times to keep production processes a secret; at other times, a company can profitably share its expertise, that is, trade it for the know-how of others. Leaders should think through these considerations carefully and incorporate them into the total business game plan.

The Trade Secret as a Competitive Advantage.   A trade secret could be any special expertise, system, or formula that provides a company a production advantage or gives a product a unique quality. For instance, Coca-Cola has been able to maintain a leading position in soft drinks with a combination of aggressive demand creation, geographic roll-out, and, most importantly, a well-kept secret formula for making Coke. Competitors have tried and failed to replicate the Coke formula. Many colas are on the market, but only one has the distinctive taste of Coke.

International Flavors & Fragrances is the world's leading independent producer of synthetic tastes and smells. Most of the fragrances are sold to makers of perfumes, cosmetics, and household cleaners, including famous clients such as Procter & Gamble, Estee Lauder, Calvin Klein, and Halston. Most of the company's flavors are used in foods, drugs, tobacco, and pet food. The company was founded in 1909 by A.L. van Ameringen and William Haebler and acquired the Dutch firm of Polak & Schwartz in 1958, changing its name to International Flavors & Fragrances at that time. IF&F works with clients to develop unique flavors and fragrances to meet specific market and demographic profiles. Its competitive advantage resides not only in this talent, but in the ability to keep processes and formulas special and secret.[7]

Drug and chemical companies have used the trade secret approach to gain and maintain market position. Their innovative difference is not just the end product but the process of making the product. Factors include the way ingredients are mixed, when ingredients are added, and the way temperature is precisely controlled. Think of a successful restaurant that is able to difference itself from the competition even though the recipes are much the same. Distinction is achieved through the *process of cooking* as performed by a skilled chef. The same is true in wine making; the skills of the wine master make the difference between good and poor wine.

The preceding two examples lead to an important point: The company's trade secret may be the expertise of its employees. Management often does not give them enough credit. Especially in trades and professions, the superiority of a product may be only in the minds and experiences of key employees. Production leaders should take the time and make the effort to capture this expertise or special knowledge. In fact, the efforts of expert systems or artificial intelligence have been directed toward capturing know-how by replicating best practices and sharing them with the less skilled or untrained. Production leaders must also demonstrate trust and confidence in their professionals and other key workers, providing them with the knowledge and training they need to do their jobs effectively.

Play 7. Avoid Ego Trips and Complacency

Sometimes the leader's trade secret engenders a false sense of superiority. I've harped on this serious flaw in earlier sections of the book, usually in terms of admonishing leaders not to believe their own press releases. Production leaders, usually caretakers, must maintain their concentrated efforts over the long haul; complacency is their deadly enemy. Building and operating a unique and superior production facility is a time-consuming proposition. Modern plants can take years, or even decades, to construct.

Play 8. Keep Current and Reinvest

Production leaders must make a continuing investment in their systems, practices, and people. They must monitor the state of the art in such areas as production equipment, motivational techniques, and material substitution so that they are prepared for change. They must constantly be aware of what their competitors are doing, but avoid slogan and fad management. Don't replicate or follow just to be fashionable.

As obvious as these practices are, they have been neglected by many major companies, and this neglect has contributed to the firms' decline. It may be, as some argue, that short-term management is responsible. Almost all the giant steel, aluminum, chemical, and automobile companies in the United States have learned this part of the production strategy too late. General Motors has spent over $5 billion to redesign its production process and implement changes in an attempt to draw even with the Japanese, and we still cannot tell whether it has indeed caught up. The steel industry waited too long to invest and moved too slowly. These manufacturers have failed to regain the dominant position they surrendered to Japanese and European producers.

Caterpillar has always been the leading company in heavy earth-moving equipment. In 1986, to defend its position against Komatsu, a Japanese company, Caterpillar launched a $1.8 billion plant modernization program that was designed to cut manufacturing costs by 20 percent through flexible automation. Caterpillar also invested in a worldwide electronic information system that would link together its 30 plants, suppliers, and dealers. By 1989, the program was over cost and behind schedule. Nonetheless, CEO George Schaefer was determined to continue, despite the uneasiness of the investment community that was worried about Caterpillar's flat earnings. He understood the investments were needed to keep the company competitive and allow it to sell smaller equipment.[8] In 1991-1992, Caterpillar was willing to endure a UAW-led strike to maintain its cost position and flexibility. It won its battle and the union was forced to retreat from its industry wage strategy.

Emerson Electric, under the leadership of Charles Knight, has remained successful because it, too, continues to invest in low-cost production facilities and methods. The company uses such established techniques as statistical process control, "just-in-time" inventory (described later in this chapter), and total quality control. Knight constantly challenges his management to be the best and continually tracks his competitive cost position. He studies his managers' strategies and monitors their implementation.[9]

Play 9. Make Vendors Partners

Another lesson that many production leaders have learned the hard way is the value of forging a strong, lasting partnership with their key vendors. Historically, producers and vendors have been adversaries. Producers have attempted to reduce their costs by cutting their vendors' margins and profits. They also have asked vendors to take many risks but offered few rewards. Vendors have been pressured to reduce their prices when producers' costs were increasing. If they hesitated or failed to respond, they were threatened or replaced. This win/lose mentality strained relationships, and both parties suffered.

The major producers in the period from the 1930s through the 1950s solved their vendor relationships by becoming totally integrated. GM, for instance, acquired and operated the suppliers of all major components of its cars. GM acquired Fisher Bodies to make the auto frames and external metal parts. Delco provided radios, ignition systems, electronic components, and batteries. GM even had an equity position in U.S. Rubber, for tires and rubber products. These captive suppliers focused internally on the parent and opportunistically added external sales to fully utilize their production capacity. They were also used to help GM gain leverage against new vendors.

However, in the 1980s and 1990s, vertical integration has decreased, and most large producers have resorted to using external suppliers to provide either the commodity, easy-to-produce components, or parts that require unique processes or expertise. Although the major producers still control the critical product components, the changes require new ways of managing and leading the vendors.

The "Just-in-Time" Philosophy and Practice.   One of the key elements of today's production strategy is to minimize inventory at all
stages without reducing the ability to provide quality products on time.
Many firms are using an approach that translates from the Japanese
(*kanban*) as "just in time" because it involves having parts, components,
and materials arrive at the assembly plant just in time (not early and certainly not late) to be used. The philosophy of "just in time" is sharing. In
practice, that means vendors must be part of the production team. They
must be privy to strategic directions, priorities, and even key programs
and timing. They need to know what the product and sales plans are so
that they can produce and deliver their parts and components just
as they are needed. In Japan, major firms have created product team
families, called *keiretsu*. Nissan and Toyota have brought many of their
key suppliers to the United States, and these firms have increased production here. The suppliers provide all the key components for the cars
and are highly dependent on their "family partners" for their success. In
many cases, the suppliers are partially owned by the producer.

The Wichita Partnership for Skills Development.   Wichita, Kansas,
is the home of Cessna, Beech Aircraft, Gates LearJet, and the military
aircraft division of Boeing. Other manufacturers include NCR (computers) and Coleman (camping equipment). Hundreds of high-tech tool
and die shops grew up in the area to service these high-tech industries.

These suppliers and subcontractors had serious difficulty in hiring
and training skilled people. An organization of local small and large
businesses, called the WI/SE Partnership for Growth, helped start the
Center for Technology Application at Wichita State University. The focus of this venture was to train people how to use new computerized
equipment so that they could take their place in the Wichita labor force.
Not only has the project met that goal, it has brought together vendors
in partnerships that go beyond inventory management.

The Integration Decision and Vendor Relationships.   In 1988, the
James River Corporation of Virginia was the second largest paper company in the world, with revenues of $5.1 billion from 133 plants world-
wide. Prior to 1980, the company's strategy was to become a force in the
fragmented market for small order, custom-designed papers. James
River kept its capital costs low by acquiring obsolete little mills from
large companies at bargain prices. The company also bought its raw material, pulp, from vendors. In 1980, however, James River decided to
change what had been a winning strategy and integrate production by
adding pulp-making capacity in advance of demand. As of early 1989,
the change had proven costly because the company had added capacity

when pulp supply exceeded demand and the buyer had a purchasing advantage. Leadership at James River was convinced, nonetheless, that becoming a self-supplier would work out in the long run.[10] The depressed market for specialty paper has kept earnings low, but the lower costs position the company well for an upturn in the market.

The lesson here is that the integration decision changes relationships with vendors. When a company integrates, becomes a self-supplier, the vendors are no longer allies, but competitors. Integration assures a source of supply and increases control. It is, however, economically risky. Success depends on the leader's ability to forecast demand and not be stuck with too much or thwarted by too little inventory.

Play 10. Keep the Game Plan Simple So Everyone Can Understand It

The production-driven strategy, more so than others, is dependent on the game plan being simple and understandable. Rather, the leader must be able to make the game plan seem clear and simple to team members. The plan itself may be complex and require the extensive use of "queuing theory," PERT (Program Evaluation and Review Technique) charts, and critical path analysis. This information must be translated so that all the players know what is expected of them because they must execute with precision and efficiency. Good communication begins with trust and sharing. Leaders must let the work force know what is happening and why. While that is difficult in a unionized shop, enlightened union leaders have increasingly been willing to reciprocate trust from management and share responsibility for the company's success. In that environment, the game plan can be implemented and everybody can win.

THE PRODUCTION LEADER'S
TEAM AND TALENTS

Clearly, production leaders must be skilled in production, which may mean they should be "hands on" leaders who have worked in the plant as forepersons or superintendents. At one time, this experience was required for most senior executives; now, however, conventional wisdom has it that the boss need only be able to read, question, analyze, and observe. In fact, many leaders have been chosen primarily for their financial acumen and their ability to make deals or do financial analyses. That notion will not cut it for production-driven companies. At a minimum, their leaders must appreciate the manual skills that go into making the product and understand not only how the product is made but how it could be improved. No matter how many production experts the leaders may have around them, they still must be at home with the language and concepts of production. Normally, production leaders are not financial wizards or MBAs who only understand the numbers of business. They have a background in production and know how to motivate production people in a straightforward manner.

Productivity and Harmony through Team Building

During the 50 years from the 1930s through the 1970s, the prevailing belief in business was that unions/workers and management had to be combative rather than cooperative. The great awakening occurred in the 1980s when aggressive foreign competitors simultaneously were able to reduce costs, improve quality, and make customers happy. American firms scrambled to discover their secrets. They found that one factor in the competition's success was teamwork.

Companies began forming teams to improve quality and every aspect of the production process. For instance, ATT Credit Corporation, of Morristown, New Jersey, used teams of employees to process applications from companies that wanted to lease computer equipment. Profits improved in a GE plant in Salisbury, North Carolina, when supervisors were persuaded to increase team involvement. In fact, GE's Jack Welch developed a team approach "work-out" that empowered teams to determine what work needed to be done, who should do what, and what tasks could be eliminated.[11]

The concept of tapping the talents of employees is not new, of course. As I gained experience in manufacturing and human resources management, I learned that workers had a great number of excellent ideas that merited adoption. In my companies, a sound suggestion program stimulated creative employee input. In addition, the more enlightened supervisors and workers ran meetings to elicit ideas. Unfortunately, the militancy of unions and the defensiveness of management often prevented openness and teamwork.

Teamwork is really a set of values and common sense. It must be viewed as a win/win opportunity for management and employees. Employees are not enemies; the enemies are the competitors outside the company. When seen in this light, the cooperation of employees and management becomes a powerful concept. However, if either workers or managers see it as a gimmick or a way for bosses to manipulate employees, it will not only fail, but create more conflict. The strategic leader must understand that honesty and trust form the soul of teamwork.

A.O. Smith is one company that has built its strategy on the teamwork concept. After six years of experimentation, it introduced production teams in 1987. Workers were motivated to participate because they were concerned that the company would not survive and thus they would lose their jobs. What were termed "participative systems" consisted of problem-solving committees on the shop floor and advisory committees with union representatives at the plant level. Employees recognized that the traditional piecework system, which had been in place for over 50 years, was a barrier to efficiency. Since eliminating the system would reduce employee earnings by $3 an hour, management agreed to freeze wages. Another important development was the workers' agreement to rotate from one job to another; this change permitted a reduction of the supervisor-to-worker ratio from 1 to 10, to 1 to 34. Supervisors were also trained to be more participative and less autocratic. A.O. Smith has benefited from the new cooperative procedures, but both management and workers realize that they have just taken the first step in a long road together.[12]

Employee Training

Whether or not a company forms employee/management teams, whether or not the employees are represented by a union, the production leader must create an equitable climate that honors the rights and expectations of workers. And a productive work environment for all concerned is one in which workers are properly trained for their responsibilities. Training is especially critical because of the demands placed on employees by participatory, problem-solving teams and by the nature of today's jobs.

Unfortunately, companies cannot count on the public-supported education system to produce trained or even literate workers, particularly at the entry level. Many companies, with the assistance of state and local governments, have invested in creative training programs.

There have been four major thrusts used to upgrade the quality of education in the United States. Adopting schools has been used by some companies. In this situation, the company provides tangible goods and services to the schools including guest speakers, employee tutors, small grants, and computers. Other companies establish specific projects with schools. This includes management training for administrators or providing specialized technical training programs. In addition, business leaders are seeking school reforms and policy changes to assure that there is a supply of the most critical resource of all—trained, qualified and motivated employees.[13]

The Total Systems Approach

To understand the total production system from the beginning to the finished product, the team must recognize where the most critical phases of production are and where the bottlenecks are likely to occur. Since most companies rely on vendors to supply materials, components, and parts, the production team must be able to evaluate the health of its suppliers. As I stressed earlier, the production company wants to develop strong relationships with its vendors. That means fostering win/win attitudes with fair prices and sacred commitments to schedules. If the vendor does not make a reasonable profit, the company will suffer in the long run.

Location Selection

Selecting the production site is a vital skill that requires an understanding of the company's business strategy and its competitive and market positions. Production-driven companies are not only geared to cost reduction and high volumes but are dedicated to achieving competitive advantage through flexibility, responsiveness, and reliability. These last qualities may not be achieved if the plant is located in an area with the lowest labor costs. As I described earlier, too many companies rushed to the Far East for cheap labor and found they could not control quality or a variety of hidden costs when doing business at a distant location. For instance, Korea today presents a very unstable environment because of strikes by increasingly discontented workers. China is an even more uncertain area for investment. The turbulent world situation points to the need for people with sociopolitical expertise on the team. Even in the United States, several firms that moved to the Sunbelt are returning to the Northeast for the quality of life and the skilled work force.

Technological Expertise

The team needs people who are experts in manufacturing technologies and methods, who are up to the minute on equipment, systems, and practices. At times, the real difference might be the company's customized and proprietary production equipment. For instance, more than 20 years ago, Procter & Gamble gained a competitive edge by developing a process for producing a softer, more attractive toilet tissue, Charmin. In a different arena, IBM and many semiconductor companies are very concerned about the availability of special process equipment that can provide certain levels of tolerance and throughput. The production team may need to establish a manufacturer's applications lab that can determine how well available equipment performs and whether some degree of customization in machine tools, punch presses, and near-net shape equipment is necessary.

Normally, thoughts of clothing manufacturers bring to mind the old garment district in New York, primitive production, and low-cost labor. An example of a progressive productive leader is Gruppo GFT, based in Turin, Italy. In 10 years, the company has used innovative technologies to establish a strong position in the high end of the men's clothing market. Because the cutting task is a major part of the production of clothing, Gruppo has invested in a computer graphics machine. The outline of each piece of clothing is positioned electronically on an oversized, black television screen, arranged on the screen for minimum waste, and the configuration is electronically printed on white paper. That paper is placed on top of a bolt of fabric, where the cutting is done with a laser beam. This efficient system has helped make the company profitable.[14]

Laser technology has also improved welding sufficiently to give some firms a competitive edge in production. In the Chevrolet Beretta plant in Lindon, New Jersey, for example, lasers are used to weld new materials, from ceramics to fiber-plastic composites, to coated steels. Currently, laser technology is focused on heavy-duty applications, such as welding transmissions and drive shafts. In the future, fiber-optic lasers may become an effective way of joining advanced materials.

Supportive Skills

Even in a production-driven company, more is involved in doing business than just making the product. Among the key "support" people are experts skilled in product design. Product designers must be familiar with the factory, the equipment, and the best level of utilization. Because this strategy requires the company to be the most efficient producer, product designs and specifications must be appropriate for and make the fullest use of the production facilities.

The production leader's sales force should be primarily "right" order takers, that is salespeople who get orders that fit the production systems and not just orders for the sake of orders. Salespeople should be aware of the levels of equipment utilization and plan their sales to optimize plant capacity. A force that makes sales beyond the plant's normal capabilities or overpromises on deliveries to customers forces leaders to make costly adjustments in production to meet those commitments. Thus, the leader should consider implementing a "real time" information and tracking system that will let the sales force and senior management know on a daily, or at least a weekly, basis how sales fit with the utilization needs of the factory.

Pricing authority may have to be controlled at centralized locations to assure that the sales force does not reduce prices to make sales that the most efficient production cannot handle profitably. Advertising should be used selectively. There is no benefit in advertising aggressively if the factory cannot meet the demand that will be created. Advertising should be used to help stimulate sales of the right products at the right time for best plant utilization.

Inventory can be the hedge for the production leader. Often in the mass consumer markets, such as automobiles and household major appliances, it is more efficient to produce one type or model and inventory the excess then to intersperse different models or sizes on a single run. Thus, inventory management skills and systems are a must for the production team, which needs to answer such questions as: How much should be stored in advance of demand? Where should the products be warehoused? What is the correct mix to minimize stockouts? In some cases, the company must risk selective stockouts to optimize utilization of the factory.

Flexible computerized manufacturing skills and techniques, supported by modeling, can be highly effective in solving these inventory problems in the current manufacturing environment. There are now computerized machine tools that can be adjusted easily, rapidly, and efficiently to fit different sizes and shapes. As a result, smaller runs are now possible, which reduces significantly the need for extensive inventories.

The team will also need people with the financial skills to determine how to finance the capital equipment, the facilities, and the inventories. These are major decisions with long-term ramifications. The leader must bring the financial planners into the game early and establish strict measures. The financials are a way of keeping score, of determining the appropriate levels of investment. Again, sophisticated computer simulations and analysis techniques can help financial specialists fine-tune their projections.

Relativity

As I mentioned under Play 5 of the game plan, team members must recognize that in competitive situations, nothing is absolute. It is how well the company compares with competitors in meeting customer expectations that counts. The leader as well as the team members can too easily become internalized and forget about the external environment. Just because the company has reduced failure rates or increased productivity does not mean it is doing well. Not if the competition is doing better.

That was the problem with U.S. auto companies. They were content to have a certain number of defects in the cars they shipped because it was economical for them to fix them later in the field or at the dealership. In fact, the dealers liked the arrangement because it helped them build a profitable service department. The Japanese, on the other hand, could not ship cars thousands of miles and expect to fix them on the spot, especially without a large dealer network. So they concentrated on zero-defect autos. The customers were amazed and pleased. Their expectations raised, they began to demand better quality cars. When U.S. companies could not meet those expectations, the public began to buy Japanese. And we have not caught up yet, at least in the minds of the customers.

RISKTAKER, CARETAKER, SURGEON, UNDERTAKER

Most production leaders are caretakers. They are conservative incrementalists, craving success without deviations. They evaluate the past and present carefully and know what to expect from the future. They seek evolutionary improvements in the production process and facilities through cautious and calculated additions of new equipment, tryouts of new methods, and steps to reduce waste or improve quality. They like models and simulations to test ideas before putting them into practice. They will take risks but only for major problems. American leaders who moved their plants offshore were risktakers. As I reported earlier, many realize that was a mistake and are coming home. The caretakers never left or moved rapidly to return.

Similarly, Japanese companies setting up production in the United States are taking a risk, and many, as I suggested earlier, are struggling with differences in culture, language, and work habits. Nonetheless, leaders at such firms as Honda, Toyota, and Nissan feel they have little or no choice. They believe the U.S. government will be pressured by the American public to reduce imports to preserve jobs. Therefore, the only way Japanese carmakers, in particular, can maintain their market position is to manufacture in the United States.

Surgeons and undertakers are often production-driven leaders because they are by nature and by training conservative and inward looking. Sadly, such leadership too often harvests company assets too early or lets the company die prematurely. Surgeon and undertaker production leaders tend to believe that if something does not work quickly and profitably or does not meet their standards, then it should be discontinued. And they are willing to make the tough decision to stop production. They are much more liable than product innovators, problem solvers, or sales leaders to feel the need to cut the fat, reduce the labor force, cut back on the product line, or move to other facilities.

Sometimes that is what's needed; sometimes surgeon leaders do not give their enterprises enough time to grow and become profitable.

It seems to me that it has become too easy to take out the knife and cut into the organization. Some of what is being called fat is really bone, muscle, and vital organs. Like the heart. People, the heart of any organization, cannot be treated as a pure investment or resource. Indeed, the concept of "human resources" may be contributing to America's manufacturing decline. People are vital partners in any enterprise, and leaders must strive to make their people feel appreciated and necessary. A leader who wants a loyal team that will energetically work to implement the game plan needs, in turn, to be loyal to them. People cannot be expected to change because short-term profits are down or because senior management took a gamble and lost. Companies that take the short view and treat their workers as expendable commodities foster rebellion. That is what is happening in the auto industry. Many workers appear to be wiling to give up on hard-nosed American employers and take their chances with the Japanese.

TIMING

When should a company adopt a production-driven strategy? Here are four situations when the time may be right for the production leader.

Situation 1. When the Production Technology Really Makes a Difference

"Flexible automation" has always seemed a contradiction in terms to me. I envision "automation" as a fixed process that does not allow deviation. Yet, the reality is that computerized factories can change rapidly and efficiently from one product configuration to another. Those companies that managed to adopt this new approach early were able to combine the best of both automation and job shop and so gain a competitive advantage. Toyota and Nissan are combining flexible automation and handcrafting to gain cost advantages in their thrust into the ultra-high-end auto markets. Once they establish a lead, they may be difficult to overtake.

Situation 2. When the Current Leader Is Complacent

I mention this opportunity in every chapter. Entrenched leaders are always reluctant to change because the system in place is working and they can reap enormous rewards by maintaining the status quo. Three factors are at work here: (1) The current system is likely to provide stability and enable the company on top to reach new levels of quality; (2) the system in place will yield high returns; (3) it fits the leader's culture and management style.

On the other hand, an aggressive challenger has every reason to change the ground rules and threaten the status quo. One approach is to change the way the product is made or how the system is integrated. Production innovation provides an opportunity. A company can invest in new processes and equipment that the established leader will be reluctant to match and so achieve a competitive advantage that will catapult the challenger into the lead position, displacing the complacent incumbent.

Situation 3. When External Factors Impact the Valued-Added Chain

We all remember the impact of the energy crisis on automobiles, home heating, and other energy-related markets. It also changed the economies of manufacturing. For instance, the cost of plastics increased because they are oil based and their production is energy intensive. The cost of transporting goods and materials altered the desirability of production locations, and some energy-deprived areas became less attractive sites. All these disruptions in the external environment provided opportunities for producers that had ample sources of energy or knew how to use energy efficiently. Similarly, government health and safety regulations in mature, industrial nations have altered or even eliminated some production processes, thus offering opportunities for developing nations that do not have those restrictions.

Situation 4. When You Have a Production Genius

Certain individuals and groups have an innate ability to make things work. These talents are very apparent in the craft or trade skills industries such as housing or general construction. I have seen individuals build houses in ways that no one else can duplicate. Perhaps they can lay a foundation in marshland or add unique features to a home. In the mass-production side, breakthroughs in modular designs and systems may be able to supply badly needed moderate and low-cost housing.

The same genius is often available to production leaders but they must seek it out, support it, and reward these production geniuses.

PART
SIX

LEADERSHIP
PAST AND FUTURE

In Chapter 13, we examine leadership practices of the 1980s that need to be avoided in the future. The asset stripper was eulogized; corporate CEOs, charitable institutions, and government officials forgot their responsibilities to their stakeholders and became too greedy; leaders didn't prepare for their succession; winning at all cost became accepted. In addition, management placed too much emphasis on short-term fixes and too little on long-term plans and commitments. Managing by the numbers rather than by strategy became the rule. These are poor leadership practices.

Chapter 14 looks ahead to leadership in the 1990s. Strategic leadership in all phases of society will be essential in this decade. It will include risktakers who can capitalize on emergence of the "global village" and drug problems, caretakers who can develop a long-term commitment and reverse the short-term mentality of the 1980s; surgeons who are willing to attack the debt issues of government, business, and other institutions; and undertakers who are willing to make the tough choices in the collapsed "planned economies." Leaders need to learn from past successes and failures while avoiding trend extrapolation.

Chapter 15, the final chapter, considers the responsibility of companies and other institutions to develop the different leadership types among their personnel and to place these leaders in situations that require their unique talents. The General Electric model should be evaluated; it has worked successfully for over five decades.

13

Leadership Lessons of the 1980s

The opening chapters of this book set out four basic tenets of strategic leadership, which I would like to review briefly now.

- The leader's primary mission and objective is the *continuing, long-term* prosperity of the institution she leads; she must look beyond short-term profitability. Therefore, the leader needs to balance the interests of *all the key stakeholders,* including the employees, the community, and society, as well as the investors.

- No single leader is best for all situations. Different types of leaders are required at different phases of the institution's life cycle. A risktaker is needed in the beginning when things are changing rapidly and growth is the major objective. A caretaker then assumes command to provide stability and promote long-term prosperity. When the company becomes too broad and unfocused and starts to decline, a surgeon is called to attempt to restore it to health. Finally, the undertaker's time has come when the company must be liquidated and brought to a dignified end.

- Leaders must excel at something and not try to be best at everything. They must identify their unique talents and build (and lead) from strength; they must avoid trying to be "all things to all people." Some will lead by introducing innovative products, others by selling, others by solving complex problems, still others through production expertise, and so on.

267

r must put together a team with compatible skills and
understandable game plan for them to follow. The di-
nd guidance inherent in the implementation of a strate-
plan is the essence of leadership.

Those principles represent the structure of strategic leadership. Throughout the book, I have drawn on my years as a practitioner and consultant to flesh out this framework with case histories of leaders and their institutions. You've no doubt noticed the reappearance of several themes from chapter to chapter. I would like to crystallize this material by identifying and elaborating on six key lessons of leadership. They are:

1. *Don't confuse asset stripping with leadership.* In the 1980s, too much press and praise was given to these deal makers. They were generally lauded as tough minded, but few recognized what they were really doing.

2. *Don't be greedy and self-serving.* Too many CEOs and top executives have been given huge bonuses and "golden parachutes" while their companies were in declining, unprofitable positions.

3. *Plan for leadership succession.* Leaders must accept that they cannot go on forever and so be ready for, and plan for, the day they must turn over the company to someone else.

4. *Develop a tolerance for failure.* Leaders will not always achieve what they set out to accomplish. Even good leaders fail. In many cases, the positive results of their leadership may not appear until after they have left the organization.

5. *Avoid change for the sake of change, but don't avoid change.* Change for its own sake is the by-product of management by slogan or management by fad. The future success of an organization depends on substance, not catch phrases. It also depends on realizing when true change is necessary.

6. *Learn to lead by strategy.* Financials are important, but only in the service of the defining quality of the organization that is its strategic driver.

LESSON 1. DON'T CONFUSE ASSET STRIPPING WITH LEADERSHIP

The past decade demonstrates graphically the consequences of having too many creative lawyers and financial experts in influential positions. Somehow, we have encouraged most of our talented youth to assume careers in which they spend their time thinking about how to take over companies and strip them apart or to restructure them with so much debt that they cannot survive. Many asset strippers seem to be motivated by the goal of making a quick fortune and then retiring at age 35. In addition, we have become so litigious that we spend more time worrying about being sued or defending ourselves than we spend creating new products, systems, or plants. Many great leaders from the past probably would be as reluctant as we are to take risks today.

Because we have lost the true risktaking spirit, many of our leaders have become defensive, premature, unplanned undertakers. Many caretaker leaders have become preoccupied with losing their jobs or losing their companies to a raider. Thus, instead of pursuing a strategy of innovation and growth, they sell off assets prematurely, just to survive for the sake of surviving. Not only have they sold their future for an uncertain present, they have lost technological expertise, unique products, and capable people to foreign competitors—and at bargain prices.

Therefore, we need to reestablish a climate in which leaders will again have the desire and the ability to take risks to create new products or to solve some of the tough problems of society (see Chapter 14). In addition, we should encourage and praise the caretaker evolutionaries who are needed by businesses if they are to grow and prosper over the long haul. That means giving these leaders the job security to make and implement long-range strategic plans. Leadership requires confidence. However, that does not mean golden parachutes and excessive compensation for executives. All the key stakeholder groups should be rewarded in a balanced way.

We also must continue to be objective and tough minded. Surgeons and undertakers have their roles. Those parts of the enterprise that no longer fit the overall strategy or cannot produce adequate returns must be pruned away. However, surgeons still must be concerned with assuring the prosperity of the firm, rather than with becoming rich by selling off assets. There have been too many liquidations for the sake of liquidation and too much emphasis on the short-term numbers.

LESSON 2. DON'T BE GREEDY
AND SELF-SERVING

CEOs who accept huge salaries and bonuses when their companies (including non-profit institutions like hospitals, United Way, even churches) are in poor financial and strategic condition are merely occupying leadership positions and are not true strategic leaders. Many of these leaders are guilty of milking their companies rather than investing in the future. Some create the appearance of profitability and growth, but the financials will not stand up to scrutiny. The major business magazines are alert to this situation and print performance charts relating management compensation to shareholder returns. That is one useful measurement, but it does not encompass all the nonfinancial aspects of business health.

Able and effective leaders certainly should be compensated for their efforts, but on a scale consistent with the state of their organizations. We cannot have those at the top rewarded for implementing destructive strategies. Nor is it good policy for a few greedy individuals to prosper when the average American's standard of living is declining.

LESSON 3. PLAN FOR LEADERSHIP SUCCESSION

Over the past three decades, we have witnessed risktaker innovators in all categories who were unable to prepare for the transition to the next leader. As I have pointed out many times, risktakers succumb to their egos and are unable to separate themselves from the business; they can't believe it will go on without them. Leaders have stayed too long in private companies and nonprofit organizations such as Howard Johnson, Wang, CBS, WR Grace, ITT, RCA, and even the Triborough Commission.

In late 1991, the *Economist* ran an article entitled "The Ten Year Itch" that emphasized the need for political leaders to get out gracefully before they are thrown out. The article cited the experiences of Margaret Thatcher (11 years in power) in England, Charles de Gaulle (11 years) and Francois Mitterrand (in trouble after 10 years) in France, and Heinrich Kohl (struggling after 9 years) in Germany to conclude that modern democracies tolerate leaders for only about a decade. What goes wrong? Political palsy sets in. Common symptoms include delusions of grandeur, aversion to criticism, boredom, and obsession with one's place in history.[1]

Leaders of all types can learn from the retirement of Johnny Carson. Johnny Carson departed while he was still a leader. He timed his exit when his rating and his advertising dollars were dropping but not at the low point. He retired and was not thrown out of this job. He told his audience "Everything comes to an end, nothing lasts forever. Thirty years is enough (far more than most leaders can last). It's time to get out while you are still on the top." Carson developed his successor and didn't worry, like many leaders, that his protege would eclipse him. He shared his success with his long time associates, Ed McMahon, Doc

Severinsen and his producer, Fred De Cordova. Carson looked to the future and not to the past. His departure is what I have described that most leaders should try to emulate.[2]

With no designated successor in place for the leader, key players on the team become disenchanted; many leave, sometimes for the competition. The risktaker should begin to look for a successor when growth starts to slow. That is a signal for the reign of the caretaker, who has the patience to succeed over the long term in a maturing market. Of course, company founders have a particularly difficult time letting go. As I related in an earlier chapter, An Wang tried to pass the business on to his son Fred. When that did not work out, he was forced to bring in a surgeon leader, Richard Miller, from outside, who unfortunately was unable to save the patient from bankruptcy.[3] Steven Jobs had the foresight to turn over operations at Apple to John Scully, a caretaker type. Scully found it necessary to purge Jobs entirely from the company to resolve conflict. Planning for succession may not be easy, but it must be done.

When I was at GE, succession planning was a critical part of the CEO's job. The story of the race at GE to succeed Reg Jones has been told often. Jones's succession system produced six candidates to replace him. Each candidate was assigned a leadership position in a sector outside his experience. For instance, Jack Welch from materials and chemicals was put in the consumer sector, and Stan Gault from consumer products was assigned to the industrial sector. Fortunately, GE was sufficiently prosperous to give the potential heirs time to meet or succumb to these challenges. All the candidates were monitored and evaluated on their ability to lead and to implement strategies, often ones that they had not developed themselves. Welch, of course, prevailed in this tough and complex contest.

Although bold and successful, the succession process was risky and not without cost, because many of the other candidates left the company. Gault successfully took over Rubbermaid (and recently undertook another risky situation as CEO of Goodyear), Vanderslice went to GTE, and Frederick moved to RCA. Nonetheless, this sort of planning is necessary, although GE's model could probably be implemented only by a strong caretaker innovator like Reg Jones. A risktaker would probably be too egotistical and insecure; a surgeon would not likely have the time and resources for such a system of trials.

In the past decade, most large U.S. companies have had to call on the talents of surgeon and undertaker leaders to refocus strategy and undo much of the diversification that was popular in the 1960s and 1970s. In the 1990s, however, successful firms will require a mix, that is, a succession, of all leadership types: risktaker, caretaker, surgeon, and undertaker. I have already described the need for risktakers in Lesson 1. We will need caretakers in the tradition of the great leaders of the 1930s and 1950s as well. America can't become just a servicer and retailer. We must have new and better ways of producing and of rebuilding our entire infrastructure. Finally, surgeons must become more precise in their restructuring; we can't afford another generation of rampant asset strippers.

LESSON 4. DEVELOP A TOLERANCE FOR FAILURE

Applauding to the point of canonizing leaders who are successful is destructive, because it makes those who fail look like idiots. Of course we need winners, but we must also recognize that they can't win all the time.

I recently read an article that was critical of Fred Smith of FedEx because his Zap Mail innovation did not meet expectations. Although Smith's timing was off and he did underestimate the growth of low-cost facsimiles, his moves were still characteristic of a capable strategic leader.[4] We must recognize such well-directed efforts if we want leaders to continue to take risks. Over the years, I have witnessed a number of individuals who bet on an innovation, lost, and never got a second chance. Some left their companies; some were demoted never to rise again; some simply withered professionally.

That is why the 3M model of venturing deserves all the accolades it receives. 3M encourages risktaking and permits individuals to try a second innovative venture if their first attempt doesn't yield the desired results. Even if they choose not to step forward again, they are not thrown away or forced out of the company. More firms might adopt 3M's policy.

Caretaker and surgeon leaders often declare that they encourage venturing but then fail to live up to their rhetoric in practice. For instance, IBM has shown signs of stagnation by being too slow to change a long-time winning strategy. Despite press coverage to the contrary, however, caretaker style leader John Akers does seem to be trying to take decisive action to transform his middle-aged company. His game plan includes decentralizing the company and making each business unit more responsive to its markets and competitors. As I described in an earlier chapter, Akers is employing a consultative and applications driven strategy. At this writing, it is impossible to tell whether Akers will succeed or whether a more dramatic surgeon type leader will be required to restructure and refocus IBM for the 1990s. Perhaps, Akers' major contribution to IBM will be to select a successor with a new game plan that will be a better fit for the company.

The medical surgeon who loses a patient is not popular, and neither is the surgeon leader who tries and fails to refocus a company and move it into the future. I've described Lee Iacocca as a surgeon leader. He was very successful in saving Chrysler in the mid-1980s, but he could not complete the job before turning it over to a successor in the early 1990s. This "apparent failure" (remember, the scorecard is not final until some time after the leader leaves) should not detract from his past accomplishments. Iacocca's career demonstrates that success is a product of the proper leadership, game plan, and timing.

The public must learn that no one can be a hero and a winner all the time. If we don't develop that understanding, we will continue to be seduced by slogans and the champions of the moment and fail to encourage leaders of all types and styles, in all organizations, to chance pursuing their visions and implementing their innovative game plans.

LESSON 5. AVOID CHANGE FOR THE SAKE OF CHANGE, BUT DON'T AVOID CHANGE

Related to management by slogans is the inclination to do things differently, without a substantial reason, just for the sake of making a change. Americans love gimmicks and catch phrases, and U.S. managers and professionals are susceptible to the allure of the latest business fads, as I detailed in Chapter 1. That is not to say that searching for excellence, focusing on quality, or trying to be entrepreneurial are not sound principles. However, when promoted but not examined in sufficient depth, or when chanted but not understood, or when officially endorsed by leadership but not implemented as part of the game plan, these principles fail to reap what they promise.

The Japanese and the Germans, on the other hand, have worked out the details of implementing these principles and have created systems and processes to make them part of the ongoing way they do business. Our foreign competitors have changed when it was appropriate and not just to follow a management slogan or to be in style. Leaders in the United States also need to develop implementable, team game plans that are specific enough to provide guidance but not so "cookbook" restrictive that they inhibit creativity. Ultimately, each key team member needs to know what the leader expects of her. Teamwork is the key to success in U.S. business. As American Airlines Chairman Robert Crandell has expressed it: "The very finest products and services are going to be produced with a team effort, rather than through the more hierarchical management that has tended to characterize this country."[5]

Leaders need to translate general strategies into specific actions. That includes specifying the skills and talents to successfully implement the game plan. Leaders can't just say they want a productive or quality-oriented work force. What does "quality" really mean and how do we produce and measure it? Slogan managers will make the speech and assume they have made a strategy change without truly understanding what they have said or providing the guidance a team needs to put the words into operation.

For instance, a number of people have come out for just-in-time (now called "quick response" by some) inventory management without really appreciating what the organization must do to put the system into place. Just-in-time management requires the company to have a strong market forecast and the ability to translate the forecast into the exact parts, components, and materials that will be needed at the exact time they are called for. As we have seen, the new system also requires close partnerships with vendors, whose trust and cooperation must be earned. In short, the company faces a tough job, involving in-depth planning and good communications both inside and outside the organization.

But whatever the management slogan or fad, *actually achieving* customer satisfaction (as opposed to just proclaiming the principle) is the only thing that really matters. In the 1970s and early 1980s, many companies apparently lost sight of their customers. Firms discovered the hard way that foreign competitors could provide satisfactory products and services. U.S. enterprises suffered from too much internal thinking and management by objectives. Almost all U.S. companies have lost in the global, and even the home, markets because they failed to monitor customer satisfaction and consistently meet customer needs. In the coming decade, international competition is likely to intensify as the nations of Eastern Europe and what was the Soviet Union find their way in democracy and free market operations. Leaders in the United States must not underestimate the skills, education, and drive of this soon-to-be-liberated work force.

The global face of competition is just another reminder that leaders can't become overconfident and lose sight of the relevant positions of their organizations. That means recognizing the abilities of risktaker innovators who are offering new products or services that can substitute for the existing lines. The creative, disruptive force often comes from outside the industry. It was not the gas industry that offered a new way to heat and light homes and businesses through electricity. It was not the steel industry that developed aluminum. Thus, the leader must look far in the distance for competition on the horizon and be willing to defend against it or lead in developing the new technology or approach.

I have been working with several clients in this area. My goal has been to have them first accept that the new offering or approach might be equal to, or even better than, what is currently available. Second, I want them to understand that they must be willing to take risks. Leaders in these situations tend to be caretakers or surgeons who are not oriented toward taking chances. One solution is to establish a *venturing program and teams,* led by risktakers in the organization, to pursue these new opportunities without inhibition. These venture leaders need the freedom to gamble on their game plans and the authority to hire and reward the right type of team.

LESSON 6. LEARN TO LEAD BY STRATEGY

Although the concept of strategic planning and thinking gained acceptance during the 1970s and 1980s, most companies still adhere to the tenets of management by objectives (MBO). The MBO school of thought holds that making the objectives is the most critical act. Adherents argue that it does not matter *how* a team wins, so long as it *does win.* Many quote the legendary football coach Vince Lombardi, who is reputed to have said, "winning isn't everything, it's the only thing." In fact, Lombardi did care *how* he won. He devised a simple but highly effective game plan and built and trained a team to execute it with intensity and precision. He was much more a strategic leader than a manager by objectives.

Let me pause here to make an important point about slogan management. This form of management is not related to *method,* but to *depth of understanding and commitment.* "Strategic leadership" can be a slogan, and executives would be practicing slogan management if they simply marched behind its banner proclaiming their allegiance. I have spent hundreds of pages detailing how to actually practice strategic leadership through integration of vision, competitive difference, game plan, teamwork, and timing that is appropriate for an organization in its particular competitive environment during its particular life cycle phase. Anyone can claim to have a "strategy," but without the commitment to those particulars, all the leader has is another slogan.

Management by strategy proclaims that *how* something was achieved is as important as *what* was achieved. Suppose a leader announces that she is going to grow the business, but instead focuses on increased earnings through a defensive or harvest strategy. She may have achieved short-run results by sacrificing long-term prospects. That is what most U.S. companies did in the 1980s. Now suppose the leader did grow the business, but by offering new products instead of solving customer problems, that is, with a different strategic driver than was promised. Does that matter? I believe it does have long-term consequences, because if the driver is different than planned, the company's people and skills may also have to be different.

We need leaders to do what they say. If they do not, they must explain why they changed and how the changes will impact the future. The success of the Japanese is based on their willingness to concentrate on their strategies and on their commitment to make their objectives and results consistent with those strategies.

We need to stop winning battles and losing wars on the business front. Short-term objective setting is a plan for a battle, not a war. It gains profits but sacrifices the vitality and future success of the company. *Committed strategic leadership wins wars.*

Understanding the lessons of the 1980s is just the beginning. In the next chapter, I will identify the significant trends and problems of the 1990s and describe the leadership responses they will require. Entrenched leaders are always motivated to maintain the status quo. Sometimes that desire can cause them to ignore the warning signs of change or underestimate the power, the inevitability, of change. We have witnessed this dynamic in the affairs of nations, as well as business, throughout this century. True leaders are aware of the forces of change and can sometimes direct them to their advantage. That will be the challenge for this decade.

14

Problems and Trends of the 1990s: Challenges and Opportunities for Strategic Leadership

I am not so presumptuous as to claim that I can predict the future. The events of 1991 and 1992 in the Middle East as well as the collapse of the Soviet Union and Eastern Bloc demonstrate that no one can predict the future. I can, however, identify several major trends and problems that are either at hand or on the immediate horizon and that are having or will have an impact on the leadership requirements of our organizations. In this chapter, I will discuss the following propositions within the context of strategic leadership.

1. Communication advances make the world a true "global village"—need for system risktakers.

2. There is a scarcity of qualified, motivated, and educated workers—need for education risktakers.

3. Too many leaders focus on the shareholders and not the stakeholders—need for long-term caretakers.

4. The drug culture impacts all aspects of society—need for tough minded problem solving risktakers followed by caretakers.

5. The United States continues to be a debtor nation—need for surgeons to set priorities.

6. The unexpected, dynamic collapse of the "planned economies" creates both chaos and opportunities—need risktakers to capitalize on undertakers of Russia and Eastern Europe.

7. Rebuild the infrastructure and the way of life—need for another Robert Moses.

COMMUNICATION ADVANCES MAKE THE WORLD A TRUE "GLOBAL VILLAGE"— NEED FOR SYSTEM RISKTAKERS

Individuals can now communicate, interact, and transact business and personal affairs with nearly anyone in the world without leaving their homes—by utilizing technological advances in radios, telephones, televisions, facsimile machines, and personal computers. They can work at home and perform services and make products that could only be done in the confines of an office or a factory just a decade ago. Thus has the world become a global village.

The power of communications and information technologies has also made an enormous impact on political history in the past decade, turning the world into a global village. Three major events dramatically illustrate this process.

The first consists of all the popular uprisings against restrictive Communist governments—the ones that were frustrated in China and succeeded in Eastern Europe. Many people believe that the critical mass for change was achieved through modern electronic communications. Television and radio images of prosperity and freedom in Western societies prompted a growing exodus of escapees and mounting insistence on reform within borders that could no longer be kept closed. Ultimately, the outside free media could not be controlled.

The second event was the 1991 war against Iraq ("Desert Storm"), which was essentially seen live around the world. CNN correspondents broadcast the hostilities from Beirut and gave us pictures and on-the-spot reports of incoming missiles and bombs. Reporters were waiting in Kuwait to welcome the allied armies. In a sense, everyone in the world saw and participated in the war.

Finally, the aborted coup against Gorbachev in the Soviet Union in the summer of 1991 was also covered continuously, live by CNN and other broadcasters to the world at large and, more importantly, to the Soviet people. The revolt was halted by a mass citizen protest, symbolized by the blockade of the government buildings in Red Square, and by aggressive world opinion. Even Gorbachev, incarcerated far from Moscow, kept up with events by listening to Voice of America.

The way that technology—the broadcast networks, electronic data banks, and so on—have changed how we live and work will become even more profound in the future. In the next few years, many people will have their own personal communication devices that they can put in their pockets or pocketbooks, or wear around their waists, so that they will always be reachable and always be able to reach others. Remember, in the chapter on systems leaders, that Craig McCaw predicts that every one will have a permanent personal communication number as part of a new portable, convenient communications system. The technologies to provide these services are now available, but their full implementation will be delayed until systems are operational, prices are lowered, and demand is created.

Experts have also forecast that the majority of the correspondence, bills, and advertisements currently delivered by the Post Office will be transmitted over telephone lines via facsimiles or computer-to-computer communications. In short, electronic mail will become as pervasive as the ordinary analog telephone, and it too will change the way we work and play. People will be able to make their own reservations, pay their bills, and get product and service information instantaneously, and they will not be restricted by the actual physical locations of service providers.

What do these changes mean to us and what are their implications for strategic leadership?

The world will become even smaller and more interdependent, as we are able to link up directly with people in all parts of the world in written, video, and oral communications. Thus, companies in one part of the world may be able to sell their products directly to consumers or businesses in another without using distributors or retailers. Consumers can request and receive information, transact the order, and pay the bill electronically with no physical exchange of paper. Debt cards, personal identification, and automatic withdrawals will make the process easy and convenient. With the improvement of the express carrier networks, led by Federal Express and United Parcel, the goods can even be delivered in a day or a few days. The size and complexity of the products may increase transaction time, but it is conceivable that cars, televisions, and furniture could be shipped by plane if speed is important.

The shrinking world will create a number of new businesses and change existing ones. Products must be designed to meet global and multinational needs. They may have to be made lighter and more durable to withstand airline shipping. Innovations in style, features, and materials will provide the competitive advantage and so offer new opportunities to the product-oriented risktaker leader. To a great degree, the Japanese have already addressed and solved some of these issues. They have demonstrated their ability to make high-quality, high-performance products that can be sold in other developed nations with considerable customer satisfaction. American leaders will have to adopt the Japanese "island mentality." They need to think of the United States as a large island, or chain of islands, on which exports are critical for survival. Thinking globally does not mean, however, believing you can develop a global product that can be sold everywhere without modifications. The concept of a global car, for instance, is destructive, because it is based on the faulty assumption that there is a true global production and product opportunity. It reminds me of Henry Ford's conviction that he could produce one or a few car models and sell them anywhere. Leaders must realize that consumer markets are highly segmented. People are no longer satisfied with plain vanilla products and services.

In the past two decades, communications and information networks based on a mixture of satellite, fiber optic, and other technologies have proliferated. In the 1990s, these nets will become more efficient, lower cost, and highly competitive. There will be opportunities to consolidate and integrate systems. McCaw's concept becomes quite feasible. Recall, from an earlier chapter, that he wants to build a national, or even international, personal communications system that would be based initially on cellular technology but later would encompass additional approaches. This idea can be applied to all areas of information and communication systems.

McCaw apparently believes he can duplicate the success of Theodore Vail. Indeed, we do need more "Vail-type" leaders in this world, individuals who will add value by integrating independent networks. In a sense, this is the approach of Rupert Murdock in print media and Ted Turner in broadcasting. High-density television is an opportunity waiting for someone to set standards and spur the growth of this technology, just as Sarnoff did for color television. Morita of Sony appears to have the vision and game plan to be a major player in electronic systems; other Japanese, and European, firms have targeted this area also. Companies in the United States seem to be lagging, although AT&T and smaller risktakers have been refocusing their efforts on these opportunities.

I have discussed the apparent failure of the videotext and home information systems to develop and prosper, and I have pointed out that Sears and IBM have invested heavily in their Prodigy system. I am not sure whether this joint venture will work; it is cluttered, slow, and difficult to understand. I am certain, however, that there is a place for risktaking followed by caretaker leadership to develop a total system or network that will permit the consumer and the home business operator to have access to the information they need. Opportunities exist for innovators to provide equipment, software, access to telephone lines, programming, and information. Many try but few win. Successful leaders must combine product innovating and marketing talents. They must try to satisfy customer needs and not simply offer an electronic version of what already exists in various print forms. Thus, the leader must combine the characteristics of the system innovator and the problem solver.

Risktaker and caretaker leaders face new opportunities to offer new products, create new systems, identify and solve new problems, and provide new ways of selling and making transactions. Surgeon and undertaker leaders may be required, in some situations, to sort things out and to refocus companies on future opportunities.

THERE IS A SCARCITY OF QUALIFIED, MOTIVATED, AND EDUCATED WORKERS— NEED FOR EDUCATIONAL RISKTAKER

For the past two decades, experts in academia and in business have advised leaders of all organizations to protect and develop their most critical resource: people. I was working in the field at GE many years ago when "personnel departments" became "human resource departments" in response to the seriousness with which we were supposed to be taking staffing. Despite the name change, however, there has been little real progress. Too much time and attention is still spent filling out forms and going through the rituals of succession and manpower planning. Too often, human resource professionals are by-the-numbers, for-the-numbers people who do little to help their organizations prepare for future needs.

Leadership at the top is no better. CEOs make speeches about developing people and then downsize the organization and cut the very professionals they said were critical to success. Politicians decry the loss of our talents and dropout rates but then reduce the budgets and eliminate staff who can make the desired improvements. However, I am convinced that the problem is not money. Rather, it is a lack of a consistent game plan that stimulates the desire and the commitment to learn. Learning is tough work that requires discipline, not gimmicks and slogans.

Deficiencies also result from the early (sometimes forced) retirement of senior people. In the past decade, millions of skilled workers and experienced professionals have been literally bought out of their jobs by accepting the generous offers of CEOs looking for a humane way to reduce payrolls. From a short-term, expedient perspective, these early retirements offer an effective solution. However, they do generate some significant long-term consequences that should be considered. Most importantly, people are leaving who play key roles on the team that is responsible for the implementation of the leader's strategic game plan. Why are vital people pushed out? Because most company manpower systems are political and functional and not based on strategic needs. And that's because human resource staff are not part of strategy development, a practice that obviously must change if better personnel decisions are to be made.

That is the exit problem. At the entry end, the school systems are not preparing our youth for a productive future. Students receive inadequate training in reading, writing, and arithmetic. Business leaders have even harsher assessments of the U.S. educational system. We face several decades of poorly educated people to operate our businesses and run our government. In other words, we have not progressed from the beginning of the 20th century and are not prepared for the 21st century. The difference is the people at the turn of this century wanted to learn but often lacked the opportunity, while today they have the money and the opportunity but lack the ability and the motivation. We have lost the learning ethic.

Strategic leaders of all types (risktakers, caretakers, surgeons, undertakers) are needed to help solve these problems. For instance, risktakers can develop systems to enhance the educational process. William Norris, founder and long-time leader of Control Data Corporation, dedicated his abilities and the resources of his company to develop a computer-based educational system called Plato. The project required significant funding and entailed the development of special computers, workstations, and software. Plato worked, but when Norris retired, the project was sold. Although Norris was called a dreamer and criticized for his lack of attention to maximizing "shareholder value," he is the type of leader we need, one who takes a personal financial risk. We need leaders like William Norris to create products that enhance learning rather than replace learning. For instance, calculators and electronic spellers can be valuable if they require users to understand the principles and not just be human input devices. I think the vision of the Edison Project envisioned by Christopher Whittle, CEO of Whittle Communications and Benno C. Schmidt, ex-president of Yale University reflects the type of risktaking required to change education.[1] It is not the total answer and we need caretaker educators who give continuity to the system, who keep the fundamental winning approaches to teaching and not try gimmicky changes for change sake. The caretaker educator is the teacher I remember from the 1950s and 1960s who motivated by demanding results and was willing to explain and teach. There are still some teachers who have dedicated their lives to learning, and we—as citizens and as business leaders—must encourage and support them at all levels of the education system.

The National Science Foundation predicts a shortage of 540,000 scientists and engineers by the year 2000. Too many of our best minds are going into the financial and legal services areas. Strategic leaders with the drive and ability to sell need to encourage people to be teachers, engineers, and scientists, to be producers and creators rather than mere manipulators of the way we buy and sell assets and stocks. Such leaders may be inside companies as well as inside the schools. Foundation money has been invested, with some success, to get educators and business leaders talking to each other, but more efforts are needed.

We need leaders who understand that teamwork entails company commitment to its people and not just employee loyalty to the organization. That means people must be given an opportunity to learn and develop. When I started at GE, we had training programs at all levels and for all purposes. There were apprentice programs that permitted high school students to learn a trade and get a degree. GE offered entry-level training in finance, marketing, sales, manufacturing, purchasing, and human resources. The best students were selected and given a chance to learn and grow. There were no guarantees, no free lunch. We had other programs for MBAs and graduate lawyers. In short, GE invested in the individual, and the individual became part of the team. Those programs should be established in companies across the country.

We need surgeon or undertaker leaders in schools and business to review the effectiveness of instructional programs and make changes when necessary. Continuity is valuable, but academics and industrial trainers can get stuck on approaches that have lost their vitality. Many tend to become lazy and teach what is convenient or easy. Surgeon and undertaker strategic leaders must attack the sacred cows of instruction, including the occasional beloved professor, who may have lost his or her teaching ability and professional know-how.

Overall, the educational arena requires a blending of creativity and stability; it is fertile ground for problem-solving leadership. Leaders must do a thorough assessment and then seek alternatives. For example, if the talents of those now in the work force are inadequate, leaders must look elsewhere in the short term. Many early retirees have become third-party vendors, providing service and know-how on a contract or temporary basis. This arrangement gives more freedom to both the companies and the individuals. It is not, however, a long-term solution for the employer.

The communication technologies that are turning us into a global village provide another solution to the human resources problem. Leaders can sometimes tap into talents at distant locations, even in foreign lands, through telephone, video, computer, and fax if the actual physical presence of the expert is not critical.

If the people must be on the scene, perhaps they can be imported from another country. Many U.S. citizens are angry because top business and technical schools have a high percentage of foreign students. Their argument that this influx restricts opportunities for Americans is not justified, however. In some cases, U.S. students don't have the interest or the background. The schools are merely recruiting the best and most motivated candidates they can find, which is both logical and legal. If a school is merely filling out quotas, however, that is wrong and illegal. Competition is good, but it needs to be a level playing field where the rules are the same for everybody.

TOO MANY LEADERS FOCUS ON THE SHAREHOLDERS AND NOT THE STAKEHOLDERS— NEED FOR LONG TERM CARETAKERS

I've talked about the problem of short-range thinking throughout this book. Most commentators place the blame on the prevailing measurement system in business and the pressure on CEOs to make decisions that optimize short-term profits. The concept of "maximizing shareholder value" has come to dominate the thinking of management. It is a "slogan" recited with little understanding of its real meaning and what it is doing to the future of our institutions. We must realize who the shareholders are and think about why their interests should be paramount. Today, the vast majority of company equity is owned by institutions. These sophisticated, highly computerized, financial players are not real shareholders. They are short-term investors, motivated only to achieve short-term gains. Their time horizon might be only days, hours, or even minutes. They use stocks to balance their portfolio. Some stocks are considered speculative; others are viewed as "parking lots," that is, as a place to store funds as long as they produce average returns and are safe. Should leaders be making decisions on the basis of whether or not they will do the most for these investors?

Do not underestimate this problem. Aggressive, short-term, large-volume investors incite fears of corporate takeovers in the minds of top management, and not without reason. We have seen CEOs make some destructive moves to counter the threat, including taking the company private through leveraged buyouts. The company takes on major debt to pay off the shareholders and hopes it can come up with enough cash to pay the bills. As a result of such activities, "between 1980 and 1988, the ratio of corporate debt to net worth at American companies climbed from 30 percent to 52 percent." Buyouts and takeovers lead to bidding wars, in which the winners get in over their heads and can't make the payments. In 1990, Robert Mercer, the former CEO of Goodyear, complained, "We're spending $1 million a day in unnecessary interest expense that is going to 17 banks around the world." This was a result of having to fight off a raid by Britain's James Goldsmith. Goodyear was forced to take on $2.6 billion in debt. He continued "I fail to see what the interest payments add to the total development of this company."[2]

Short-term thinking is not just a business phenomenon; it has become a U.S. trait. Our schools teach students by example to seek short-term goals. The grading system often does not measure knowledge; it measures the ability to satisfy a specific professor or teacher. Entrance exams measure the ability to make a quick response and not to solve problems. In fact, Americans have little patience with problems that are too complex or that require long-range solutions. We are enamored with the "one-minute manager" or the "one-minute problem solver." We reward managers, as we do sports and entertainment stars, for providing instant gratification.

Our society teaches us to go for the big hit and then move on. The "best" CEOs and senior managers have learned that lesson well. They were put on the fast track and moved rapidly through their organizations, staying just long enough in positions to see the challenges but not meet them. Worse, they were told to solve complex problems with quick fixes. That is why so many businesses are in trouble today. Managers who initiated changes often were not around when they were tested and, frequently, failed. In many cases, these individuals had been promoted to positions that permitted them to hide the problems or even get rid of them by selling the business or the product line.

Senior managers should make the commitment to take on longer term assignments. They should remain in a post long enough to be measured on how well a strategy works. The few examples of GE leaders I have used (Charles Reed, Gerhardt Neuman, and Willard Sahloff) demonstrate what I mean. These individuals literally dedicated their careers to the development and implementation of strategies and were in leadership positions long enough to have the results known. They were given latitude to make the tough decisions and the authority to select a team and successors to work for the long haul.

Establishing a long-term perspective means developing human resources at all levels. That will require a return to basics in education, the use of new systems and technology to enhance learning, and a commitment to lifelong learning so that we continue to grow. We must utilize the talents of all our people, including the prematurely retired. If we do not, our competitive position will decline even further.

In addition, it may be possible to make more productive use of the increasingly large amount of capital, estimated at over $2.6 trillion, stashed away in pension funds. Why can't a significant percentage of this money be used by caretaker leaders to invest in their organizations's future? This assistance would be similar to that provided by Japanese banks to their companies. Of course, caretaker leaders must commit themselves to producing a yield sufficient to meet the payment obligations of the pension funds. These funds can't be a windfall for the greedy manager or a target of the unscrupulous asset stripper.

THE DRUG CULTURE IMPACTS ALL ASPECTS OF SOCIETY—NEED FOR TOUGH-MINDED PROBLEM SOLVING RISKTAKERS FOLLOWED BY CARETAKERS

Drug abuse contributes to the low level of educational achievement in America and elsewhere in the world; it has a negative impact on the way people work, their motivation, and their ability to learn and benefit from training. Drugs have had and will continue to have serious implications for the marketplace and the overall competitive environment. And don't forget that alcohol is part of the drug problem. We need risktaker leaders to solve this problem in every area of society. We need leaders in government willing to take action to curtail the use of drugs beyond just punishing sellers and distributors.

Those who operate the drug trade are very good businesspeople. The Colombian drug cartels and their U.S. criminal distributors consistently implement a classic logistical strategy. They understand how to create demand by offering free samples to get new users hooked. They pay their distributors and retailers very well and "terminate" them if they show disloyalty. They price low and continue to experiment with methods for increasing yields. Enforcement personnel are bought off or scared off. In short, the drug dealers have installed a total system, which they maintain well. They are very bottom-line oriented but are willing to take the long-term view.

Since the only way they can make money is to sell the product, the lasting and effective way to stop them is to cut off the business and the market. Thus, we need risktakers in government willing to identify users and get them to stop. Such a strategy would include effective advertising and promotion displaying the problems associated with drug and alcohol use. A similar campaign focusing on drinking and driving has had some success. The primary objective is to reduce the demand for drugs and thus shrink the market and the profitability of the business.

A different solution has been proposed by those who cite the lessons of Prohibition; namely, that it increased rather than reduced the nation's consumption of alcohol. The thinking here is that drugs could be controlled by licensing their distribution and sale, as is done with alcohol today. This program will require the efforts of the same sort of risktakers who have made the liquor and beer business socially and economically feasible. Once the system is developed, caretaker leaders can manage it effectively for the long run. Many companies, including those in (legal) drugs, beverages, and liquors, are positioning themselves for this possibility.

There is no simple solution to the drug abuse problem, and any simple proposal isn't worth consideration. To resolve this complex situation, we need real leadership.

THE UNITED STATES CONTINUES TO BE A DEBTOR NATION—NEED FOR SURGEONS TO SET PRIORITIES

The philosophy of "buy now and pay later" has been both a positive and a negative force in U.S. economic history. Spending borrowed money has enabled companies and industries to grow more rapidly and has increased the opportunities for individuals to enjoy a much higher standard of living. If people waited to make major purchases such as a home, car, or college education until they had enough saved to pay for them, our market size and growth rate would be much smaller. However, the benefits of buying on credit are threatened if the practice is taken to the extreme. In the past two decades, every government, all institutions, and most people seem to have decided that carrying a large amount of debt is fine. Advertisements portray individuals making spontaneous purchases using VISA, American Express, or some other form of plastic money. Financial experts advise us that we are foolish to have a large equity in our homes and that it is smart to take out loans on that equity. Our consumer society appears dedicated to living only for the present.

Our government has become extraordinarily adept at deficit spending. Our leaders proclaim that we must reduce the national debt, but they lack the political will to take the heat and do the job. (Our three most recent presidents have promised to eliminate the debt, but it has increased during each of their terms in office.) Government officials use every accounting gimmick to hide the debt, some of which, like off-balance sheet financing, are, if not unethical, at least not good business practices. Many state and city governments can't legally run deficits, but they too use questionable accounting practices and issue bonds as a form of borrowing. At the national level, the cost of paying the interest on the debt, and of making social security and other entitlement payments, has caused the decline of the value of the dollar, which has made U.S. assets such bargains that they are swooped up by foreign investors. We owe the debt not just to ourselves, but to other nations, and our children will owe it, too.

To solve this problem we will first need a surgeon leader strong enough to make the tough decisions and trade-offs. Programs that by any standard are "pork barrel" must be eliminated. Although these are relatively small and have little impact on balancing the budget, cutting them will send a message that the leader is serious. Next, low-priority programs must be reduced. Defense spending must be managed better. We need to determine whether we must continue to act as the world's unpaid police officer. If Japan wants protection, it should pay for it. (If Japan decides to rearm, however, it may be necessary to monitor its military growth.) The same holds true for Europe. One of the lessons of the breakup of the Communist bloc is that military defense is powerless without a strong national economy. Our politicians do not seem to have grasped this truth.

The surgeon leader will need widespread popular support to make these reforms. Unfortunately, the history of our country indicates that a major crisis is necessary to mobilize the populace. Franklin D. Roosevelt was able to capitalize on the fear generated by the Great Depression to take decisive action. And I believe that sort of crisis is coming. We may see more local and state governments go into default. At that point, let us hope we have a leader who can take charge.

Once the surgeon has restructured spending, reset priorities, and lowered the deficit, then caretaker leaders can carry on with the job. These will be professional managers who can install workable systems and programs. We will need leaders like Robert Moses to rebuild the country's infrastructure and install sound management. They will be systems builders and problem solvers who can motivate a work force to do big jobs. They must be supported by salespeople who can present reality not pipe dreams.

After the system is in order, we can afford risktaker innovators to create new social programs (reversing the usual life cycle sequence of risktaker to caretaker to surgeon). However, we cannot follow the example of Lyndon Johnson, who tried to do everything at once and wound up in despair. Johnson wanted to fight the war in Vietnam and the domestic "War on Poverty" simultaneously. Two fronts was too many. Both "wars" were expensive and risky; neither worked, and the budget suffered. Timing and realism are critical to this phase of leadership.

Individuals, local governments, and businesses must follow the national leader's example and get their financial houses in order. That will require leadership of the best sort everywhere.

There are profound implications to increasing savings and decreasing credit. The markets are likely to grow slower, and consumers are likely to demand better quality products that last. We can learn from the past when Americans were more savings oriented, or, perhaps better, from the savings tendencies of Japan and some European nations in the present. Because Japanese savings rates have been very high and interest rates low, Japanese companies have had access to low-cost capital, which has permitted them to build and improve production facilities and invest in R&D. Thus, they have the longer term perspective that we have wished for our government and business leaders. However, slower growing markets will lessen our competitive aggressiveness and our ability to reduce costs from volume production and the learning curve. On the other hand, it will force a broader market perspective and encourage more international development. Further, the use of planned obsolescence to entice buyers to trade in and up will become increasingly difficult.

THE UNEXPECTED, DYNAMIC COLLAPSE OF THE "PLANNED ECONOMIES" CREATES BOTH CHAOS AND OPPORTUNITIES—NEED RISKTAKERS TO CAPITALIZE ON UNDERTAKERS IN RUSSIA AND EASTERN EUROPE

The dramatic, unexpected events of the late 1980s and early 1990s in what was once the Soviet Union and its Eastern European allies will impact the world for decades. The critical issue is whether the new governments will be able to solve some of their major problems and avoid bloodshed. I am not knowledgeable enough even to guess at what will happen next. However, I can offer an analysis of the situation from the perspective of strategic leadership.

Clearly, Gorbachev was an undertaker leader, even if he did not fully comprehend all the ramifications of his actions. His "restructuring" of the Soviet Union had a ripple effect across Eastern Europe that was strong enough to bring down governments and shred the Iron Curtain, as several nations disassociated themselves from Communism. Many have tried to hold free, multiparty elections and establish more capitalistic economies. These enormous changes will present significant opportunities for risktakers with the ambition to fill the void.

Opportunities for Development

First, the area will need innovative, quality products that are reasonably priced and convenient to buy. Some Western companies have already established a foothold in the consumer market. For instance, GE has acquired 50 percent of Tunsgrum, a Hungarian company that makes low-priced electric lamps. Tunsgrum was once a licensee of GE and, in fact, helped GE develop the tungsten required for the early electric lamps when GE had an equity position in the company prior to World War II. Tunsgrum is well positioned in Europe and has even exported low-priced electric bulbs to the United States. Jack Welch said, "We're trying to position ourselves for the decade ahead. It's a prudent risk for this point of history." Other major firms are launching themselves into the Eastern European market, including the German firm Triumph-Adler and the Swiss/Swedish multinational ABB Asea Brown Boveri Ltd.[3]

Any ventures in this turbulent region are, of course, quite risky. In an article printed late in 1989, *Business Week* suggested that the "model for the East could be such neutral countries as Austria and Sweden, with free markets but some state ownership and cradle to grave social safety nets." The goal is some happy combination of social stability and economic freedom that will allow development without chaos.

The Russian market will also probably grow quite rapidly. Leaders venturing here will need an understanding of the history and culture of the people and at least a staff of translators and foreign language experts. They will also have to possess or hire the talent to decipher the laws.

If history is repeated, U.S. companies will not be able merely to export to these countries; they must make acquisitions, produce in the host country, and form alliances with local vendors and barter rather than just sell. The Europeans and the Japanese have demonstrated better skills in these areas and should have the competitive advantage. The Japanese industrial giants are all allied in some manner with trading companies and understand how to barter and trade. Further, they have the resources to offer low-cost, long-term loans. The United States was once the master at financing, but we have lost our position because we can't control our own debt.

The second opportunity will be to help solve major national and business problems. These nations need to construct modern efficient factories, rebuild their national infrastructures, and train productive work forces. They will need technical help in all these endeavors. This is one of the most significant rebuilding opportunities since the end of World War II. The United States was the only real player in the reconstruction of Japan and Western Europe; now we will have to compete with them in the restoration of Eastern Europe and the republics of the former Soviet Union. In addition, U.S. firms will be at a disadvantage because they are less skilled in forming alliances with firms from other nations, which will be critical to problem solving in this area of the world. Successful alliances require unselfish leadership willing to allow all the partners to achieve their goals and become winners. Unfortunately, Americans are taught to compete and not to share; we are used to win/lose rather than win/win situations. Further, U.S. antitrust laws may inhibit the sort of multinational relationship needed.

The third major opportunity involves creating new, and improving existing, sales and distribution channels. State-controlled economies are highly bureaucratic. Russian retail stores are notorious for long lines and shortages; it almost seems as though the system were designed to limit goods and restrict sales. If the capitalist system is adopted and consumer spending increases, U.S. selling and marketing leaders may prosper. For instance, McDonald's Moscow operation is currently flourishing, and, as I described in an earlier chapter, Avon has successfully applied its home direct selling approach in developing nations, in former Communist states, and even in China. Large department stores such as Sears and JC Penney and discount stores such as Wal-Mart and KMart will likely find opportunities to open outlets or ally themselves with merchants in these countries. Risktaker leaders can be winners there.

REBUILD THE INFRASTRUCTURE AND THE WAY OF LIFE—NEED FOR ANOTHER ROBERT MOSES

In Chapter 11 I described the leadership achievements of Robert Moses. The United States, possibly the entire world, needs more civil servants of the talents and abilities of Robert Moses. I recognize that he was not the most popular man of his time and that he was a tyrant in many ways, but this does not mean that his leadership skills should not be cloned. Let's examine some of the tasks that a risktaker innovator could attack.

First, the highways are in complete disarray. Many of the roads and bridges are in virtual collapse. Though billions of dollars are being spent to fix them, they are being repaired with little creativity and a lack of urgency. Those in charge seem to be interested in spending time and money and not in getting the job done.

Second, mass transit is still not popular. Most people are not interested in using the systems, even after they have been upgraded. There is a concern for safety and the feeling that those who operate the systems don't care about being on time or even safe.

Third, the airports are congested and often unsafe as well. The frequent traveler and tourist is subjected to long delays, inadequate parking, and in many cases, unpleasant personnel.

The list can extend to water supplies and garbage, as well as deterioration of our parks, beaches and so on.

We need a risktaker leader to develop a long term plan and make it work. Moses demonstrated that roads, bridges, beaches, and parks could be built on a business and quick payback basis. His Henry Hudson Parkway was profitable in less than five years. He was a man of vision and this is what we need in the coming decade.

Beware of Trend Extrapolation: All Changes Do Not Proceed as Anticipated—Need to Transition Leadership and Not Permit Them to Stay Beyond Their Time

In a volatile geopolitical environment, forces set in motion may not remain on the path they first follow. The old guard Communists may, for instance, stage a counterrevolution and retake power. The Chinese leaders have certainly been able to reassert control, at least for the time being. If the new leaders in Eastern Europe cannot rebuild their countries and give their people what they want, violent civil unrest could result.

The collapse of the Soviet Union and the creation of a rather loose federation of republics has produced a very unstable situation. Recall that Russia suffered through a civil war in the early 1900s after the Czar was overthrown and before Lenin's forces assumed control. (Civil wars are particularly destructive to the fabric of the country; the American Civil War inflicted wounds that took 100 years to heal.) The former Soviet republics are a diverse collection of hundreds of nationalities and languages. The Moslems identify more with Iran and Iraq than they do with Moscow. Nationalistic and religious passions have been stifled for decades; many groups bitterly resent the European Russians and view them as conquerors rather than countrymen. On the other side, past rulers of the Soviet Union, especially the military, no doubt resent their loss of power and privilege. Conditions are ripe for unrest and possibly even civil war.

If there is a war, all the consumer and industrial opportunities will not materialize. However, the demand for war equipment and weapons will grow dramatically. In that event, as the leader in war materials, the United States is well positioned. Major hostilities in Eastern Europe and the former Soviet Union would reconfigure the world. The Japanese may feel compelled to rearm. Besides the military and political aspects of that decision, it would mean they would have less to invest in consumer businesses and industry, their economy would decline, and they too might be burdened with major debt.

The point of these *speculations* (they are *not* predictions) is that while leaders must make assumptions about the future in order to plan and implement strategy, they must realize they are dealing with uncertainty. Assumptions are only assumptions. Leaders who become too arrogant about their ability to predict events are headed toward disaster. They must have the good sense and humility to plan for contingencies and build flexibility into their systems.

PARALLELS TO THE PAST—NEED LEADERS THAT UNDERSTAND HISTORY!

One excellent way to improve your power of prediction of the future and acquire a little humility is to study history. Many conditions of today are similar to those of the 1920s and 1930s. In both eras, for instance, we see an unstable Europe. Immediately after World War I, many new and idealistic governments formed. In Germany, leaders tried to do too much too soon, and the economy fell apart. In the resulting hyperinflation, the Mark became so worthless that people had to carry around bags of money to buy food and other basic essentials. In the social turmoil, a little-known paperhanger came to power—Adolf Hitler. In Russia, the first socialist government, led by Alexander Kerensky, was proceeding with some well-conceived, moderate changes when it was overrun by events. Lenin and the Communists took control, and they held it tightly for over three generations.

In the 1920s and 1930s, the Germans sought to regain the territories they had lost in World War I. Today, Germany is reunited after 45 years of separation, and it threatens to become the most powerful military and economic force in Europe. During Stalin's long reign, the Soviet Union acquired vast territory by swallowing small independent states in the Baltics and to the south of Russia. Today, these are the republics that have seceded or are in the process of secession.

The second parallel involves the atmosphere in the United States. Then as now, many people were willing to bet their savings and live beyond their means. Governments were and are in debt; too many people were and are out of work and without shelter. The gap between rich and poor was and is large and growing. The nation's infrastructure was and is in disarray.

Third, in the 1920s and 1930s, the Japanese were feeling strong to the point of invincibility. They conquered China, Burma, and Korea easily. Their leaders told them they were the chosen race whose destiny was to rule the world. The Japanese had little respect for the United States and its ability or will to fight. Today, the Japanese are again winning at will, this time on the economic battlefields. Their business managers and technocrats are moving around the world and taking market share. They often express little regard for the United States' ability and will to work hard, that is, to fight. A *Business Week* poll conducted in late 1989 indicated, "The Japanese think America's growing dependence on Japanese technology gives Japan more clout in dealing with the U.S. A plurality expect their country to eventually replace America as the world's leading economic and political power."[4]

Americans have also come to fear the Japanese. Many Americans resent them acquiring U.S. land and key properties—so much so that there is talk of limiting Japanese investment, and even production, in America. We still like Japanese autos and consumer electronics, but we are beginning to feel uneasy about buying them. More and more Americans are working for Japanese managers in Japanese-owned plants in the United States. So far, relations have been largely amicable, but, as I have pointed out earlier, that natural initial positive response may turn negative as workers get frustrated in boring jobs or face layoffs.

Japanese Miscalculations: History Forgotten

Japanese youth have not experienced the pains of war or the distress of the postwar period. They may begin to believe their own press releases or, even worse, accept the gloom and doom of the U.S. press. If so, they will likely overestimate their own strengths and force the United States into open economic warfare. According to *Business Week*, "A number of experts worry that a modern form of nationalism could turn hostile if the Japanese and the U.S. government mismanage their increasingly fractious relationship. . . . A majority of Japanese think they should rely less on the United States for military security."[5] The *potential* parallel with the 1930s and 1940s is frightening.

Strategic leaders of all nationalities need to understand history to avoid repeating the mistakes of the past. That many strategic leaders have not been personally affected by the Great Depression and World War II is a concern. The past 40 years have been prosperous, and the people who will be running governments and businesses in Europe, Japan, and the United States have not experienced hard times. They will have less inclination to temper the emerging global economic competition. The struggle for market share cannot become a real "war" with conquering "winners" and devastated "losers." The world needs long-term strategies consistent with the talents and personality characteristics of caretaker leaders. We need strategic leaders with the maturity to accept that they don't know all the answers and the patience to manage both the upswings and downswings of fortune.

WILL WE HAVE ENOUGH ENERGY
AND ELECTRICITY?—NEED "INFRASTRUCTURE"
RISKTAKERS ESPECIALLY IN THE ENERGY SECTORS

Just a decade ago, the United States was in a crisis mode. Motorists were forced to wait in long and frustrating lines for gasoline. The price of heating oil and gasoline went through the roof. Since most electrical power was generated by oil, the price of electricity also skyrocketed. Politicians panicked. They advocated the creation of new alternative forms of energy and openly expressed concern about the potential world domination by the OPEC oil cartel. In time, however, the gas lines dwindled, prices fell, and OPEC proved unable to control its own members. Crisis talk faded and so did plans to prevent a recurrence. In fact, the United States is probably now more dependent on imported oil from the Middle East. Conservation has declined, and consumers are more interested in the horsepower of their cars than gas mileage. Domestic oil production is in a slump, and the country has no real alternatives to oil. History again seems ready to repeat.

Consequently, strategic leaders in business and government must examine their energy dependencies. For instance, those planning the development of new, or the improvement of existing, products must consider what would happen should oil again become scarce or rise steeply in price. How would big-ticket items be affected? Would people build massive new homes if they could not afford to heat them? Would they want fuel-efficient cars again? What about labor-saving appliances, would they be cost effective?

When we ask energy-related questions, however, we frequently ignore one resource more critical than oil to our prosperity, or even to our survival, because we take for granted that it will always be available in abundance. That energy source is electricity. From my long association with GE, I have grown to respect the wisdom of the long-range planning of the leaders in the electrical industry. I have described the leadership skills of Edison, Westinghouse, Swope, and others. I have also stressed several times in this book that the electrical industry is in trouble.

U.S. electrical equipment companies have not been aggressively investing in new forms of generating and transmitting equipment. In fact, there is only one committed nuclear equipment and systems company. The use of nuclear power has not grown; instead, some of the plants that were scheduled to come on line have been mothballed or converted to fossil fuels. Mario Cuomo and other political leaders have tried to rip down the plant on Long Island. Cuomo contends the plant is not safe and that inadequate plans have been made for the evacuation of the island. This is a legitimate concern, but simply abandoning the plant does not solve the energy problem.

Managers of electrical utilities have been forced to buy power from others and promote conservation. Their actions represent the implementation of a harvest strategy, an understandable approach for individuals who are responsible to their shareholders and who have not been rewarded for taking risks. Nonetheless, harvesting does not help alleviate a potential energy shortfall.

One solution to the difficulty of building power-generating plants in populated areas is the use of high-voltage transmission to move power from plants in more desolate regions. The power grid permits companies to purchase power from distant sources when they need it. For instance, New York purchases from hydro plants in Canada. Hydro is an excellent source of power because it is not polluting and the water is not really "consumed." However, conservation and consumer groups are protesting against the use of high-voltage lines. The recent scare involves the electro-mechanical ring that emanates from the lines and is injurious to the health of people living near them. Of course, that is a problem that must be addressed, but it also gives us another reason to be concerned about the shortage of electrical power in the future.

Many people, including business and government leaders forget about our dependence on electricity. The great New York City area blackout of 1966 was a severe disruption, and there have been the "inconveniences" of smaller electrical outages and "brownouts." In the darkness, the streets belong to the gangs and the looters. Stoplights don't work, and traffic is snarled worse than usual. Railroads shut down. Office and apartment buildings don't have functioning elevators or air-conditioning. Nor do we have oil or gas heat, because electricity is needed to start the pumps. In some places water is pumped with electrical power, too. Certain buildings do not have phone service because the PBXs work on electricity. In short, without electricity nothing works, and we can't survive for long.

Although some argue that we have ample electricity, the data indicate our reserves are low. By the year 2000 and beyond, many locations will be forced to ration electricity or be without it altogether. Offices may close, factories may shut down, and the quality of life may decline. Nor is this a global problem, as some would insist. The Japanese and Europeans have made major investments in nuclear plants and have become less dependent on oil and gas. The United States will need decades to catch up.

We need major efforts from risktaker and caretaker leaders to improve the prospects. We will need alliances between the government, business, and the electrical industry. We will have to find new ways of generating and transmitting electricity. We must also address safety concerns and give the public a realistic overview of our energy capacity. People deserve to know the trade-offs. The United States must have a healthy electrical industry to survive and grow. Indeed, we should evaluate carefully the availability of all our resources. Strength comes from honest awareness; vulnerability is the product of self-delusion and ignorance.

CONCLUSION

I started with the premise that different types (product innovator, problem solver, system builder, seller, and so on) and styles (risktaker, caretaker, surgeon, undertaker) of leaders are required for different situations. Each of the trends and problems I have outlined in this chapter will require the right mix and sequence of each of these leaders. The real issue is whether we will have the right type and style of leader at the right time.

I have real concerns in that regard. I have seen too much attention paid to risktakers and those whom I would term "great pretenders." I know there is no one answer to any problem and there is no such thing as a "leader for all seasons." I hope that this book will encourage risktakers not only to take additional risks but also to recognize that they must groom a successor and turn their enterprise over to that caretaker leader at the right time. We must honor the caretakers and the surgeons and undertakers who follow. We should appreciate that these leaders must eliminate the parts of the organization that are not doing their jobs. But those cuts must be made for sound strategic reasons. We can't afford more asset strippers who only act for themselves.

15

Leaders for
All Seasons

Throughout this book, I have asserted that there is no one style or type of leader for all seasons. Different types and styles of leaders fit different business (and nonbusiness) situations depending on the organization's nature, life cycle phase, and particular competitive environment. As I have researched and written the book, I have sought examples of individuals who could be the exception to this rule. I was hoping I could nominate at least one person who had the characteristics of the risktaker, caretaker, surgeon, and undertaker and who had excelled in several of the strategic drivers.

I have been impressed with Stanley C. Gault, who has served as a caretaker, risktaker, and surgeon during his highly successful career, while exhibiting many characteristics of the strategic leader. I first knew Stan Gault when he was the leader of General Electric's Major Appliance Group. In this position, he was a strong evolutionary caretaking leader, who grew the business profitably. In 1980, he recognized that he would not become the CEO of General Electric and so assumed the leadership of Rubbermaid. In his decade at Rubbermaid, Stan became a dynamic risktaker and grew this company from $300 million to $1.3 billion, while maintaining over an 8.5% return on sales and 21% return on equity. Recognizing the need to have a successor, Stan selected Walt Williams and retired in 1991. During his tenure at Rubbermaid, Stan initiated systems and practices that have made the company a recognized marketing and product leader. Stan is a skilled marketing innovator and understands how to meet customer needs consistently. Upon retirement, Stan assumed a new challenge. He has taken over as CEO of a lagging Goodyear. In this role, Mr. Gault is likely to have to assume the characteristics of a surgeon as well as stabilize and grow the company. In short, Stan has shown the ability to lead in a variety of situations and exhibited many of the leadership styles we have discussed.

Even though there may be other examples of leaders for multiple seasons, I am still convinced that no one person can be the all-purpose leader for every occasion. Those individuals who do change style often appear to have been coerced and to have lost some measure of effectiveness. Thus, I must stand behind my original basic premise.

There may, however, be institutions and companies that can be described as "organizations for all seasons." Because I have spent much of my life (30 years, in fact) working for General Electric, I have described several people from GE to exemplify various types and styles of leadership. I have come to see GE as remarkable in its ability to tolerate and even encourage a wide variety of leaders. General Electric is an eclectic institution, a diversified company with a mixture of mature, rapidly growing, and embryonic products and services. Its markets cover all aspects of the gross national product: consumer, industrial, military and aerospace products; financial and business services; chemicals, materials, and many other substances of this world. Thus, it should not be surprising that GE's sundry leaders represent every type and style.

GE's current chairman, Jack Welch, is able to handle and promote this leadership diversity. In fact, Welch himself might be a candidate for the unattainable title, "Leader for All Seasons." But I think he is more a calculated risktaker than any other type. He is an inspiring missionary, with a strong talent and appreciation for both growth through innovation and the creative financial efforts necessary to produce good bottom-line results. Welch's defining gift, however, is his ability to appoint leaders to, and maintain them in, the businesses for which they are most suited.

That aptitude has also defined GE over its history. Most leaders of GE businesses have been on the job for a long time and thus have been able to develop and implement long-term game plans. Although the company has the long-term perspective, it also holds managers to short-term objectives and goals. GE evaluates quarterly the numbers and how the numbers are achieved. I witnessed on a number of occasions, during Reg Jones's leadership, when managers had not met the projected numbers, but the long-term strategy was on course and so still continued. Why? Because the deviation was based on real data and not excuses, emotional appeals, or rationalizations. "Trust me" was not an adequate reason to continue. Likewise, I saw the numbers achieved and the strategy not implemented. In this situation, the business unit management was required to justify itself. If the data backed them up, they were given the go-ahead to continue. Though I have not been part of GE for nearly a decade, I believe this approach is still practiced.

Jack Welch, during his multiseasonal leadership of GE, has made decisions in support of leaders who were risktakers, caretakers, and even surgeons or undertakers. GE in this period has been highly selective in what it wanted to do and where it wanted to go. It has been a strategically planned portfolio company, in the positive sense of the concept.

Welch has had to perform skilled surgery in certain cases. Utah International, for instance, had been a major coal, copper, and uranium producer and looked financially promising when it was offered to GE by one of the board members during Reg Jones's reign. Unfortunately, after GE made the acquisition, the coal and copper markets declined, and because much of Utah International's assets were in South Africa, the uranium also suffered. Welch cut the company's losses and got out. He also sold Housewares, the Sahloff innovation, to Black and Decker. Then he was able to trade television and audio electronics to Thompson Houston of France for its medical systems business, which was considered very attractive by GE.

These last two transactions demonstrate the leadership and strategic genius of Jack Welch. For the first time in its history, the company sold the "GE" monogram. Welch was willing to sell the monogram to the purchaser of a GE business unit on a time-phased basis. In the case of Housewares, Black and Decker was allowed to sell under the GE name for three years and then revert completely to its own brand. B&D was thus able to phase in its brands successfully, and at the same time, GE was able to reap some extra profit by selling its reputation, that is, the use of its name. The strategic change was a calculated risk, which previous leaders had declined to take for fear that the purchaser would not maintain quality and so tarnish the GE monogram. Welch protected the company by limiting the time the name could be used. In contrast, Westinghouse did not place time constraints when it sold its monogram, and now the Westinghouse name is on low-end appliances and products, which may cause the company long-term problems.

The trade with Thompson Houston came after GE had acquired RCA at a bargain price. After careful strategic portfolio analysis, Welch kept cash-rich NBC and RCA's aerospace business but sold RCA's record company and satellite business. Then he invested in RCA and created the impression that GE was interested in continuing to be a leader in this market, which was consistent with the long-running company policy of being number one or two in an industry. Thompson Houston was attracted to the television business (which does not include NBC broadcasting) and was willing to trade its medical systems business, plus cash.

GE has taken a number of other product/market risks during the past decade. Brian Rowe has bet billions on his division's ability to gain share in the commercial jet engine business. Glen Hiner of the Engineered Plastics Division (now CEO of Corning Fiberglass) has gambled on new applications and the development of new materials on a global basis. But the company's biggest risks have been in financial services. GE Credit was originally designed to help sell appliances. It is now a global multi-billion-dollar business and a major player in leasing, credit cards, receivables management, insurance, reinsurance, auto auctioning, venture capital, and investment banking. Growth has been achieved through a skillful combination of internal development, asset leveraging, and acquisitions. Although GE Credit (now G.E. Capital) has been a highly profitable business, it also faces major risks because it has become more a bank and global financier than a credit company.

Despite these risktaker ventures, GE is, and always has been, a caretaker style company. All the major divisions—Lighting, Medical Systems, Major Appliances, Industrial and Power Generation, and Communications—have been led by people who believed in and practiced evolutionary growth. They continue to evolve their markets but focus on making the bottom line. They continue to prosper, maintain, even grow market share and remain major predictable earnings generators.

GE has been able to develop, reward, and encourage leadership of all types. The company has had product innovators, missionary salespeople, and cost-oriented production people. The financial arm has produced financial leaders.

GE believes strongly in education and development. Crotonville, its management development institute, was created by Ralph Cordiner to develop general management skills critical to his decentralization moves. It was used by Fred Borch to develop strategic thinking and management skills. Borch was the leader who introduced strategic management to GE. I was part of this major effort to convert GE people from operating to strategic managers. Reg Jones employed the institute to develop skills in cost and productivity areas when these became critical in the 1970s. Crotonville is now part of Welch's efforts to change the corporate culture. His latest thrust is to teach people to set strategic priorities and create realistic game plans to reach their objectives.

GE has also a tradition of leadership succession planning. However, as I pointed out earlier, all the key GE businesses have been led by the same management team since Welch assumed command, although some with problems have had new leaders take over. Thus, succession planning is one of the major unknowns in GE today. Welch is breaking with the company history of 10-year leadership cycles. We will need to watch the situation closely to see whether a 20-year reign creates the leadership problems other firms have experienced when the top individual stays around a very long time.

Nonetheless, GE has demonstrated over the years, and in particular under Jack Welch, that it is adaptive and is a model company for developing leaders for all seasons. In the coming decades, companies must look for individuals who fit the particular needs of different businesses or products. Even organizations without the breadth of GE have products or services in different phases of their life cycles that require different types and styles of leadership. There is no one leader for all these situations. The company should establish a system or method to match the right leader with the right position at the right time.

I hope this book has not only demonstrated the truth of that proposition but described in sufficient detail how to make the best choices, or at least provided the basis for doing so. Proper selection and placement of strategic leaders is the solution. Good luck.

Notes

CHAPTER 1

1. Thomas J. Peters and Robert H. Waterman, Jr. 1982. *In Search of Excellence* (New York: Harper & Row).

CHAPTER 3

1. Glenn Rifkin. "Digital Equipment Founder Is Stepping Down," *New York Times.* 17 July 1992, D.1.

CHAPTER 4

1. *Hoover's Handbook.* 1990. (Austin, TX: The Reference Press) 218.
2. "Steve Jobs: Can He Do It Again?" *Business Week.* 24 Oct 1988.
3. *Hoover's Handbook.* 1990. (Austin, TX: The Reference Press) 440.
4. Brenton R. Sclender. "Couch Potatoes! Now It's Smart T.V." *Fortune.* 20 November 1989.
5. *Hoover's Handbook.* 1990. (Austin, TX: The Reference Press) 500.
6. Amy Borrus. "Sony's Challenge." *Business Week.* 1 June 1987, 64.
7. "Picturetel Is Opening Quite a Few Eyes." *Business Week.* 1 June 1987, 82.
8. Gary Slutsker. "Whose Invention Is It Anyway?" *Forbes.* 19 Aug 1991, 114–118.
9. Anthony Ramirez. "The Games Played for Nintendo's Sales." *New York Times.* 21 Dec 1989, D5.
10. Akio Morita with Edwin M. Reingold and Miksuho Shimomura. 1986. *Made in Japan.* (New York: E.P. Dutton).
11. Anthony Ramirez. "The Games Played for Nintendo's Sales." *New York Times.* 21 Dec 1989, D1.
12. Jay Finegan. "Banker's Suits." *INC.* Nov 1989, 113.

13. John Byrne. "Donald Burr May Be Ready to Take to The Skies Again." *Business Week*. 19 Jan 1989, 74–75.

14. Anthony Ramirez. "Boeing's Happy Harrowing Times." *Fortune*. 17 July 1989.

15. *Hoover's Handbook*. 1990. (Austin, TX: The Reference Press) 440.

16. Keith H. Hammonds. "Inventor, Teacher, Economist—and That's Just for Starters." *Business Week*. 18 Dec 1989, 81.

17. Methew Schifrin. "Living Off the Fat of the Land." *Forbes*. 13 Nov 1989, 186–196.

18. Gifford Pincholt III. 1985. *Intrapeneuring* (New York: Harper & Row).

19. Russell Mitchell. "Masters of Innovation." *Business Week*. 10 Apr 1989, 58.

CHAPTER 5

1. John Holusha. "How Harley Outfoxed Japan with Exports." *New York Times*. 12 Aug 1990, 2.

2. Barnaby J. Feder. "Formica: When a Household Name Becomes an 'Also-Ran'."

3. Keith Hammonds. "How a $4 Razor Ends up Costing $300 Million." *Business Week*. 29 Jan 1990, 82.

4. Subrata H. Chakravarty. "We Had to Change the Playing Field." *Forbes*. 4 Feb 1991, 82.

5. Keith Hammonds. "How a $4 Razor Ends up Costing $300 Million." *Business Week*. 29 Jan 1990, 83.

6. Methew Schifrin. "Living off the fat of the land." *Forbes*. 13 Nov 1989, 196.

CHAPTER 6

1. *Hoover's Handbook*. 1990. (Austin, TX: The Reference Press) 395.

2. Roy Furchgott. "A Sick Insurer, a Bitter Dose of Medicine and Mr. Nice Guy." *New York Times*. 2 Aug 1992, 3-1.

3. "Brain Drain at Chrysler." *USA Today*, 14 Aug 1991, B 6b.

4. Doron P. Levin. "It's Official at Chrysler; G.M. Man Will Be Chief." *New York Times*. 17 Mar 1992, D1–5.

5. Jeff Cole. "General Dynamics Comtemplates Selling Its Remaing Units." *The Wall Street Journal*. 3 Nov 1992, A1 & A5.

6. James B. Treece. "Doing It Right, till the Last Whistle." *Business Week*. 6 Apr 1992, 38–39.

CHAPTER 7

1. Joan Hamilton, Emily Smith, Larny Armstrong, Geoffrey Smith, and Joseph Weber. "Biotech: America's Dream Machine." *Business Week*. 2 Mar 1992, 68–69.

2. *Hoover's Handbook*. 1990. (Austin, TX: The Reference Press) 130.

3. *Hoover's Handbook*. 1990. (Austin, TX: The Reference Press) 298.

4. Barnaby J. Feder. "The Sponoff Strategem." *New York Times*. 11 Nov 1990, 4/5.

5. Leslie Helm with Alice Cuneo and Dean Foust. "On the Campus: Fat Endowments and Growing Clout." *Business Week*. 11 July 1988, 70–2.

6. Carla Rapoport. "Great Japanese Mistakes." *Fortune*. 13 Feb 1989, 108–111.

7. *Hoover's Handbook*. 1990. (Austin, TX: The Reference Press) 347.

CHAPTER 8

1. Joel Dreyfuss. "Reinventing IBM." *Fortune*. 14 Aug 1989, 87.

2. *Hoover's Handbook*. 1990. (Austin, TX: The Reference Press) 102.

3. Methew Schifrin. "Living Off Fat of the Land." *Forbes*. 13 Nov 89, 186–196.

4. *Hoover's Handbook*. 1990. (Austin, TX: The Reference Press) 122.

5. Julianne Slovak. "American Express Service That Sells." *Fortune*. 20 Nov 1989, 84.

6. *Economist*. 2 Sept 1989, 60. Ginz Street W1.

CHAPTER 9

1. *Hoover's Handbook*. 1990. (Austin, TX: The Reference Press) 103.

2. James P. Womack, Daniel J. Jones, and Danile Ross. "How Lean Production Can Change the World." *New York Times Business Magazine*. 23 Sept 1990, 20.

3. "Natures Sunshine." *Fortune*. 5 Dec 1988, 140.

4. Gary Strauss. "Monaghan at crossroads picks Church." *USA Today*. 14 Sep 1989, B1.

5. *Hoover's Handbook*. 1990. (Austin, TX: The Reference Press) 397.

6. Eugene Carlson. "Patterson's Machine Age Remedy for Pilferage." *Wall Street Journal*. Centennial Edition, 6, 1989.

7. *Hoover's Handbook*. 1990. (Austin, TX: The Reference Press) 309.

8. *Ibid.*, 499.

9. *Ibid.*, 385.

10. Gail De George. "Home Shopping Tries a Tonic for Its Sickly Stock." *Business Week*. 25 Apr 1988, 110.

11. Subrata H. Chakravarty and Evan McGlinn. "This Thing Has to Change People's Habits." *Forbes*. 26 June, 150.

12. *Hoover's Handbook*. 1990. (Austin, TX: The Reference Press) 492.

13. Carole J. Loomis. "State Farm Is Off the Charts." *Fortune*. 8 April 1991, 79.

14. *Hoover's Handbook*. 1990. (Austin, TX: The Reference Press) 578.

15. Wendy Zeller. "OK, So He's Not Sam Walton." *Business Week*. 16 Mar 1992, 56.

16. Andrea Rothman. "AP Is Thriving—So Why Is James Wood Still Around?" *Business Week*. 10 April 1989, 90.

17. Michael Sansolo. "Stew Leonard's Search for Excitement." *Progressive Grocer*. Special reprint.

18. *Hoover's Handbook*. 1990. (Austin, TX: The Reference Press) 69.

19. *Hoover's Handbook.* 1990. (Austin, TX: The Reference Press) 538.
20. Julia Lielich. "If You Want A Big, New Market." *Fortune.* 21 Nov 1988, 181.
21. Neal Santelmann. "Armchair Auctions." *Forbes.* 29 May 1989, 316.
22. John Huey. "WAL-MART: Will It Take Over the World." *Fortune.* 30 Jan 1989, 52–60.
23. Joshua Levine. "I Never Learned Anything from Another Car Dealer Except What to Do Wrong." *Forbes.* 26 June, 148.

CHAPTER 10

1. John Huey. "WAL-MART: Will It Take Over the World." *Fortune.* 30 Jan 1989, 54–5.
2. *Hoover's Handbook.* 1990. (Austin, TX: The Reference Press) 438.
3. Wendy Zellner. "OK, So He's Not Sam Walton." *Business Week.* 16 Mar 1992.
4. Bill Saporito. "Is Wal-Mart Unstoppable?" *Fortune.* 6 May 1991, 58.
5. Richard Stevenson. "Watch Out Macy's Here Comes Nordstrom." *New York Times Magazine.* 27 Aug 1989, 34–40.

CHAPTER 11

1. John Keller and Mark Maremont. "Bob Allen Is Turning AT&T into a Live Wire." *Business Week.* 6 Nov 1989, 140.
2. Robert A. Caro. 1975. "The Power Broker." *Robert Moses and the Fall of New York* (New York: Vintage Books).
3. Seth Lubove. "Vindicated." *Forbes.* 9 Dec 1991, 198.
4. Dean Foust, Jonathan Kapstein, Pia Farrell, and Peter Finch. "Mr. Smith Goes Global." *Business Week.* 13 Feb 1989, 66–72.
5. Fleming Meeks. "Winning Is Only the First Step." *Forbes.* 25 Dec 1989, 80–89.
6. "AT&T Plans to Buy McCaw Cellular Stake." *New York Times.* 5 Nov 1992, D1.
7. *Hoover's Handbook.* 1990. (The Reference Press: Austin Texas), 545.
8. William Symonds and Susan Duffy. "John Malone's New Strategy: Divide and Placate." *Business Week.* 5 Feb 1990, 32.
9. Michael Lev. "Media Impresario Is Selling Movies Via Satellite Dish." *New York Times.* 23 June 1991, B5.
10. Christoper Knowlton. "Want This Stock Its Up 91,000%." *Fortune.* 31 July 1989, 104.
11. Kenneth Auletta. 1992. "The Three Blind Mice." (New York, Random House).

CHAPTER 12

1. Ralph King Jr. "Let the Growth Come By Itself." *Forbes.* 17 Apr 1989, 98.
2. *Ibid.,* 98–104.

3. Eugenec Carlson. "A Gallery of the Greatest Who Influenced Our Daily Business." *The Wall Street Journal, Centennial Edition.* B 17–22.

4. *Hoover's Handbook.* 1990. (Austin, TX: The Reference Press) 205.

5. Louis Uchitelle. "Only the Bosses Are American." *New York Times.* 24 July 1989, D3–5.

6. Carla Rapoport. "How Japan Will Spend Its Cash." *Fortune.* 21 Nov 1988, 198.

7. *Hoover's Handbook.* 1990. (Austin, TX: The Reference Press) 310.

8. Brian Bremner. "Can Caterpillar Inch Its Way Back to Heftier Profits?" *Business Week.* 25 Sept 1989, 75–6.

9. Bill Saporito. "Companies that Compete Best." *Fortune.* 22 May 1989, 40.

10. Janet Novack. "We make dozens of mistakes, but they're all little." *Forbes.* 28 Nov 1988, 186.

11. Thomas A. Stewart. "GE Keeps Those Ideas Coming." *Fortune.* 12 Aug 1991, 42.

12. John Hoerr. "The Cultural Revolution at A.O. Smith." *Business Week.* 29 May 1989, 66.

13. Troy Segal, Christina Del Valle, David Greising, Rena Miller, Julia Flynn, and Jane Prendergast. "Saving Our Schools." *Business Week.* 14 Sept 1992, 71.

14. Jeffrey A. Trachtenberg. "Designers are made as well as born." *Forbes.* 11 July 1988, 86.

CHAPTER 13

1. "The Ten Year Itch." *Economist.* 17 Aug 1991, 17.

2. Jeffrey A. Sonnenfeld. "Johnny Carson's Classy Exit." *New York Times.* 7 June 1991, F 13.

3. Adam Bryant. "Wang Files for Bankruptcy in Plan to Slim Down." *New York Times.* 19 Aug 1992, D1.

4. Gary Slutsker. "ZAP." *Forbes.* April 1989, 193.

5. Joseph Nocera. "What Went Wrong at Wang." *Wall Street Journal.* 26 Feb 1992, A10, Bookshelf.

CHAPTER 14

1. Troy Segal, Christina Del Valle, David Greising, Rena Miller, Julia Flynn, and Jane Prendergast. "Saving Our Schools." *Business Week.* 14 Sep 1992.

2. Ruth Simon, Graham Button. "What I Learned in the Nineteen Eighties." *Forbes.* 8 June 1990, 102.

3. Johen Templeman, Thane Peterson, Gail Schares, and Jonathan Kapstein. "A New Economic Miracle?" *Business Week.* 27 Nov 1989, 58.

4. Robert Nieff. "Japan's Hardening View of America." *Business Week.* 18, 1989, 62.

5. *Ibid.,* 64.

Index

DATE DUE